HIS APPEARING AND HIS KINGDOM

His Appearing
and
His Kingdom

THE CHRISTIAN HOPE IN THE LIGHT OF ITS HISTORY

T. FRANCIS GLASSON

M.A., D.D. (London University)

LONDON
THE EPWORTH PRESS

PUBLISHED BY

THE EPWORTH PRESS
(FRANK H. CUMBERS)
25–35 CITY ROAD, LONDON, E.C. I

*

New York . Toronto
Melbourne . Cape Town

*

SET IN MONOTYPE BASKERVILLE AND PRINTED IN
GREAT BRITAIN BY WESTERN PRINTING SERVICES LTD.
BRISTOL

PREFACE

Since the publication of *The Second Advent* in 1945 I have received repeated requests to write a sequel on more positive lines and I have also been asked to present something more adapted to the general reader. The former work was concerned with 'the *origin* of the New Testament doctrine'. Whether the case propounded on this matter of origins be accepted or not, the question remains as to what exactly we are to put in the place of the traditional forms of the great doctrines of Advent and Judgement. On what lines are we to construct a Christian eschatology without forsaking our New Testament basis and at the same time allowing for the framework which modern knowledge has created for us, a framework which makes it impossible to cling to the precise form in which these matters were presented to our grandfathers.

On the whole I have been greatly encouraged by the reception given to my earlier work, particularly by private intimations of help it has given to those who were troubled with this particular problem. The long-accepted view that in the time of Christ the Messiah's descent from the sky was a familiar Jewish doctrine is still unsupported by evidence. And if, as I maintain, such a view is untrue the subject has certainly taken a new turn even for those who do not follow the alternative answer to the problem which I submitted.

In the following pages I have addressed myself to the question: What is a Christian in the twentieth century to believe about the return of Christ and the Last Judgement; how is he to find his way through the variety of conflicting pronouncements on these subjects; is he to be prepared for a winding-up of the universe at any moment by divine intervention, or is the story of man's earthly life to continue for a very long period; and if the latter is likely, what should he expect in the coming centuries and how will the whole process terminate?

I do not wish to suggest that I have a clear answer to these questions. But I have tried to show how Christian thought has dealt with them in the past, in the belief that a flood of light is thrown on the whole question by a consideration of what representative writers have had to say in past centuries. By following certain tendencies to be traced through this development, we shall, I think, be able to indicate the kind of answer which the Christian of today will find of help.

I have made a point of giving quotations from Christian thinkers of many different periods. We make a mistake in confining ourselves too much to recent utterances; it is important to know what living authorities are saying, but it is equally valuable to know what Origen said in the third century and Aquinas in the thirteenth. Anyone who reads the book carefully should have a fairly good idea of the kind of beliefs about the Last Things which were current in the early Church, in the Middle Ages, at the Reformation and after, and the very varied views which hold sway at the present time. Again, many of the quotations are from works not readily accessible to the 'general reader'; for example, a footnote reference to Lactantius' *Divine Institutes* would be meaningless and not one reader in a hundred would take the trouble to search out the actual reference. The quotations from such writers also carry the advantage of allowing them to speak for themselves; too often writers have eschatological views ascribed to them which they did not hold. I have not confined myself to theologians; very often a work of poetry or of general literature is of value not only for what it tells us about its immediate period but also for its spiritual discernment.

In the first part, a number of Advent problems are discussed, among them questions of Judgement and Resurrection and various adventist movements. In the second part, Christian views about the Kingdom of Christ are discussed more or less in historical sequence, with particular reference to the Millennium and the hope of Christ's ultimate victory through the world's conversion to the faith. It may be noted here that the word Chiliasm means the same as belief in the Millennium; the former comes from the Greek word for thousand, while the word millennium is from the Latin (*mille*, thousand; *annus*, year). Curiously enough, millenarian is usually spelt with one 'n' and millennial with two.

The opening chapter is a summary of my book *The Second Advent*, which I was asked to contribute to the *Preachers' Magazine* two or three years ago, and is reproduced by kind

permission of the editor, the Rev. Dr Leslie F. Church. It will
serve to refresh the minds of those who have read the earlier
work, and will indicate my general standpoint to others. Those
who find themselves in disagreement on this particular point
about origins may nevertheless appreciate the more historical
sections which follow.

I am indebted to the Oxford University Press for permission
to quote from Arnold Toynbee's *Study of History* and to Messrs
Burns Oates & Washbourne Ltd for two brief quotations from
the section by Abbot A. Vonier in *The Teaching of the Catholic
Church*, edited by Canon G. D. Smith. In Chapter 4 I have with
the consent of Canon H. D. A. Major repeated the substance
of a few sentences from an article which I contributed to the
Modern Churchman (March 1949) on 'Jesus Christ and Christian
Apocalypticism'.

T. F. G.

HORLEY
   SURREY

CONTENTS

Part Two
His Kingdom

Part One
His Appearing

The signs mentioned in the Gospels do not all refer to the Second Advent which will happen at the end of the world, but some of them belong to the time of the sack of Jerusalem, which is now a thing of the past, while some, in fact many of them, refer to the advent whereby He comes daily to the Church, whom He visits spiritually when He dwells in us by faith and love.

St Augustine

I should have felt more nervous about the late comet, if I had thought the world was ripe. But it is very green yet, if I am not mistaken; and besides, there is a great deal of coal to use up, which I cannot bring myself to think was made for nothing.

Oliver Wendell Holmes

In reinterpreting the New Testament idea of the Parousia (and, as we shall see later, all other ideas dealing with the relation of history and super-history, such as resurrection and judgement) it is important to take biblical symbols seriously but not literally.

The symbol of the Second Coming of Christ can neither be taken literally nor dismissed as unimportant.

Reinhold Niebuhr

Section A—*The Advent Message*

From thence He shall come

CHAPTER I

RÉSUMÉ OF *THE SECOND ADVENT*

THERE is no part of the Christian message more difficult and baffling than the section known as Eschatology, the doctrine of the Last Things. In recent years there has been a tendency for preachers to concentrate on the application of the Gospel to the present life and the present world—a reaction from an over-emphasis on the future made by our grandfathers. The result has been that we have given too little attention to these subjects and have allowed them to become the happy hunting-ground of the crank.

We are all familiar with those who spend their time working out prophetic charts of the future. Every few years we are assured that the Advent is about to occur. I remember meeting some time ago a writer and speaker who pointed to 1927 as a year which would almost certainly mark the end of the age, and, failing that, things could hardly go on longer than 1934, a date which had been independently arrived at by many Bible students! The main thing to note about all these attempts, which are still flourishing, is that this kind of thing has been going on for centuries. A thousand years ago men were saying: 'Antichrist is just round the corner.' All previous attempts to fix dates and make detailed prophecies have failed and been discredited by the mere lapse of time.

Other factors, too, have influenced the thoughtful Christian to fight shy of the subject. The old scheme of things was based upon belief in a three-story universe: heaven was 'up' and Christ was to make a visible descent to Jerusalem. 'Up' has ceased to have any meaning to those who have cousins in New Zealand! Their 'up' is our 'down', and our present conception of the solar system makes some traditional interpretations meaningless. Again, the vast aeons of time now known to be involved in the creative process and the incredible patience of God in the fashioning of man make it very unlikely that at such an early stage He will destroy His handiwork.

All this means that some restatement or reinterpretation is essential. It means too that we shall be content to remain agnostic concerning many matters 'which the Father hath set within His own authority'. We shall preserve a reverent silence on some matters about which our predecessors were so cock-sure. At the same time we shall find that the spiritual values which the Advent doctrine has represented and preserved through the centuries still remain—the final victory of Christ in the scene of His humiliation, the fact of judgement, and the certainty of reunion.

WAS JESUS MISTAKEN?

Another serious difficulty linked with this subject is that in the Gospels as we now have them Jesus Himself is represented as uttering prophecies which, if taken literally, were plainly unfulfilled—for example Matthew 16_{28}: 'There be some of them that stand here, which shall in no wise taste of death, till they see the Son of man coming in his kingdom.' See also Mark 13 and the reference to 'this generation' in verse 30. Early this century a young German theologian, Albert Schweitzer, wrote a book which caused a good deal of stir (rather more in this country than in his own). Its English title was *The Quest of the Historical Jesus*. In this book, Schweitzer, who is also a famous organist and a heroic missionary in equatorial Africa, maintained that the key to the life of Jesus was that He lived and died in the firm expectation of an immediate return in glory from the sky (known as the *Parousia*, a term which should be noted as it is a useful abbreviation and will occur in the sequel). His announcement that the Kingdom of God was 'at hand' meant that the end of the world was imminent and that very soon God would crash in with irresistible might, would destroy the evil world and create a new one with Christ as the King. Schweitzer, of course, had a great admiration for the moral teaching of Jesus and he maintained that His marvellous ethic was made possible by His eschatology. His vivid expectancy gave Him a detached view of life and He was thus saved from the fashions and atmosphere of the times and lifted into the eternities.

The details of Schweitzer's interpretation of the life of Jesus have not commended themselves to many students; but his main point is widely accepted, that Jesus lived in expectation of the speedy end of the world and of His own Parousia. There are, of course, a few touches in the Gospels which support this view, but surely the main trend of our Lord's teaching is against it. As one who has found in the Gospels his daily food for twenty years, I personally cannot reconcile the impression they make upon me with this picture of a mistaken fanatic bringing the message that millions now living will never die.

In considering the teaching of our Lord on these subjects there are several points which should be borne in mind.

LITERAL OR SYMBOLIC?

Our matter-of-fact Western outlook makes it difficult for us to appreciate the highly pictorial language of Eastern writings. The Bible shares this pictorial element and we may be creating needless difficulties by pressing symbolic expressions too literally. Let us consider, for instance, the reply of our Lord to the question of Caiaphas. Mark 14 $_{61-2}$: 'Art thou the Christ, the Son of the Blessed? And Jesus said, I am: and ye shall see the Son of man sitting at the right hand of power, and coming with the clouds of heaven.' In Matthew 26$_{64}$ and Luke 22$_{69}$ the sentence begins with the words '*From now*'. (In our English versions, the milder word 'Henceforth' is used; but the original Greek is quite simply 'From now'. The Basic English version for the Matthew passage reads: 'From now you will see the Son of man . . .'.) It is of interest that there is some manuscript evidence that Mark also originally had the phrase 'From now'. Our Lord's words in Mark and Matthew combine two Old Testament passages, Psalm 110 and Daniel 7$_{13}$; Luke has the former only. Both these Old Testament passages describe a kind of coronation; in the psalm 'my Lord' is called to sit on God's right hand; in Daniel 7 the Son of man is described as approaching the throne of God and receiving from Him authority and dominion. (The coming in Daniel 7 is not a descent to the earth, but an approach to God— 'he came to the Ancient of days.') In the light of all this, it seems clear that to take the words of Jesus literally is impossible. But if He meant that the moment of seeming defeat was the beginning of His triumph, that His reign and exaltation would begin from that point, we have something profoundly true and moving, something that Paul has expressed with greater fullness in Philippians 2$_{8-11}$. Some words of Bishop Gore may be quoted:

If Jesus, standing among His disciples, speaks of some among them who, before they die, shall have 'seen the Kingdom' or 'seen it come with power', and if, standing before Caiaphas, He declares that 'henceforth' or 'from this moment' they shall see realized Daniel's vision of the Son of man in divine power, His words are satisfied by the events which followed His death and gave the Church that sense of glory and power reflected from Christ, which was the secret of its surprising success, and which inspired in its adversaries a kind of terror.

Another line of thought of some importance is concerned with our Lord's prophecies about the nation and its future. It is clear that Jesus foretold the destruction of Jerusalem and with prophetic vision saw that the tendencies then present in the national life could only lead to destruction. There are words of His (particularly in Luke 17 and Matthew 24) which are usually regarded as referring to His final coming, but which seem more applicable to Jerusalem's fall. When He told His followers not to return to their houses to collect their belongings, and to remember Lot's wife, was He not warning them to flee from the doomed city when the time came? Such sayings could hardly refer to the Last Day and the Final Judgement.

Another very important consideration in the present connexion is what is known as

THE SYNOPTIC PROBLEM

There can be no real doubt that the Gospels present reliable accounts of the works and the words of our Lord. An inventor of this teaching would be as great as Jesus, for never man spake like this man. But this does not mean that every word in the Gospels can be accepted as an infallible record; I once believed this, but closer study of the Gospels has convinced me that it is untenable. They do not claim to be inspired or inerrant, but they set out to record genuine reminiscences of 'all that Jesus began to do and to teach' and they may be confidently accepted as such. It has long been recognized that in the Fourth Gospel we have a greater measure of paraphrase and devotional expansion than in the other three, which are of course known as the Synoptic Gospels. Jesus spoke Aramaic, a Semitic tongue allied to Hebrew (Hebrew at this time being a dead language); our Gospels were written in Greek, a language which belongs to quite a different family, the Indo-European. It is obvious that a certain amount of interpretation and para- phrase is to be expected in all the Gospels, as without this no translation would be intelligible.

After one hundred years of study and debate, it is now fairly widely agreed that Mark is the earliest Gospel and that the writers of Matthew and Luke made use of it, reproducing most of its material. Matthew and Luke also appear to have used in addition a common source containing some of our Lord's teaching, and a little narrative; this is generally known as Q. (See F. B. Clogg, *Introduction to the New Testament*; Vincent Taylor, *The Gospels*; and B. H. Streeter's *Synoptic Problem* in Peake's *Commentary*.)

Study of the Synoptic problem is sometimes regarded as a harmless and unimportant pursuit suitable for those who are interested in such things, and it is not always recognized that it may have important doctrinal repercussions. In connexion with the present subject it can be shown that some references to the *Parousia* in the Gospels are 'secondary'. Let us look at this in more detail.

Matthew and Luke in their use of Mark frequently alter his language, usually for compression; and at times words are modified or added, in perfectly good faith, to clarify the meaning. The motive for these slight changes can often be seen. (See Mark 4_{15} and Luke 8_{12}; Mark 6_3 and Matthew 13_{55}.) Now if we turn to Mark 13_{1-4} it will be observed that this passage is concerned solely with the destruction of the Temple. The parallel in Matthew 24_{1-3}, which is derived from Mark, contains references to the *Parousia* and 'the end of the age'— two expressions found only in Matthew among the evangelists. In fact the word *Parousia* occurs only in this chapter in all the four Gospels. Mark 13_4: 'Tell us, when shall these things be? and what shall be the sign when these things are all about to be accomplished?' Matthew 24_3: 'Tell us, when shall these things be? and what shall be the sign of thy coming (Greek: *Parousia*), and of the end of the age?' It is difficult to avoid the conclusion that Matthew is responsible for these additions and modifications.

Again, let us look at Mark 9$_1$: 'There be some here of them that stand by, which shall in no wise taste of death, till they see the 'kingdom of God come with power.' Matthew 16$_{28}$ reproduces this as follows: 'There be some of them that stand here, which shall in no wise taste of death, till they see *the Son of man coming in his kingdom.*'

Not only are we able to compare Matthew's and Luke's versions of certain sayings with the Marcan version on which theirs was based, but at times we have a saying in Q which we can compare with some other rendering: e.g. see Matthew 10$_{32-3}$ = Luke 12$_{8-9}$ (Q) and the parallel in Mark 8$_{38}$ (= Matthew 16$_{27}$ = Luke 9$_{26}$). It is a great advantage to have these dual renderings, because they enable us to distinguish the core of the saying and thus to get a clearer idea of what Jesus meant.

Some of the considerations we must bear in mind in studying the Gospel material have been briefly mentioned, such as the allegorical elements and the Synoptic question. For fuller discussion and for further similar points I must refer to my book, *The Second Advent*, pages 63–105, where all the Gospel references to the subject are considered. The conclusion reached is that while Jesus foresaw the fall of Jerusalem and the ultimate triumph of His cause, He did not Himself expect a literal descent from the sky in glory, either in the near future or later.

Now, two criticisms of this conclusion may be made: (*a*) Were not the Jews looking for a glorious Messiah to descend from the sky and did not Jesus accept this conception and apply it to Himself? (*b*) How can the clear teaching of the Epistles be explained unless it represents the teaching of Jesus? Let us look at these two points.

WHAT WERE THE JEWS EXPECTING?

The Jews, it is said, had advanced beyond the Old Testament view of a Son of David who should be born on the earth (as in Isaiah 11$_1$) and were now expecting the Messiah to come in glory from the sky in accordance with their apocalyptic writings. Middleton Murray in his *Life of Jesus* says it is impossible to understand the thought of our Lord unless we recognize that the Jews had abandoned belief in a Messiah who belonged to the order of humanity and expected the dramatic and spectacular advent of a transcendental figure. This of course is in line with what has been taught for many years, and similar statements could be cited. Schweitzer and others take it for granted that Jesus took over current Messianic expectations. But what evidence is there that the Jews believed no longer in a Son of David who should be born on the earth, but in a Messiah who was to descend with clouds, or that the two views were both current at the time when our era opened?

Some years ago I began to examine the Jewish apocalypses which were alleged to give this teaching and to my surprise I failed to find it in their pages. Some had no mention of a Messiah at all and those which did refer to him spoke of a Son of David in familiar Old Testament language. The Psalms of Solomon which are specifically cited by Schweitzer as giving the 'apocalyptic' view prove on examination to do nothing of the kind; instead, there is the familiar picture of a warrior king. I wrote to a leading biblical scholar asking for evidence for the statement that the Jews expected the Messiah to descend with clouds; in his reply he quoted (as far as I recall) only one passage—2 Esdras 13 (2 Esdras is an apocalypse which may be found in the Apocrypha). Now two observations may be made about this passage: (1) The date of 2 Esdras is round about A.D. 100. A book produced a century after Jesus was born is not good evidence for the teaching extant when He lived. (2) The passage makes not the slightest mention of a descent from the sky, but describes the Messiah ascending out of the sea!

ENOCH

It is the *Book of Enoch*, however, which needs special notice for unlike other apocalyptic works of its period it does describe a transcendent Messiah and great importance is attached to this apocalypse, which in its entirety only exists in the Ethiopic language. The famous traveller Bruce brought the book back with him from Abyssinia in the eighteenth century. This work is alleged to present that view of the Messiah's advent which Jesus adopted, interpreting His own Messiahship in accordance with its teaching. (In *The Second Advent*, pages 25–62 are devoted to it.) It consists really of five books, written at different periods and giving widely different teaching; they became associated in one collection because of their supposed connexion with the patriarch Enoch. Only in one section, the Similitudes (Enoch 37–71), is the Messiah a superhuman figure; in the other four parts he is either omitted altogether or spoken of as born within the community. In the Similitudes the coming of God to judge the world is described, and with Him come multitudes of angels and also the Son of man, the supernatural Messiah, who carries out the judgement. A brief passage may be quoted to illustrate the style of this work:

And there I saw One who had a head of days, and His head was white like wool, and with Him was another being whose countenance had the appearance of a man, and his face was full of graciousness, like one of the holy angels. And I asked the angel who went with me and showed me all the hidden things, concerning that Son of Man, who he was, and whence he was, and why he went with the Head of Days? And he answered and said unto me: This is the Son of Man who hath righteousness, with whom dwelleth righteousness, and who revealeth all the treasures of that which is hidden, because the Lord of Spirits hath chosen him, and whose lot hath the pre-eminence before the Lord of Spirits in uprightness for ever. And this Son of Man whom thou hast seen shall raise up the kings and the mighty from their seats, and shall loosen the reins of the strong, and break the teeth of the sinners (Enoch 46_{1-4}).

The phrase 'Son of man', so familiar to us from the Gospels, is the strongest argument for the contention that Jesus derived His teaching from this apocalypse. But the following points should be noted. (1) Jesus' use of the term 'Son of man' can be otherwise accounted for; and many would agree with the words of Dr Vincent Taylor: 'In all His references to the Son of man there is no certain trace of dependence upon the ideas of Enoch.' (2) The Son of man in Enoch apparently accompanies God at His coming; the picture is in important respects different from the teaching found in the New Testament about the final advent of Christ. (3) Many features of the *Book of Enoch* are quite out of harmony with the ruling ideas of the Gospels and are crude and fantastic in their descriptions of God. (4) In Enoch 71 the Son of man is identified with Enoch himself. (5) While four of the five parts are probably pre-christian, the date of the Similitudes is doubtful. Some authorities have with good reason suggested that this section comes from the middle of the first century A.D. (that is, years after the Crucifixion). This, however, is a matter of some doubt and the other points are not affected by the question of date. In any case, the Similitudes are unique among Jewish writings; nowhere else is the Messiah spoken of as judge and it has even been suggested that they reveal traces of Christian thought.

The current Jewish view today is that the Messiah is to be a human descendant of David, born on the earth, and this has been the main doctrine on this subject throughout the centuries, both B.C. and A.D. It should be noted that when Jewish writers apply Daniel 7_{13} to the Messiah, they usually regard the clouds as symbolic and as referring to 'the great magnificence and power which God shall give unto the Messiah'.

The importance of all this is that it disproves the common assumption that the Messiah's *Parousia* was a current Jewish conception which was ready for Jesus to 'take over'. Those who might agree that He expressed Himself in the thought-forms of His time would, I think, hesitate to say that He originated the idea of a literal descent from the sky. This disposes of objection (*a*) mentioned earlier. We turn now to (*b*).

THE ORIGIN OF THE EARLY HOPE

The early speeches in Acts do not reveal any expectation of a speedy end of the age; but the epistles show that it was not long before this expectation came to hold a prominent place. There is no doubt that by the middle of the first century the Church believed that Christ's return was imminent and that it would take the form of a dramatic and visible descent from the sky; He would come 'with the angels of his power in flaming fire, rendering vengeance to them that know not God and to them that obey not the Gospel' (2 Thessalonians 1_{7-8}). This theme with its wealth of vivid detail and its prophecy of the Man of Sin cannot be accounted for from the teaching of Jesus; yet it holds a prominent position in the Thessalonian letters, written about A.D. 50. How are we then to explain it?

First of all let us consider the background and atmosphere of the period. For many years the Jews had been looking forward to the Messianic age, a time when God would intervene on their behalf, destroy their enemies, and set up a kingdom of peace and prosperity. Jesus preached about the Kingdom of God and clearly regarded Himself as the Messiah; but how different His interpretation was! He announced that the Kingdom had arrived; what prophets and kings had longed to see was now in the midst of men (Luke 11_{20}, 10_{23-4}, 17_{20-1}). God had interposed, not with the immediate destruction of evil, but with the injection into the world situation of a new divine life which He had brought. This seed would grow into a great tree; this leaven would permeate the whole mass. This Kingdom was so different from anything men had expected that even John the Baptist began to doubt if Jesus really were the Messiah; had they in their disillusionment to look at the distant horizon once again for the new age and for 'him that should come'? The early Christians evidently shared this feeling; they did not 'look for another' but they looked for 'this same Jesus' to come back and fulfil the main part of His task in a more realistic spirit. Jesus was such a strange King— born in a stable, working at a bench, crowned with thorns, enthroned on a Cross. At best this could only be the prelude to the real thing. And so the spirit of expectancy passed over into the Church, and instead of seeing that Jesus had transmuted their hopes, they projected them into the future. They had looked for so much, the overthrow and destruction of evil, the establishment of a righteous kingdom, a new order. What they had already witnessed surely could not be the whole story of the divine intervention. Several other factors would contribute to the hope of some new interposition in the near future: (1) misunderstanding of our Lord's words about the life-time of the apostles; (2) the prophecy of Jerusalem's fall within a generation; (3) the taking over of the Jewish Antichrist doctrine, which maintained that the end of the age would be marked by the emergence of some outstanding monster of iniquity; (4) the behaviour of the Roman emperor Caligula (i.e. his desecration of the Temple at Jerusalem in the year 41, which seemed to suggest that the spirit of Antichrist was already in the world; see 2 Thessalonians 2_7)—all this would tend to encourage a spirit of great excitement and anticipation about the middle of the first century. This is exactly what we find in the Thessalonian correspondence.

THE ADVENT IMAGERY

It was natural that this spirit of expectancy should link itself with the Old Testament descriptions of the Day of the Lord, and it is to these that we must turn to find the origin of the pictorial details so prominent in the Advent teaching of the New Testament. Let us consider a few of these passages: Psalm 50_{3-5} ('Our God shall come, and shall not keep silence. . . . He shall call to the heavens above, and to the earth, that he may judge his people: Gather my saints together unto me . . .'); Isaiah 66$_{15}$ ('The Lord will come with fire, and his chariots shall be like the whirlwind; to render his anger with fury, and his rebuke with flames of fire'); Zechariah 14$_5$ ('The Lord my God shall come, and all the holy ones with thee'). The actual phrases used in these Old Testament accounts of the coming of the Lord turn up again in the New Testament accounts of the coming of Jesus.

The following features concerning the Day of the Lord appear in Isaiah 26–7:

1. The Lord's coming (26$_{21}$).
2. The Judgement (26$_{21}$).
3. The Resurrection (26$_{19}$).
4. The gathering of the saints (27$_{12}$).
5. The great trumpet (27$_{13}$).

All these five elements reappear in the Thessalonian letters in connexion with the Advent of Jesus (see 1 Thessalonians 4$_{13ff}$; 2 Thessalonians 1$_9$, 2$_8$). It is most important to observe that the development of the advent imagery sprang from the conviction that Jesus was Lord, not (as has been thought for many years) from the conviction that He was Messiah. It was of course quite a familiar usage in the early Church to apply to Jesus Old Testament passages about God.

Other references which should be consulted because of their influence on the New Testament doctrine are Isaiah 2 and 63. In 2 Thessalonians 1$_9$ (in the original Greek) a dozen consecutive words are taken from the Greek version of Isaiah 2$_{10}$; they were originally written concerning God and His Advent, and they are here applied to Christ. Thus, all the pictorial details attached to Christ's Advent in the epistles are derived from the doctrine of the coming of the Lord. '*Broadly speaking, the Christians took over the Old Testament doctrine of the Advent of the Lord, making the single adjustment that the Lord was the Lord Jesus*' (*The Second Advent*, p. 176). We can thus account both for the spirit of expectancy and the advent imagery without modifying what was said earlier about the teaching of Jesus Himself.

PAUL AND JOHN

We have been referring to the Thessalonian letters, which are possibly the earliest of the epistles and indeed of any of our New

Testament books. It is of great interest to notice that while
Paul began with this note of intense expectancy, he did not
remain at this stage. If we read his letters in chronological
order we find great development in his thought on these
subjects. In Romans he appears to expect that the final consummation will not take place until the Jews as a body turn
to Christ (see $11_{12, 26}$). But later still comes the great epistle
to the Ephesians, where we probably have Paul's maturest
thought. Here the Jews as such are not given any definite role
in the future, but a great process of reconciliation through
Christ is envisaged. God's purpose is 'to sum up all things in
Christ' (1_{10}), and in this cosmic process the Church is His
instrument. Even now the barrier between Jew and Gentile
has been broken down, and finally harmony in the whole
universe is to be achieved. No mention is made of the Second
Advent at all, but some future consummation is hinted at in the
phrase 'the day of redemption' (4_{30}). Paul had come to see
that the true manifestation of the power of God was the Cross
(1 Corinthians 1_{18-25}). It is instructive to observe how in his
writing fervent apocalypticism recedes and the great message
of a spiritual kingdom centred in the Cross gradually comes to
the fore.

This final message of Paul is in harmony with what we find
in the Fourth Gospel. Here it is made plain that the real
inbreaking of the divine into the world has already taken place
in the Incarnation. 'Lifted up' Christ draws all men unto
Himself (12_{32}). It is highly significant that in this Gospel the
Last Discourse of Jesus with His disciples is not of an apocalyptic character as in the other Gospels. The *Parousia* is mentioned in 14_3 but the main thought is of a coming of a very
different kind: 'If a man love me, he will keep my word:
and my Father will love him, and we will come unto him,
and make our abode with him' (14_{23}). More prominent still
is the coming of the Holy Spirit, who at times seems to be
Jesus Himself coming in a new way. It may be that in some
matters John is trying to correct the imperfect views of the
early Church (see 12_{16}: 'These things understood not his
disciples at the first').

If we reject some of the traditional forms of the Advent hope,
we are thus moving in line with the maturer development of
New Testament teaching and we are also in my opinion closer

to the original mind of our Lord. Our discussion has been mainly the tracing of origins; the question as to what we are to believe and teach about the future and climax of human history is a wider one. But in the light of the foregoing it may be maintained that if we regard the traditional imagery of Advent and Judgement as *symbolic* rather than *literal* we shall not be guilty of disloyalty to the teaching and spirit of Jesus. The great spiritual realities which have been preserved through the centuries by these conceptions are still valid today and they include the final victory and vindication of Christ, the certainty of judgement and the assurance of reunion. Even though there may not be a literal assize at which all the millions who have ever lived will stand one by one before a visible great white throne, it is nevertheless true that we are accountable to God, that character and destiny are linked together, and that Christ is the Judge both of nations and men.

As to the future of human history, even the atom bomb has not entirely invalidated some words which Archbishop Temple wrote years ago: 'The earth will in all probability be habitable for myriads of years yet. If Christianity is the final religion, the Church is still in its infancy. Two thousand years are as two days.' There is much to encourage us in the belief that Jesus looked forward to a long period during which the New Covenant, sealed with His blood, would operate and to the final victory of His cause. The meek shall inherit the earth and the day will come when God's will shall 'be done on earth as it is in heaven'.

CHAPTER 2

ADVENT TEACHING OF ST THOMAS AQUINAS

So MANY different conceptions of the Second Advent have been
put forward that, in order to determine what we are talking
about, it will be a great advantage to consider one great
classical presentation. We could not be better served than by
St Thomas Aquinas (c. 1227–74), who deals at length with this
subject in his famous *Summa Theologica*. He died before completing this voluminous work and the final parts concerning
eschatology have actually been supplied from another of his
works, the commentary on the *Sentences* of Peter Lombard.
There are many reasons why Aquinas should be chosen to help
us in the present connexion. His teaching is set forth with
admirable clarity. No reader can fail to admire the fairness
with which he presents the views of opponents or heretics, or
the ingenuity which he shows in solving the most difficult
problems. His great work rises with the majesty and sublimity
of a noble cathedral. Again, he stands at a mid-point in the
development of Christian thought. On the one hand, he
follows in the tradition of Augustine whom he constantly
quotes as an authority, and is conversant too with such teachers
as Bede the Englishman and John of Damascus and with the
revived Aristotelianism which he weaves into his system. On
the other hand there is his dominant influence in succeeding
centuries. His teaching has been singled out by the Roman
Catholic Church for special commendation. This does not
mean of course that every part of his work is equally authoritative. Most theologians would agree that his doctrine of God
and his general philosophical standpoint are of far more
importance than the eschatological sections; and it was the
former which were undoubtedly in the mind of Pope Leo the
Thirteenth when by his Bull he drew attention to the value of
St Thomas's teaching. The neo-Thomism of the present time
is also mainly concerned with his philosophical theism. Nevertheless, in trying to trace through the centuries the development
of Christian thought on the Last Things we shall be wise to

14

give special attention to this leader of the Schoolmen. But our immediate purpose is to find some definite presentation of what has been meant in Christian tradition by the Second Advent of Christ.

THE CELESTIAL ROTATION STOPS

To begin with we must remember Aquinas' conception of the structure of the universe. The earth was regarded as stationary and at the centre. It was spherical and hell was in its interior. Around the fixed earth revolved all the heavenly bodies in accordance with the Ptolemaic astronomy. The planets had particular movements, but the fixed stars formed a kind of outer sphere enclosing the whole system. Outside this sphere was Paradise, the abode of God and the angels and the souls of the blessed. The great sphere was continually revolving, and it was the movement of the heavenly bodies which caused the processes of life and growth upon the earth, as Aristotle taught. But while Aristotle maintained that this great circular movement had been going on from eternity and would do so for ever, the earth having no beginning and no ending, Aquinas believed that 'in the beginning God created the heaven and the earth'. He admitted that this could not be proved by reason; it was a part of revealed truth. But he agreed with Aristotle's view that the whole process of becoming and corruption was caused by the movement of the heavenly bodies around the earth.

Just as Aquinas held that this process had a beginning so he maintained that it would end—not by some natural cause, but by divine decree. There was nothing in the nature of things to prevent the movement continuing for ever; but God had revealed that the process would one day stop, there would be an end. But this would not mean the annihilation of the world; rather God would stop the revolution of the heavens—He would as it were put His hand on the great wheel. This in itself would entail the ending of all life on the earth. One is reminded of the words of Marlowe's Faustus as he awaits the fearful moment when the devil is to come to claim his soul:

> Stand still; you ever-moving spheres of heaven,
> That time may cease, and midnight never come.

But this stopping of the celestial rotation was to be accompanied by more important events. Christ Himself in glorious majesty was to descend from heaven accompanied by hosts of angels and was to come to a place on or just over the earth where He would be seen by all in order to conduct the Last Judgement of 'the quick and the dead'.

Another event to take place about the same time as this glorious descent was the great conflagration spoken of in 2 Peter 3_{10-12}. This did not mean that the whole universe was to be burnt out until nothing was left but a cinder; it was to be a purifying rather than a destroying process. Just as the earth had once been cleansed with water by Noah's Flood, so it would be cleansed with fire, and the fire would extend to the same height as the waters of the Flood, fifteen cubits above the top of the mountains. Some authorities had suggested that the cleansing flames would extend to the starry heavens; but Aquinas does not agree with them. The distant stars have not been polluted by man's sin; the fire is only needed where this pollution extends. St Bonaventura thought that the fire would rise to the summit of the space containing the four elements, but Aquinas disagreed.

One remarkable factor entailed by this fire is that all who are alive on earth at the time are burned to death by it. Here Aquinas is following the rather pedantic literalism of Augustine. Although Paul had definitely said, 'We shall not all sleep, but we shall all be changed' (1 Corinthians 15_{51}), it was pointed out that elsewhere he had written: 'As in Adam all die, so also in Christ shall all be made alive' (verse 22). All must therefore die, and the final conflagration will reduce to ashes those who are alive at the time of the Second Coming. Nevertheless, the Resurrection would immediately follow; and all the dead great and small would stand before the Judge. The fire 'will act in like manner on the wicked and the good who will be alive, by reducing the bodies of both to ashes'. This astonishing item in the programme of the 'blessed hope' is still retained in Roman Catholic teaching today. 'It is certain', we read in *The Teaching of the Catholic Church* (ed. G. D. Smith),

that the Resurrection of the dead will precede the judgement, properly so-called; there is more room for doubting the sequence of happenings with regard to the universal conflagration, but it would seem that the fire in which all men then living will find their death will be the first act in this tremendous drama. Out of the ruins of the world that was till then, a new world will be created which will be truly part of the Resurrection. It will be in that new world that the judgement will take place' (p. 1136).

Aquinas admits that the point about all dying without any exception was disputed: 'The saints differ in speaking on this question, as may be seen in the text. However, the safer and more common opinion is that all shall die and rise again from the dead . . . human nature cannot return to immortality save by means of death.' He finds confirmation in the argument that when the movement of the heavens ceases, the living must depart from this life . . . as the members die when the heart ceases to move. This may be found under Question 78 in the third part of the *Summa*. (Here and elsewhere I follow the standard translation by the English Benedictine Fathers, with the kind permission of Messrs Burns Oates and Washbourne):

It is also in keeping with the order of nature for another reason, as it it stated in Phys. 8, text 1 [here he quotes Aristotle],
'the movement of heaven is as a kind of life to all existing in nature', just as the movement of the heart is a kind of life of the whole body: wherefore even as all the members become dead on the heart ceasing to move, so when the heavenly movement ceases nothing can remain living with that life which was sustained by the influence of that movement. Now such is the life by which we live now: and therefore it follows that those who shall live after the movement of the heavens comes to a standstill must depart from this life.

Augustine's teaching on this point may be found in the *City of God*, Book 20, xx.

In Question 74 Aquinas deals with the conflagration. He points out that that part of the world which is given to our use contracts from men's sins a certain unfitness for being glorified, wherefore in this respect it needs to be cleansed. In like manner with regard to the intervening space, on account of the contact of the elements, there are many corruptions, generations, and alterations of the elements, which diminish their purity; wherefore the elements need to be cleansed from these also, so that they be fit to receive the newness of glory. It is unnecessary for the fire to cleanse the higher heavens. There is no need to take anything away from the substance of the higher heavens, but only to set its movement at rest. Peter himself in

c

2 Peter 3$_{5-7}$ explains to which heavens he refers; the heavens to be cleansed are those which before were cleansed by the waters of the deluge, namely the aerial heavens.

Now it is clear that the waters of the deluge did not rise to the summit of the space occupied by the elements, but only fifteen cubits above the mountain tops, . . . that fire will not rise higher than the waters of the deluge.

THE JUDGEMENT AND ITS SEQUEL

The conflagration would be followed by the General Judgement and at this all human beings who had ever lived would be assembled in their resurrection bodies. The resurrection body was conceived in the most literal fashion and in spite of St Paul's teaching that flesh and blood cannot inherit the kingdom of God, Aquinas followed Augustine in maintaining that the resurrection body would have flesh, blood, hair, nails, and so on—each point being discussed at some length.

The place of the Judgement is said to be in all probability the valley of Jehoshaphat. Article 4 of Question 88 is devoted to this question: 'Whether the Judgement will take place in the valley of Josaphat?' Some had objected that the whole promised land would not be large enough. Their opponents quoted Acts 1$_{11}$, 'shall so come', which they applied as follows: 'Now He ascended into heaven from Mount Olivet which overlooks the valley of Josaphat. Therefore He will come to judge in the neighbourhood of that place'. Aquinas, after giving the two sides of this debate, concludes: 'We cannot know with any great certainty the manner in which this Judgement will take place, nor how men will gather together to the place of Judgement; but it may be gathered from Scripture that in all probability He will descend in the neighbourhood of Mount Olivet, even as He ascended from there, so as to show that He who descends is the same as He who ascended.' He points out that a great multitude can be enclosed in a small space. Christ will be raised in the air and will be visible from a great distance.

After the Judgement, men proceed either to Paradise or to Hell. Paradise is the empyrean heaven beyond the stars; and this was originally intended to be the destiny of man even if he had not sinned in Eden. Adam would have been immortal and after a definite time would have been transferred to the blessed life (Part 1, Qu. 97). 'He was not placed from the beginning in the empyrean heaven, but was destined to be transferred thither in the state of his final beatitude' (Part 1, Qu. 102, A. 2). The lost would on the other hand spend eternity in a hell of fire situated in the centre of the earth. Hell would thus be at the central point of the universe. The universe with all its planets and stars would continue for ever, though now they would all be stationary, and their brightness would be increased. This last point is dealt with in Part 3, Question 91, 'Of the quality of the world after the Judgement'; according to Article 3 'the brightness of the heavenly bodies will be increased'. Aquinas inclines to the view that 'man's sin wrought no change upon the state of the universe'. The minishment of light which resulted from the Fall was not a real lessening of light, but a lessening in reference to man's use, 'because after sin man did not receive as much benefit from the light of the heavenly bodies as before'. After the resurrection, however, there will be a real increase in the light of the heavenly bodies. 'After the resurrection . . . when the light of the moon will be increased in very truth, there will be night nowhere on earth, but only in the centre of the earth, where hell will be.'

With regard to the time when the advent might be expected to occur Aquinas has some wise things to say, particularly about those who even in his day were trying to fix dates. His teaching is that the Advent may occur at any time, it may be very near or centuries ahead. He held that first Antichrist would appear, a man in whom evil was to be concentrated; the usual view was that Antichrist would reign for three and a half years (time, times and half a time, as in Daniel). In Question 77 he quotes Augustine's words: 'As to the last age of the human race, which begins from our Lord's coming and lasts until the end of the world, it is uncertain of how many generations it will consist.' After another quotation from Augustine, 'He scatters the fingers of all calculators and bids them to be still', Aquinas continues:

For what He refused to tell the apostles, He will not reveal to others: wherefore all those who have been misled to reckon the aforesaid time have so far proved to be untruthful; for some, as Augustine says, stated that from our Lord's Ascension to His last coming four hundred years would elapse, others five hundred, others one thousand. The falseness of these calculators is evident, as will likewise be the falseness of those who even now cease not to calculate.

OLD AND NEW ASTRONOMY

It is obvious that the teaching of Aquinas is tied up with certain conceptions of the physical universe, conceptions which have long been obsolete. Copernicus, reviving the teaching of Aristarchus, dislodged the earth from the centre of the universe and since then we have arrived at the rather frightening representations of modern astronomy. We are told that the sun, around which the earth and the other planets turn in their elliptical orbits, is one of some thousands of millions of suns which make up the Milky Way; and that the Milky Way itself is one of many millions of nebulae. One writer (M. Davidson, *The Heavens and Faith*) has put the matter in this way. If our Milky Way or Galaxy which is bun-shaped were reduced to a diameter of 1,000 miles, the 80,000 million specks which would move about its centre would each measure a ten-thousandth part of an inch. Our sun would be one of these specks, situated about three hundred miles from the centre of the system. The earth would on this scale measure a millionth of an inch in diameter and would be invisible even with the aid of a powerful microscope. The next great nebula, Andromeda, would be 9,000 miles away, and the most distant one and a half million miles. Actually the Andromeda Nebula is 900,000 light-years away, i.e. light from it, travelling at 186,000 miles per second takes 900,000 years to reach us. The most distant nebula is 1,000 million light-years away. Thus the whole conception of a fixed earth at the centre with all the heavenly bodies revolving around it has completely gone. This does not affect the fundamentals of the Christian faith; great spiritual and divine realities are not affected by material factors; but the old eschatological framework has been broken for ever. We must do in our day what Aquinas did in his—use the best knowledge we have of the nature of the universe and weave it together with the great realities of our faith. Thomas Aquinas himself recognized that even in the scientific teaching which he adopted man was in bulk very small; and his words on this subject are still valid today as we face the same problem in a more acute form. He agrees with an objector that 'man is a very small thing in comparison with the heavenly bodies, which by their huge bulk surpass the size of man almost beyond comparison: in fact the size of the whole earth in comparison with the heaven is as a point compared with a sphere, as astronomers say'. It was on the strength of this that Rabbi Moses had argued that the world was by no means made for man's use and that therefore any renewal of the world spoken of in Scripture must be metaphorical, in the sense that the sun shines brighter to one in joy. 'But this', replies Aquinas,

is not in harmony with the authority and commentaries of holy men. Consequently we must answer this argument by saying that *although the heavenly bodies far surpass the human body, yet the rational soul surpasses the heavenly bodies far more than those surpass the human body.* Hence it is not unreasonable to say that the heavenly bodies were made for man's sake; not, however, as though this were the principal end, since the principal end of all things is God (Part 3, Qu. 91).

CHAPTER 3

NEW TESTAMENT DIFFICULTIES

No DOUBT there are many who would agree that we can hardly accept the teaching of Aquinas today as outlined in the previous chapter, and who would advise a return to the less detailed doctrine of the New Testament. Admittedly, the teaching of the *Summa* is intertwined with the scientific views of its period, many of which are now obsolete. But this does not mean that we cannot return to the more reticent descriptions of the Last Day given in the New Testament.

Those who press us to accept the New Testament teaching as it stands do not appear to have faced the difficulty that an advent in the near future was expected. 'Little children, it is the last hour: and as ye heard that antichrist cometh, even now have there arisen many antichrists; whereby we know that it is the last hour' (1 John 2_{18}). 'But the end of all things is at hand' (1 Peter 4_7). 'For the coming of the Lord is at hand' (James 5_8). There is not much evidence to support the view that our Lord shared this erroneous belief; but it seems that He was either mistaken or misreported in respect of the sayings found in Matthew 16_{28} and Mark 13_{30}: 'There be some of them that stand here, which shall in no wise taste of death, till they see the Son of man coming in his kingdom'; 'This generation shall not pass away, until all these things be accomplished.' Either horn of this dilemma is fatal for those who insist that all we have to do is to accept the New Testament as it stands.

ATTEMPTED SOLUTIONS

All kinds of methods have been employed to circumvent this difficulty. The reference to 'this generation' in Matthew 24_{34} is obviously to a limited period of time, a generation being thirty to fifty years. It is obvious, too, that many of the events spoken of in the chapter were not fulfilled within fifty years of our Lord's death and have not been fulfilled even now, particularly the events in the immediately preceding verses (29–31). One way out of the difficulty is to interpret the word 'generation' (Greek: *genea*) differently. The comment of Bishop Christopher Wordsworth, a Victorian commentator and nephew of the poet, is interesting. The word *genea*, he writes, means one thing in reference to Jerusalem, another in reference to the world at large; the meaning is that 'the spiritual Israel, the generation of them that seek the Lord (Psalm 24₆) would not pass away—i.e. that the faithful seed of Abraham would survive . . . even to the end'. He continues with a point made by Origen; the generation of the Church will survive the world, but all other generations, especially that of the tribes of the earth, will pass away. On the word 'immediately' in verse 29, which places the return of Christ immediately after the tribulation, he says that we must follow not our human reckoning, but that of God to whom a thousand years are as one day. Matthew 16₂₈ he paraphrases as follows: 'Some who are standing here, viz. remain steadfastly by Me, shall not taste of death (cf. John 8₅₂), i.e. shall not feel its bitterness, for I will take away its sting, . . . they will not taste its bitterness until I come again in glory; and they will not taste of that death which alone ought to be called death, viz. "the second death", the death of the soul (Revelation 20₁₄). Thus they will not taste of death till I come. Much less will they taste of it then. They will have fallen asleep in Me, and they will rest in peace in Paradise as to their souls, till I come again in My kingdom.' By this interpretation the saying seems to be robbed of any significance.

Returning to the word 'generation' (Matthew 24₃₄) we may refer to a footnote in the Scofield Bible, an edition of the Bible which is widely read at the present time as millions of copies have been sold this century:

Greek *genea*, the primary definition of which is, 'race, kind, family, stock, breed'. [So all lexicons.] That the word is used in this sense here is sure because none of 'these things', i.e. the world-wide preaching of the kingdom, the great tribulation, the return of the Lord in visible glory, and the regathering of the elect, occurred at the destruction of Jerusalem by Titus, A.D. 70. The promise is, therefore, that the generation—nation, or family of Israel—will be preserved unto 'these things'; a promise wonderfully fulfilled to this day.

The tradition that St John never died is also to be connected with this problem. The end of John 21 appears to betray the perturbation felt when the aged apostle passed away. But as St Augustine tells us, according to one opinion in the early Church the apostle though buried was still alive, and the dust above his tomb at Ephesus could be seen moving for the old man was still breathing below! One is reminded of the legend of Barbarossa asleep in his cave. But the point was that the generation of Christ's disciples had not passed away, and one of 'them that stand here' had not yet tasted of death, since St John was still preserved in this strange fashion—a suggestion that makes little appeal to us today. Arethas mentions the tradition that St John was to live to the end of the world and connects it with the angel's charge in Revelation 10_{11}: 'And they say unto me, Thou must prophesy again.' Hippolytus and Ephraem give the tradition that Enoch, Elijah and St John the theologian are to be the forerunners of the Second Advent.

The legend of the Wandering Jew has been thought to owe its origin to the desire to keep alive someone from the generation of Christ's contemporaries. According to this legend a certain Jew was destined to continue in the world until our Lord's return. This way of solving the difficulty is as precarious as the others mentioned.

A.D. 70

Another traditional way of dealing with this question is to find the fulfilment in the fall of Jerusalem. Gibbon in his *Decline and Fall of the Roman Empire* drew attention to the unfulfilled promises of the New Testament, and numerous replies were forthcoming. J. B. Bury in his well-known edition of Gibbon gives a long list of works which attempted to deal with his chapters on Christianity and some gave particular attention to this question of the delayed Advent. One writer named N. Nisbett wrote a series of works on this point; one of his replies to Gibbon is entitled *Triumphs of Christianity over Infidelity* (1802) and he maintains that Matthew 24 and its parallels refer to no other event than the destruction of Jerusalem in A.D. 70. There is much force in Nisbett's argument in relation to this particular chapter; but the evidence of the epistles is more difficult to account for. Some apologists, as he points out, admitted a mistake on the part of the apostles and were 'not extremely solicitous to relieve them from the accusation of error'. Grotius had said that for wise purposes the pious deception was permitted to take place. Nisbett stresses the importance of allowing for symbolic and pictorial language and much help was found along this line in days before the Synoptic problem had received its generally accepted solution. In the times when such passages as Matthew 24 were regarded as the accurate reporting of a single utterance, there was strong ground for finding the fulfilment in the fall of Jerusalem.

It is of interest that Archdeacon Farrar in his *Early Days of Christianity* (1882) took a similar course. 'It was to this event, the most awful in history . . . that we must apply those prophecies of Christ's coming in which every one of the Apostles and Evangelists describe it as near at hand.' (Among other passages referred to at this point, three from the Gospels are included: Matthew 24_{34}, 16_{28}, 10_{23}.) The fall of Jerusalem and the events which followed in the Roman world and the Church 'had a significance which it is hardly possible to overestimate. They were the final end of the old Dispensation. They were the full inauguration of the New Covenant.' While we can hardly accept this as the true explanation of all the passages concerned, it was probably the best answer that could be found to the problem in the days before the Synoptic theory and Gospel study generally opened up the new ways of explanation which are available to us today.

While some have given too much prominence to the events of A.D. 70, this element should surely hold some place in a discussion of the prophetic teaching of our Lord. Bishop Gore in his *Belief in Christ* maintains that in the so-called 'apocalyptic discourse' Jesus, following the method of the great prophets, pronounces judgement upon one nation and community, but this picture of imminent judgement is thrown upon the screen of the final doom.

It is likely that at least parts of Luke 17 should also be connected with the fall of Jerusalem. It is worth noting that in *The Teaching of the Catholic Church* (ed. G. D. Smith) verses 30–2 are referred to Christ's temporal judgement upon Judaism:

The Temporal severities are announced when Christ speaks of what is manifestly the end of the Jewish people as His 'day', for by 'day' is here meant judgement: 'Even thus shall it be in the day when the Son of man shall be revealed. In that hour, he that shall be on the housetop, and his goods in the house, let him not go down to take them away: and he that shall be in the field, in like manner, let him not turn back. Remember Lot's wife' (p. 1128).

Did not our Lord Himself imply that the fall of Jerusalem would be a kind of divine advent? 'What therefore will the lord of the vineyard do? *he will come* and destroy the husbandman, and will give the vineyard unto others' (Mark 12 ₉).

We shall be wise therefore to notice that the eschatological teaching of the Gospels is not exhausted by one interpretation. This is well brought out in a saying of Augustine (*Epistle* 199):

The signs mentioned in the Gospels do not all refer to the second advent which will happen at the end of the world, but some of them belong to the time of the sack of Jerusalem, which is now a thing of the past, while some, in fact many of them, refer to the advent whereby He comes daily to the Church, whom He visits spiritually when He dwells in us by faith and love.

Allowance is thus made for the element of symbolism (mentioned in Chapter 1) not only in Matthew 24 but in other eschatological passages. The Old Testament descriptions of God riding on the sky belong to the realm of poetry and imagination and this must not be forgotten in reading the New Testament. A good illustration of the Semitic way of putting things is provided by the following epitaph on a rabbi: 'Son of Sion, before this stone weep for the sun buried beneath the dust of the earth; the firmament was clothed with darkness, the constellations were ashamed, the moon blushed; on the day when the glory and crown of the Law was buried.' This means that the death of the rabbi was a very sad event! Remembering such usages it would be possible to take even those phrases which modern critics regard as secondary and to interpret them as a poetical way of setting forth the idea of ultimate triumph.

Not all the aforementioned attempts to deal with this difficult problem can be pronounced successful. Instead of resorting to some of the rather dubious methods referred to, it might have been wiser for Christian apologists to have admitted that they were unable to solve the problem. They had not the appropriate tools, such tools as Synoptic criticism has now placed in our hands. At the same time they had sufficient 'evidences' of other kinds to assure them of the validity of their faith in Christ. This should serve as a lesson to us today. Some of the questions which disturb our faith (difficulties which did not arise in earlier centuries) may find adequate solutions in years to come; and our wisdom is to 'hold fast that which is good' even though we may be unable to give a completely satisfying account of it.

SYNOPTIC CRITICISM

The particular points from modern Gospel study which have a bearing on the subject include the following:

(1) If Matthew and Luke are in many passages dependent on Mark, it is advisable to attach most importance to the Marcan form. This is quite an objective criterion and applies to subjects which have no connexion with eschatology (e.g. Luke $8_{12}{}^{b}$—'that they may not believe and be saved'—is almost certainly a Lucan addition).

(2) The interpretations now attached to parables are regarded by many scholars as expansions of the original words of our Lord; again this view was arrived at without any thought of eschatology.

(3) When we have sayings of Jesus transmitted in two forms, along two lines of tradition, it is helpful to compare them and we shall feel more confident about the common element than about some feature peculiar to one version.

(4) There is also the question of the Little Apocalypse, Mark 13 and its parallels. Even men like Schweitzer, who interpret our Lord's teaching on purely apocalyptic lines, accept the view that this discourse contains matter which Jesus did not utter. The judgement of E. Meyer on this subject may be quoted:

That Jesus, like all the Old Testament prophets, spoke of the future and the approaching dissolution of earthly things and the establishment of the Kingdom of God is not to be doubted . . . but it is unlikely that He surrendered Himself more deeply to the traditional conceptions, or that He occupied Himself with eschatological pictures. The content of Mark 13 gives us the tradition as it took shape in the narrower circle of the leaders of the primitive community, and as it was put in the mouth of their Messiah on the ground of the expectations which they attached to Him. (*Ursprung und Anfänge* I, 129, as rendered in J. M. Creed's commentary on St Luke.)

While Moffatt regarded this theory as fairly settled, there has since been a tendency to reopen the whole question; but even those who regard all or most of the discourse as genuine, would

agree that it is a collection of sayings spoken on different
occasions, so that the total impression is not necessarily in
keeping with the teaching of Christ Himself. T. W. Manson in
The Mission and Message of Jesus (ed. Major) gives a most
valuable study of this problem. He holds that Luke followed a
different version, which was in verse and into which Marcan
extracts were later embedded by the evangelist. It is important
to notice that on this view the coming of the Son of man was
not mentioned in this non-Marcan version; Luke 21_{27} comes
from Mark 13_{26}. For a recent attempt to disengage the
genuine words of Jesus see Vincent Taylor in *Expository Times*,
January 1949, and his *Gospel According to St Mark* (1952).

Most of these points (at least in (1) (3) above) are quite
objective and are simply an appeal to literary evidence. There
is nothing subjective in noting that Matthew tends to modify
or expand Mark's words in an apocalyptic direction. The
tendency might easily have been the other way, reducing the
eschatology; in that case the appropriate conclusion would
have to be drawn.

A strong case can be made for the view that when we apply
these principles to the Gospels, not only do we find a way out of
the serious difficulties of non-fulfilment, but also there emerges
the kind of conclusion briefly summarized in our opening
chapter.

So far we have been speaking of the Gospels and the teaching
of Christ. With regard to the evidence of the epistles, there is
as far as I can see no way of evading the conclusion that the
early Church was mistaken in expecting an early return of
Christ in glory. Whatever interpretation we adopt of the
teaching of our Lord Himself, the fact remains that the New
Testament writers expected some quite literal fulfilment of
their words in the near future. We must frankly recognize
that they were mistaken. The fact that their expectations
were disappointed should make us hesitate in saying that in
the future their prophecies will yet be fulfilled to the letter.
Such a passage as Acts 1_{11} cannot be resolved into symbolism:
'This Jesus, which was received up from you into heaven,
shall so come in like manner as ye beheld him going into
heaven.' This conception belongs to a view of the universe in
which heaven is 'up', a three-story universe. If, however, the
Second Advent means a kind of Ascension in reverse, as in
Acts 1_{11}, it may be asked if the Ascension itself is not involved

in this 'obsolete' view of the universe. And on this point it is
worth noting that the Ascension is not described in Matthew or
John; nor is it in Mark, since our oldest manuscripts of Mark
end at 16$_8$ and several different endings (one of which is
usually printed in our Bibles today as verses 9–20) are found,
each being an attempt to round off the story. The remaining
Gospel is Luke and here it is suprising to find that the Western
text omits the Ascension in Chapter 24—as the Revised Version margin says: 'Some ancient authorities omit "and was
carried up into heaven"'—so that Luke may have originally
written: 'And it came to pass, while he blessed them he parted
from them and they returned to Jerusalem with great joy'
verses 51–2). It is therefore dubious if any of the Gospels
support the idea of a literal Ascension into the sky. In Acts,
Luke may have been following a different tradition from the
one adopted in his Gospel. The spiritual principle behind the
Ascension doctrine is not affected by the discarding of a literal
and visible levitation. The spiritual meaning is concerned with
the great fact that Christ shares the sovereignty and omni-
presence of God. He 'ascended far above all the heavens,
that he might fill all things' (Ephesians 4$_{10}$).

SOME MODERN ATTITUDES

We have in the preceding pages shown the difficulties which
arise if we take the New Testament teaching just as it stands,
and the unsatisfactory nature of some of the attempts made to
circumvent those difficulties. In earlier centuries there was
much force in stressing the symbolic nature of the passages
concerned and in pointing to the significance of the fall of
Jerusalem in A.D. 70. But today our approach to the Gospels
is governed by Synoptic research and as already indicated the
commonly accepted views on this matter enable us to obtain
a much juster appraisal of the Gospel evidence.

Strangely enough, however, a number of scholars whose
approach takes full account of modern Synoptic criticism
nevertheless still maintain that Jesus was mistaken, and that
the hope of an early return in glory played a prominent part
in his outlook and teaching. Guignebert, one of the most radical
of critics, may be referred to at this point. In his book *Jesus*,
while maintaining that the Master did not teach the doctrine
of His own Parousia, he holds that in the thought of Jesus the

kingdom of God in a dramatic and material form would arrive very shortly. When we consider the slender evidence by which this contention is supported, we cannot help feeling somewhat puzzled by the emphatic way in which it is put forward.

The passages which Guignebert relies on to prove that Jesus expected the setting up of the kingdom by divine intervention in the near future are as follows: Mark 9_1, 13_{30}; Matthew 10_{23}. These are quite unable to support the weight of the confident assumption which Guignebert rests upon them. He continues with the surprising statement: 'At all events, it cannot be denied that Jesus believed in the imminence of the Kingdom; his insistent exhortation, "Repent", would alone be sufficient to prove it' (p. 346). He adds two other passages in confirmation, (*a*) Luke 19_{11}, which merely states that they, i.e. either the disciples or the crowd, 'supposed that the kingdom of God was immediatcly to appear', and (*b*) Mark 14_{25}, 'I will no more drink of the fruit of the vine, until that day when I drink it new in the kingdom of God'. Comment is scarcely needed.

It is rather astonishing that so many of our New Testament scholars accept this precarious view, precarious because of the flimsy evidence on which it rests and because of the many indications which point in another direction, particularly the strong and impressive case which Dr C. H. Dodd has presented for 'realized eschatology', the view that Jesus regarded the kingdom as something which had already arrived among men. There are many writers, including some who hold orthodox beliefs about the divinity of Christ, who admit quite frankly that Jesus was mistaken in this matter, but maintain that the admission is not a serious one. All we have to do is to see the spiritual principle behind the belief and translate it into modern terms. Jesus had to put things in the terms of the day in which He lived, and His life was rooted in the historic conditions of that time. Thus Weinel says that our lives today are still limited by death, so that for each of us this is the last generation. The note of urgency found in the teaching of Jesus and expressed in the thought-forms of His time is still relevant. Bultmann suggests that behind the thought of an imminent end of the world was the perfectly sound idea of the challenge and claim of God upon our lives; he imports into the Gospel story his own theology of the Word. C. J. Cadoux perhaps puts things more persuasively in his *Life of Jesus* (pp. 219–20). He too accepts the view that Jesus thought 'that he would within that generation be divinely vindicated by being brought back from the beyond in triumph and great glory'—an event which did not take place. Cadoux continues:

It is, however, important for us to notice that it is only the *form* of His coming triumph which is here in question. The main assurance that some great vindication would come, reversing the shameful repudiation inflicted on Him by the Jews, was a true apprehension of the future. The whole story of the Christian Church from Pentecost onward is the real 'Second Coming' of Jesus. . . . Many different attempts have been made to state what is precisely the element of truth of which (the eschatological teaching of the Gospels) is the true vehicle. I would suggest that this teaching was the form—determined by the conditions, psychological and historical, under which it was delivered—which set forth the convictions, held both by Jesus and His followers, that the truths and values enshrined in His mission and message are of absolute and eternal validity. This surely is the real bearing of the tremendous words, uttered by Him in connexion with these great future events: 'Heaven and earth shall pass away; but my words shall not pass away.'

For myself I find these and similar suggestions unconvincing. It is at all events difficult to find a bridge to orthodoxy from the more extreme apocalyptic interpretation. Let us consider what it means. When Jesus reproached the northern cities for their failure to repent He was, according to the apocalyptic view of Him, admonishing them for their blindness to the signs of the times. There they were, building and marrying and planting, quite impervious to the stupendous fact that they were living in the very last days of the world; a fearful destiny of judgement awaited them for their stupidity. Now if this is a correct reading of the message of Jesus, consider what follows. It means that the lapse of time fully vindicated those Galileans who wisely went on with their regular pursuits and took no notice of this vain announcement. The event proved that they were right and He was wrong; how wise they had been to ignore Him and His threatenings! Today we are not strangers to certain self-accredited prophets who take it upon them to speak in the name of religion and announce that millions now living will never die; most of us feel embarrassed and ashamed that such men should set this forth as the Gospel. Yet can it be after all that Jesus was one of this class? That of

course is how Schweitzer describes Him, and the way in which
his main thesis has been accepted by a number of New Testament scholars is to me astonishing. For my own part I find
it difficult to escape from the conclusion of Dr Inge who, in his
Confessio Fidei (*Outspoken Essays 2*) refers to the view that Jesus
was 'an apocalyptic dreamer whose message consisted essentially of predictions about the catastrophic "end of the age",
predictions which of course came to nothing', and goes on
to define his own position if this should be the true account.
'The figure of Christ as an object of worship would be gone.
We could take no interest in a deluded Jewish peasant, who,
believing that the world was coming to an end, preached only
an *Interimsethik* of no value to a world which had thousands
of years before it.' He feels that on such a foundation he himself would be reduced to the Platonic philosophy. 'But the loss
of the "Divine Word" would be a very heavy deprivation;
and if I felt that I had lost it, I should not think it honest to call
myself any longer a Christian, or to remain in the Christian
ministry.'

Archbishop Temple took a similar attitude. In an early
letter quoted in the biography by Iremonger he wrote: 'You
are right when you say that I do not expect a catastrophic end
of the world (though of course I do not dream of denying its
possibility), but then I am quite convinced that our Lord
Himself did not expect it. I interpret the discourses as referring
partly to the fall of Jerusalem, partly to His own Passion and all
that should flow from it, partly to the eternal significance of any
moral decision. . . . Anyhow, I think our Lord definitely
rejected the Apocalyptic idea of Messiahship. And I if thought
He expected an immediate catastrophe other than His own
Death and Resurrection, I *think* I should have to renounce
Christianity.'

Temple's *Readings in St John's Gospel* show that his thought
on this issue remained fairly constant through the years. In
this work he writes:

In power the Kingdom was established when Christ was lifted up
upon the Cross. From that moment it is true that 'He cometh with
clouds'; that is present fact. He reigns from the Tree. But not all
have eyes to perceive; and the time when 'every eye shall see Him'
is still future, and this is the truth in the expectation of a Return or
Second Coming.

The progress of the Kingdom consists in the uprising within the hearts of men of a love and trust which answer to the Love which shines from the Cross and is, for this world, the glory of God—the shining forth of His very self . . . There remains a final consummation which involves a change in our mortal state and a removal of our present limitations. The Kingdom cannot come in all its perfection in this world (p. xxx).

I may be allowed to mention that it was the interpretation of our Lord's reply to the High Priest found in the writings of William Temple which gave me one of the first impulses to a study of the eschatology of the Gospels. This interpretation is given in one of his earliest writings, his essay in *Foundations*; and many years later he still advocated the same view in his *Readings in St John's Gospel*, one of his last works. The position taken up in the present chapters on the eschatological question is in its approach and conclusions in substantial agreement with his teaching.

As far as the saying before the High Priest is concerned, the view that Jesus was not speaking literally but was referring to some spiritual triumph is not a new one. It was put forward over a century ago, and in more recent times has been supported by Lagrange, Gore, Lowther Clarke, A. M. Hunter, G. S. Duncan, H. D. A. Major, and others. It is generally agreed that the reference is to Daniel 7 and there the coming of the Son of man stands for the emergence to victory of the divine community, just as the coming (verse 3) of the beasts stands for the emergence to world-power of the pagan empires. The language here is obviously symbolic and as Dr C. H. Dodd says: 'We may suppose it was equally symbolic in the mouth of Jesus' (*Companion to the Bible*, ed. T. W. Manson, p. 375).

D

CHAPTER 4

THE BOOK OF REVELATION

AMONG the books of the New Testament, the Apocalypse in particular has exerted a notable influence upon Christian conceptions of the future of history and its climax; and in view of this some special reference to this work is necessary. It is worth noting that from earliest times there has been some hesitation in admitting it as a part of the Christian Scriptures.

While it was accepted fairly early in the West, the Eastern Churches hesitated for centuries. In the time of Eusebius (fourth century) the Greek Church was saturated with prejudice against Revelation on account of its 'Jewish' millenarianism, or chiliasm. At Constantinople its position was in doubt as late as the eleventh century. It never formed part of the Syriac Bible. At the time of the Reformation, Luther placed it with a few other books in a separate division at the end of the Bible. His attitude toward it underwent certain fluctuations but at one time he wrote: 'My spirit cannot acquiesce in the book.' According to the Swiss Reformer Zwingli: 'It is not a book of the Bible.'

Anyone who goes into the question of the numbers of surviving biblical manuscripts can see that Revelation was copied least of all the books of the New Testament. Before the introduction of printing in the fifteenth century it was customary to have one book containing the Gospels, another the epistles of St Paul, another the Acts and General Epistles, and another the Book of Revelation. There are few instances of the whole Bible or New Testament being included in one manuscript. The Gospels quite rightly were copied more frequently than the rest. Half of the surviving New Testament manuscripts are of the Gospels alone. Some works on textual criticism give lists of the available manuscripts and it can be seen from these how few those of Revelation are as compared with those of the Gospels and the other books. The adoption of printing meant that all the books of the Bible (or the New Testament) were included in one volume, although even now it is true that the Gospels have the widest circulation since they are still produced separately, particularly for use on the mission field.

It is noteworthy that in the earlier *Prayer Book* lectionaries of the English Church, Revelation was hardly represented while some books of the Bible were read three times over in the course of a year. The first *Prayer Book* of Edward the Sixth (1549) included two chapters, 1 and 22; but later these were omitted. No doubt the difficulty of the book accounts for this in the main.

It is a striking fact that on account of the position in the Eastern Churches and the attitude of the Reformers, the Book of Revelation has lacked completely universal and unquestioned acceptance during a great part of Christian history. Nevertheless, millions of Christians today regard it as one of the most important of Scriptures and spend a great deal of time and ingenuity in its interpretation.

ITS MESSAGE

There is strong evidence that Revelation should be interpreted in relation to the situation at the time it was written. Its theme was suggested by the conflict between the Church and the Empire. When thus related to its time it is of value as illustrating the invincible faith of the Christians at a crisis when annihilation threatened them. Its sublime imagery and its skilful weaving together of strands taken from many parts of of the Old Testament make it a kind of triumphal finale to the Bible as when a composer gathers up the themes of his symphony in a closing burst of glorious music. We cannot altogether regret its inclusion in the Bible but there are features which tend to underline some of the misgivings mentioned above.

Those who still accept it as the inspired and authoritative word of God and as an infallible chart to the course of history should notice and consider one or two features of this writing. It claims to deal with matters 'which must shortly come to pass' (1_1). As many centuries have passed since it was written, we must surely admit that in this matter it was mistaken. The sublime faith underlying it can help and instruct us today, but as a key to the future it has already been disproved. (See H. A. Guy, *New Testament Doctrine of the 'Last Things'*, 152–3.)

Again, some of its teaching is sub-Christian—its hatred for
Rome, its spirit of vengeance, its gloating over the appalling
sufferings and judgements which await the enemies of the
Church—these things are far removed from the spirit of Christ;
they may be explained but not excused. The influence of these
features has at times been lamentable; good men like Matthew
Henry, who thought Babylon meant the Roman Church,
felt that Chapter 19 called upon Christians to share actively in
military measures against the papal Antichrist. The Christ of
the Gospels is stained with His own blood poured forth in
redemptive sacrifice; the Christ of Revelation 19 is splashed
with the blood of His enemies. Horses drive in pools of pagan
blood (14_{20}). One can understand the outburst of D. H.
Lawrence, who in his last book, *Apocalypse*, wrote that just as
inevitably as Jesus had to have a Judas among His disciples,
so did there have to be a Revelation in the New Testament.
This is going too far; but there is something to be said for the
distinction he makes between the Christianity of Jesus, Paul
and John on the one side and that of John of Patmos on the
other.

We have seen how St Paul's thought developed so that the
fervent apocalypticism of his earliest letters yields more and
more to the great message of a spiritual kingdom centred in the
Cross and the cosmic reconciliation which is to fulfil the divine
purpose. But not all in the early Church were big enough to
keep step with the apostle and the apocalyptic tendency still
flourished, reaching its final expression in Revelation. This
work and Ephesians seem to exhibit two incompatible views.
The striking contrast between them can be shown in the following way. (*a*) In Revelation there is despair of the present;
God's main activity is looked for in the future. Only after a
great cataclysmic judgement and divine intervention can the
Christian hope for the future of the world be fulfilled. At
present the earth holds only the seeds of sin and judgement.
(*b*) According to Ephesians God is even now engaged in working
out His redeeming purpose in the world; the existing community of the Church is a proof of His reconciling grace and
the organ of His activity. One can hardly hesitate in deciding
which of these two is the nobler conception and which is more
in harmony with the character and ways of God as revealed in
Christ.

One element in this book which is of some importance is its

teaching concerning the *Millennium*. Revelation 20 teaches quite plainly that after Christ's return to the earth and the slaughter of His enemies He will reign over the earth for a thousand years. After this Millennium comes the Final Judgement and the eternal state associated with the new heaven and earth. It is still the orthodox Jewish view that the reign of the Messiah will be a literal reign of limited time on the present earth and will precede the final resurrection. This temporary Messianic kingdom is taught in the *Talmud*, where various suggestions as to the length of the period are given. One period suggested is four hundred years and this is the period given in the apocalypse known as 2 Esdras:

For my son shall be revealed with those that be with him, and shall rejoice them that remain four hundred years. After these years shall my son Christ die, and all that have the breath of life. And the world shall be turned into the old silence seven days, like as in the first beginning: so that no man shall remain (7_{28-30}).

It should be noted that in 2 Esdras no resurrection is associated with the beginning of the kingdom period. This absence is normal in all Jewish forms of the temporary Messianic kingdom. The idea that all the saints who have ever lived will rise to share in it is restricted to later Christian millenarianism. The Book of Revelation itself knows nothing of this particular matter; it is martyrs who rise to share in Christ's reign in Chapter 20. Those killed in the great persecution are to rise again and reign with Christ a thousand years. 'The rest of the dead lived not until the thousand years should be finished. This is the first resurrection' (20_5).

Later on this passage was interpreted to mean that all the saints would share in the first resurrection and the millennial reign, saints of the Old Testament as well as all Christians. In the Western Church chiliasm (or belief in the thousand years reign) was a part of the Christian message as expounded by such Fathers as Justin, Tertullian, and Irenaeus. Tertullian, however, believed that the resurrection would take place in stages; some would rise at the beginning of the millennium and would thus have the benefit of the whole period; others would rise at other stages in the course of it, their period of earthly bliss being in proportion to the reward they had merited. Those who had been cleansed by the bloody baptism of martyrdom were to be raised at the beginning (*De Anima*, 58).

Most chiliasts came to believe, as they do today, that all the
saints (B.C. as well as A.D.) would rise at the beginning of the
millennium and would live throughout it upon the earth in
their resurrection bodies. There would also be upon the earth
a number of survivors from the pre-millennial period who
would live on in their natural bodies and these would still
propagate the race. At the same time Christ, it is said, will be
personally and visibly present on the earth throughout the
thousand years. Lactantius (fourth century) said of this period
that 'the nations shall not utterly be destroyed but some of
them shall be left to be triumphed over by the just and subjected to perpetual slavery'. Some of these early chiliasts
applied the prophecies of Isaiah 60_{10-13} and 61_5 quite literally.

It should be noted that these are not matters of merely
antiquarian interest. Many Christians of the present time
share this belief in the millennium. This means that upon the
earth during the thousand years, all the saints who have ever
lived will be present in their resurrection bodies, so that they
will not eat or breed or die. They will be reigning over multitudes of Jews and Gentiles still in their natural bodies, eating,
multiplying, and even dying, though the life-span will be much
longer than at present—it will be exactly as described in
Isaiah 65_{20}: 'There shall be no more thence an infant of days,
nor an old man that hath not filled his days: for the child shall
die an hundred years old, and the sinner being an hundred
years old shall be accursed . . . for as the days of a tree shall be
the days of my people' (v. 22). The same view is advocated
in the Scofield Bible, where Isaiah 65_{18-25} is said to describe
the kingdom-age: 'Longevity is restored, but death, the
"last enemy", (1 Corinthians 15_{26}), is not destroyed till after
Satan's rebellion at the end of the thousand years.' T. Hartley
in a work on the millennium written in 1764 drew a careful
distinction between the risen saints who will have a glorious
body and will not marry (Mark 12_{25}) and those alive at the
beginning of the reign who 'will go on to increase and multiply
according to the order of nature in which they stand'; the
latter die in accordance with Isaiah 65.

The imagination may well reel at the astonishing possibilities
of this conception of a world in which glorified saints of old
time live side by side with ordinary men and women. It should
be stated that according to some interpretations, the saints
rise at the beginning of the millennium but do not receive the

full glory of their resurrection bodies until its close, when they are fitted for the eternal state. This was evidently the view of Lactantius:

When the thousand years shall be completed, the world shall be renewed by God, and the heavens shall be folded together, and the earth shall be changed, and God shall transform men into the similitude of angels, and they shall be white as snow. . . . At the same time shall take place that second and public resurrection of all, in which the unrighteous shall be raised to everlasting punishments (*Divine Institutes*, VII, 26).

We shall return to the subject of the millennium at a later stage. At the moment our concern is with the Book of Revelation.

METHODS OF INTERPRETATION

Most modern authorities, as mentioned earlier, interpret the book in the light of the times in which it was written. Babylon stands for the Roman empire which in the first century began its persecution of the Church and was thus 'drunk with the blood of the saints'. The writer foretells the doom of Rome and although the empire did not fall as speedily as he expected or in the way he described, the fundamental message was ultimately vindicated—the empire did fall and the cause of Christ lived on. Moreover, the great persecutors of the first century, Nero and Domitian, can be identified in these pages. The popular fear that Nero was not finally dead but would return from the East at the head of the Parthians is reflected in one or two passages. There is wide support for the view that the number of the beast, 666 (see Revelation 13_{18}), is to be explained by the name 'Nero Caesar'. At that time each letter of the alphabet stood for a number, just as if 'a' were to equal 1, 'b' to equal 2, and so on up to 'j'$=$10, 'k'$=$20, etc. This is shown here with the English alphabet to illustrate how the Greek and Hebrew alphabets were treated. Thus any name could be turned into a number by calculating the numerical value of each letter. Now if Nero Caesar is written in Hebrew, the numerical value is 666. Thus the number, if this explanation is correct, is in line with other indications in the work.

Once, however, the book is regarded as a chart of the future

extending through centuries of history the way is open for all
kinds of identifications; and with a little ingenuity any period
and any notorious figure can be 'found' in the Book of Revelation in symbolic form. Thus the beast has been identified with
Mohammed, with the Pope or Luther, Napoleon or Hitler, and
with many others. According to Professor G. Salmon, any
name with sufficient ingenuity can be made to yield the
number 666:

There are three rules by the help of which I believe an ingenious
man could find the required sum in any given name. First, if the
proper name by itself will not yield it, add a title; secondly, if the
sum cannot be found in Greek, try Hebrew, or even Latin; thirdly,
do not be too particular about the spelling. The use of a language
different from that to which the name properly belongs allows a good
deal of latitude in the transliteration.

    Tolstoi's famous novel, *War and Peace*, contains an interesting
reference to the number of the beast. On the opening page
we have Anna Scherer's remark that in her belief Napoleon is
Antichrist; and later on the central character of the story,
Pierre, Count Bezukhov, finds that the numerical equivalent of
'L'Empereur Napoleon' (counting in the 'e' of 'Le') is 666.
He reaches this result by equating a, b, c, with 1, 2, 3, and so on;
k, l, m, with 10, 20, 30, until he comes to t=100; then he
continues, u=110, v=120, up to z=160. Pierre discovers that
his own name yields the same result, but this time he has to
omit the 'e' and to write 'L'russe Besuhof'. He draws the
conclusion that he is marked by destiny to set a limit to
Napoleon's power and later plans to kill him. Tolstoi, however,
made a mistake in saying that he was following the Hebrew
method in this numerical scheme—in the Hebrew alphabet
Qoph stands for 100, but the next letter for 200 (not 110), and
the next for 300. Such an alteration of the rules is, however,
characteristic of these attempts.

    Perhaps the best comment on all such efforts is provided by
Macaulay's encounter with someone who also held the view
that Napoleon was the Antichrist:

'Pray, Mr Macaulay, do you not think that Buonaparte was the
Beast?'
    'No, sir, I cannot say that I do.'
    'Sir, he was the Beast. I can prove it. I have found the number
666 in his name. Why, sir, if he was not the Beast, who was?'

This was a puzzling question, and I am not a little vain of my answer. 'Sir,' said I, 'the House of Commons is the Beast. There are 658 members of the House and these with their chief officers— the three clerks, the Sergeant and his deputy, the Chaplain, the doorkeeper and the librarian—make 666.'

'Well, sir, that is strange. But I can assure you that, if you write Napoleon Buonaparte in Arabic, leaving out only two letters, it will give 666.'

'And, pray, sir, what right have you to leave out two letters? And, as St John was writing Greek, and to Greeks, is it not likely that he would use the Greek rather than the Arabic notations?'

'But sir,' said this learned divine, 'everybody knows that the Greek letters were never used to mark numbers.'

I answered with the meekest look and voice possible: 'I do not think that everybody knows that. Indeed I have reason to believe that a different opinion—erroneous no doubt—is universally embraced by all who happen to know any Greek.' So ended the controversy. The man looked at me as if he thought me a very wicked fellow; and, I dare say, has by this time discovered that, if you write my name in Tamil, leaving out T in Thomas, B in Babington, and M in Macaulay, it will give the number of this unfortunate Beast.

Sometimes the significance of the number 666 has been seen in dates rather than names. Thus Innocent the Third (Pope from 1198 to 1216) declared officially that the Saracens were the true Antichrist, and Mohammed the false prophet; their power was to last for 666 years. In summoning Europe to a new crusade he used this interpretation as an incentive, since it suggested that the destined fall of Islam was close at hand.

Among Protestants the association of Antichrist with the Papacy used to be popular. Even centuries before the Reformation this identification was made by the Spiritual Franciscans. Ubertino di Casale demonstrated that the numerical value of the Greek letters *Benedictos* was 666 and therefore the reference to Pope Benedict the Eleventh was clear. Nearer our own time, Sir Isaac Newton, who busied himself with prophetic studies as well as with gravitation and optics identified 'the little horn' with the Pope in his *Observations upon the Prophecies of Daniel*. The reduction of three horns, he maintained, refers to the Pope's acquisition of authority over (*a*) the Exarchate of Ravenna, (*b*) the Lombards, and (*c*) Rome itself. Toward the end of the eighth century, he continues, the Pope emerged in his full character as a horn of the Beast and reigned with a look more stout than his fellows, times and laws being given into his hands.

A brief reference may be made here to the Futurist method of interpreting Revelation. This view has been advocated in modern times by the Plymouth Brethren and others and is adopted in the Scofield Bible. It is contended that the main part of the book, say from Chapter 4 to Chapter 19, speaks of events which still lie entirely in the future; they will take place during the last seven years of the present age and before the millennial reign of Christ.

But it is most difficult to imagine that this can be the true interpretation of the book. As A. S. Peake writes (in his *Revelation of John*, 158–9) concerning this method of exposition: 'Language can hardly express in a more definite or emphatic way the imminence of the events which are predicted. It is this which constitutes the urgency of the author's message. Alike at the opening and close of the book the message is repeated, "The time is at hand", "Behold I come quickly", and the contents of the book are described as "the things which much shortly come to pass".' It is difficult to evade this contention that the Futurist interpretation contradicts the explicit language of the prophecy's opening declaration (1_1) and its placing of the Second Advent in the near future. 'It would also be unparalleled if a prophecy stood so completely out of relation to the age and conditions in which it was uttered. . . . Moreover, the book would on this supposition be almost entirely useless to the Church in its pilgrimage through the centuries.'

CHAPTER 5

THE END IS AT HAND

THE THEORY that the Book of Revelation gives a chart of history in symbolic form has given rise to all kinds of prophecies and attempts to fix dates. Nearly all interpretations of this kind reach the conclusion that the Advent is 'at hand'. Men may be writing in the Middle Ages or the twentieth century or the eighteenth; but the writer always finds himself living in the period of the sixth vial or at some stage just before the end of the age.

Also the view that before the end there is to be a widespread apostasy and the appearance of Antichrist (ideas taken over from the Jews by the Church with little modification) has encouraged this feeling of vivid expectancy. This factor is probably of greater importance than the Book of Revelation itself in the present connexion. What age has not been described by those living in it as an age of apostasy? Such an estimate is a commonplace of the present time.

Those who feel attracted to these speculations should remember that hundreds of years ago precisely the same message was being declared with the same note of certainty. All earlier prophecies of this kind have been disproved by the mere lapse of time. In 1917 a group of English clergymen issued a manifesto expressing their firm conviction that the coming of Christ was at hand. Such messages are no less insistent today. It would be much wiser to follow the guidance of St Thomas Aquinas in his section on the thesis that the time of the Judgement is unknown (*Summa*, III, Qu. 88, A. 3); he refers to St Augustine for confirmation of the view that it is impossible to decide after how long a time it will take place, or fix the month, year, century, or thousand years. Again, he says that the last hour mentioned in scripture, and similar expressions, do not indicate a short length of time but 'signify the last state of the world, which is the last age of all, and it is not stated definitely how long this will last. Thus neither is fixed duration appointed to old age, which is the last age of man, since sometimes it is seen to last as long as or even longer than all the previous ages, as Augustine remarks.'

When a friend of mine puts outside his Church a poster bearing the words, 'The coming of the Lord draweth nigh', he intends the readers to understand that 'nigh' means 'very soon'. But if you point out to him that this quotation from St James was written nineteen centuries ago he will get over the difficulty by saying that a thousand years in God's sight is but as yesterday. But he fails to see that if that was the case in the first century it is equally true today, and 'nigh' must bear the same interpretation now. In God's sight a thousand years is a small period, and so is a million years. If all the confident forecasts of past centuries have proved wrong ought we not to hesitate before we compromise our Gospel by attaching it to forecasts which may be (and almost certainly will be) exploded in a few years?

It would no doubt be possible to provide instances from every century since the first, of prophecies of the imminent 'end of all things'. As Sir Thomas Browne wrote in the seventeenth century: 'That general opinion that the world grows near its end, hath possessed all ages past as nearly as our own.' Instead, however, of taking the trouble of exploring every single century, I will give instances from each period of five hundred years in our era.

THE PERIOD A.D. 1–500

A good illustration for this period is supplied by Montanism, which arose in Phrygia in the middle of the second century. Montanus was associated with two women disciples, Prisca and Maximilla. He claimed to be the mouthpiece of the Paraclete (the Holy Spirit) and foretold the immediate advent of Christ to set up the millennial kingdom. The New Jerusalem, they said, would descend from heaven to Pepuza in Asia Minor. Their excited followers abandoned their possessions, broke off family ties and prepared for the great event.

Tertullian, one of the greatest of the Latin Fathers, became a Montanist and in his most valuable work, *Against Marcion,* betrays here and there his apocalyptic beliefs. Thus in Book III, Chapter 24, he says that the new prophecy (i.e. Montanism) foretells that prior to the manifestation of the New Jerusalem, a picture of it would be revealed to human sight.

'This prophecy has been very lately fulfilled in an expedition to the East' (this would be the campaign of the emperor Severus against the Parthians); 'for it is evident from the testimony of even heathen witnesses, that in Judaea there was suspended in the sky a city early every morning for forty days. As the day advanced, the entire figure of its walls would wane gradually, and sometimes it would vanish instantly.'

Montanism lingered for a considerable time before its final decay. The expectation of an imminent end of the age was, of course, not confined to movements that were out of sympathy with the main body of Catholics. The severely orthodox St Cyprian (third century) wrote: 'The day of pressure is even over our heads, and the consummation of all things and the coming of Antichrist approaches.' Later St Jerome (fourth century) declared: 'He which held or withheld is removed out of the way; is not Antichrist at hand?'

THE PERIOD A.D. 500–1000

A good instance for this period is provided by Gregory the First, the Father of the Medieval Papacy. This was the pope who sent Augustine the monk to England. He became pope in the year 590 and he is generally known as Gregory the Great. In one of his sermons he declared:

Of all the signs described by our Lord as presaging the end of the world, some we see already accomplished; the others we dread as close upon us. For we now see that nation rises against nation, and that they press and weigh upon the land in our own times as never before in the annals of the past. Earthquakes overwhelm countless cities, as we often hear from other parts of the world. Pestilence we endure without interruption. It is true that as yet we do not behold signs in the sun and moon and stars; but that these are not far off we may infer from the changes in the atmosphere.

The calamities of the times, especially the coming of 'the most unspeakable Lombards' convinced Gregory that the end of the world was near.

It is often affirmed that toward the close of the tenth century there was exceptional excitement and widespread panic on account of the belief that the year 1000 would mark the end of the world and the Last Judgement. Something may be said about this, as it is a quite erroneous statement and is still being

repeated. J. H. Robinson has the following reference in his
Readings in European History (Vol. I, page 3):

A distinguished historian of the Church, Cardinal Baronius, writing
about 1600, made the statement, upon very insufficient evidence,
that, as the year 1000 approached, the people of Europe generally
believed that the world was about to come to an end. Robertson, a
very popular Scotch historian of the eighteenth century, repeated the
statement and went on to describe the terrible panic which seized
upon sinful men as the awful year drew on . . . About thirty years
ago [Robinson is writing at the beginning of the present century]
a French scholar pointed out that there was really no adequate
basis for this strange tale.

Although this theory has been repeatedly exploded since
1873, it is still current. Frank Rutter, for example, in his
interesting work *The Poetry of Architecture* maintains that during
the ninth and tenth centuries hardly any building of importance was erected in Italy (apart from Venice) or in Western
Europe; he continues:

This cessation of building was due not so much to the deplorably
chaotic condition of Europe, swept by a tide of barbarian invasions,
as to a firmly held conviction among the Christian peoples that the
world would come to an end in the year 1000. As that dread year
approached there was little disposition to set about erecting struc-
tures which the impending Day of Judgement would render
superfluous.

When the year 1001 came and passed, he says, gradually normal
conditions were restored and the business of building proceeded
as usual. Even the erudite Canon R. H. Charles gives cur-
rency to the same view in his *Studies in the Apocalypse* (p. 14),
where he describes multitudes giving or bequeathing their
possessions to the Church, a religious revival springing up and
Churches filled with ardent worshippers. 'This movement
reached its height about the year 1000.'

There is a good note on this subject in *Histoire des Conciles*,
H. Leclercq's edition of the standard work by C. J. Hefele
(Vol. IV, Part 2, pp. 901–3). This well-documented note on
the supposed agitation about the year 1000 denies that there
was any wide-spread belief in the imminent end of the world.
There is not a single reference, it is maintained, from the period
970–1000 which authorizes us to say that men left their work
and simply awaited the final catastrophe as certain historians

have alleged. Leclercq traces the origin of this legend to an architectural theory advanced in 1633; this explained the abundance of Churches built at the beginning of the eleventh century to the fact that the terrors associated with the year 1000 had passed, and there was a spirit of relief and joy which found expression in beautiful Churches. If, however, these theorists had studied their subject more closely, says Leclercq, they would have noticed that many of these edifices were erected at the very approach of 1000, several of them in 996 and 997! Once invented, the legend was taken up by Robertson, Michelet, and others, who affirmed that in 999 the entire mass of men found themselves in the position of a condemned man who had received his sentence. It is true that certain fanatics in the years 960–70 taught that the world was about to end, but their error was opposed by the Church. We have about a hundred and fifty bulls of the period 970–1000 and they make no reference to such a fear, nor do the records of synods. In 998 the Council of Rome imposed on King Robert a penance of seven years. References in bequests and other documents to the approaching end of the world can be found from the eighth century and after.

The truth seems to be that while certain prophecies of the sort can be traced, they are mostly of the kind that can be paralleled from every period of the Christian era; there was no wide and outstanding expectancy at the end of the tenth century.

THE PERIOD A.D. 1000–1500

We may refer here to Bernard of Cluny and his famous and sublime hymn on Paradise. He lived in the twelfth century and was the son of English parents, but he was born at Morlaix in Brittany and is sometimes known as Bernard of Morlaix. The great poem begins:

> The world is very evil;
> The times are waxing late;
> Be sober and keep vigil,
> The Judge is at the gate:
> The Judge that comes in mercy,
> The Judge that comes with might,
> To terminate the evil,
> To diadem the right.

In the thirteenth century many expected that the year 1260 would be a year of destiny, though there was some difference of opinion as to what exactly would happen then. This date was suggested by the book of Revelation, 11₃: 'And I will give unto my two witnesses, and they shall prophesy a thousand two hundred and three score days, clothed in sackcloth.' Revelation 12₆: 'And the woman fled into the wilderness, where she hath a place prepared of God, that there they may nourish her a thousand two hundred and threescore days.' Some of the Joachites of this period regarded Frederick the Second as Antichrist and expected him to live for seventy years. His death in 1250 came as a rude shock. Salimbene the famous Franciscan chronicler was not the only one whose faith in these prophecies was shaken: 'After the death of the ex-Emperor Frederick, and the passing of the year 1260, then I let that whole doctrine go: and I am purposed to believe no more than I can see.'

Cardinal Jacques de Vitry who also belongs to the thirteenth century looked upon the Franciscan Revival as the last flicker of an expiring world. The Franciscan Order, he wrote, 'has revived religion, which had almost died out in the eventide of a world whose sun is setting, and which is threatened by the coming of the Son of Perdition: in order that it might have new champions against the perilous days of Antichrist, fortifying and propping up the Church' (see G. G. Coulton, *From St Francis to Dante*).

William of Saint Amour, the famous opponent of the Friars, saw in them the 'ungodly men' foretold in the New Testament as a sign of the approaching end of the world. His work, *The Perils of the Last Times*, appeared in the middle of the thirteenth century and affirmed that he and his contemporaries were near the end of the world; the dangers of the last times, heralding the advent of Antichrist, were imminent.

Belief in the imminent advent of Antichrist was as strong in the fifteenth century as in its predecessors (so Lea, *History of the Inquisition*). In 1445, for example, the University of Paris was astonished by a brilliant young Spaniard. The doctors concluded that he must be Antichrist, who according to one theory would be a good Christian up to the age of twenty-eight.

THE PERIOD A.D. 1500 TO THE PRESENT

These speculations continued to flourish after the Reformation and evidence for this period is abundant. It is unnecessary to mention more than one or two examples. We are familiar with those current at the present time.

In the seventeenth century Sir Thomas Browne in his well-known *Religio Medici* affirmed: 'I believe the World grows near its end.' He was aware that a similar view had been held in all previous ages but nevertheless reiterated his belief:

Though the Number of the blessed must be compleat before the World can pass away, yet since the World itself seems in the wane, and we have no such comfortable prognosticks of latter times, since a greater part of time is spun than is yet to come, and the blessed Roll already much replenished; happy are those pieties, which solicitously look about, and hasten to make one of that already much filled and abbreviated List to come.

In the early part of the eighteenth century, William Whiston, the successor of Sir Isaac Newton and Lucasian Professor of Mathematics was, like his predecessor, busying himself with apocalyptic studies. He discovered that some prophecies in Revelation had been fulfilled by Prince Eugene's campaigns. The prince said 'he did not know he had the honour of being known to St John,' but sent Whiston fifteen guineas. Whiston, who was in holy orders, was an Arian and a Millenarian. He attempted to determine the year when the millennium would begin, first fixing upon 1715 and when that passed, on 1734. He himself survived the second date also, and for his next attempt after further study of his prophetic material fastened on 1866, making sure that he would not suffer further disappointment during his life-time.

Reference may next be made to the Millerites of America who arose last century. Their founder William Miller (1782–1849) was born in Massachusetts, U.S.A., and as a young man became interested in Bible study and Adventism. He took the 2,300 days of Daniel 8_{14} to mean so many years; and by taking the year 457 B.C. as his starting-point he reached 1843 as the date of the Second Advent of Christ. His lectures appeared

E

under the title *Evidence from Scripture and History of the Second Coming of Christ about the year* 1843. When this year passed he announced to his disappointed followers that 1844 was the year, the error being due to following Hebrew instead of Roman chronology. 22nd October was declared to be the actual day of the year 1844 when Christ would return. His followers were urged to prepare for this great day. Many left their business and, dressed in white muslin robes, they awaited the event on housetops and hills. Even when this day passed, many remained as his disciples and were known as Millerites or Adventists. Later they divided into four sects, but by far the larger proportion formed the Seventh-day Adventists. They still exist and celebrate Saturday as their sacred day. They are also vegetarians. They have about 200,000 members in the U.S.A. (figure for 1946) and are also represented in other countries.

Other attempts at date-fixing, and confident pronouncements that the Advent was to take place in the near future, will be mentioned in the following chapter.

CONCLUSION

Surely a calm review of the foregoing should make anyone pause before repeating a message which has been disappointed so frequently. It is obvious that in earlier centuries men misconceived the purpose of God; the Christian dispensation was not to last, as they thought, for a short time. Ought not this to prepare us for the possibility of a very long period during which the Gospel will continue to lay claim to every soul of man and to seek the establishment of Christ's dominion over every area of human life? Our wisdom is to recognize frankly that all previous attempts to forecast the future in this way have been discredited, and to admit the likelihood that human history will continue for many thousands of years. The outworking of a divine purpose through the reconciling ministry of the Christian Church demands a long time for its completion. But it is in this conception of divine purpose that we shall find the key to history. The first Christians did not know how vast the world was, how great the task before them.

Further, our whole conception of the universe has changed enormously during modern times. Those who believed that creation was as recent as 4000 B.C. could quite readily expect

the end of human history a few centuries after the Incarnation.
But vast aeons of time which led up to the appearance of man
make it impossible to expect the climax of history in the near
future and open the way to a far more comprehensive and
sublime conception of the purpose of God.

We must take advantage of our growing knowledge of the
universe and of the new light which God has given to us through
the painstaking researches of thinkers and scientists. The
records of geology show that life has been slowly developing
on the earth through countless millions of years. It began in
the sea and only after an enormous period invaded the land.
At length the great saurians developed and for many millions
of years were the dominant type. With a change of climate
their day declined and soon the mammals came to the fore.
Finally the time for mankind arrived; and while his story may
stretch back for 100,000 years, civilization itself is compara-
tively recent since it seems to have begun a few thousand years
ago. In the light of all this, is it credible that at such an early
stage as the present God will wind up the whole story? If
we are almost at the beginning of the story of man, as we are
in terms of the new time-scale, we must adapt ourselves to this
vaster framework. In contrast to the petty apocalyptic schemes,
how much more inspiring is the conception of God, Creator
and Redeemer, working out His purpose with infinite patience
through immense stretches of time and at length calling man
to share His creative work and in Jesus Christ gathering into
a unity all the varied strands of His great plan.

Even two hundred years ago a certain Mr Earbery, who in
1728 translated Thomas Burnet's Latin work on the Resurrection, protested against Burnet's view that the present world
could not last more than a few centuries as its allotted span of
6,000 years was nearly up:

What authority has he for so forward a conjecture? the Earth has
all the signs of Youth and Improvement on its side; there are beds
of minerals in all probability, for 40,000 years more, and the pro-
pagation of mankind is not upon the decay. . . . There have not
been since the Deluge above eighty very moderate generations; yet
near 1700 years ago, the primitive Christians were very warm for
the Day of Judgement; a hasty anticipating these Events has caused
great Mischiefs in the World . . . .

Can we believe God planted the realms of space, with so many
habitable worlds and suns, for so short a time as 6,000 years? Saturn

has made few revolutions since the world was made, and must he be dissolved, burnt, before he has made as many turns as would roast a leg of mutton? This is a very odd scheme of the Creation, and incredible to believe. New Heavens and a new earth in so short a time, is rather a Work of Sport, than the serious operation of divine Wisdom.

CHAPTER 6

FORMS OF ADVENT TEACHING

In this chapter a few different forms of Advent teaching will be mentioned. There are of course very many more which would have to be considered in a complete review of the subject. The following are among those still represented in the world of today.

SWEDENBORG AND THE NEW JERUSALEM CHURCH

One of the most interesting interpretations of the Second Advent is that put forward by the Swedish scientist Emanuel Swedenborg (1688–1772). He claimed to have witnessed the Last Judgement in 1757 and he equated the Second Advent with the new revelation which then came to him. His teaching may be studied in his book, *The True Christian Religion*, published in 1771, particularly in Chapter 14 on 'the consummation of the age, the coming of the Lord, and the new heaven and the new Church'. It is said that since the creation there have been four Churches on the earth corresponding to the four sections of the image in Nebuchadnezzar's dream. The first lasted until the Flood; 'the second Church, which may be called the ancient, was in Asia and part of Africa, and this was brought to its consummation and destruction by idolatries'. The third Church was the Israelitish, and lasted from the promulgation of the decalogue to the Crucifixion. The fourth is the Christian Church, which 'has had two epochs, one extending from the time of the Lord till the council of Nice, and the other from that council to the present time. This latter, however, in its progress, was divided into three branches —the Greek, the Roman Catholic, and the Reformed; nevertheless all these three are called Christian.' Now, he declares, we have reached the last time of the Christian Church; but this night in which former Churches have set is followed by morning, 'and the coming of the Lord is the morning'. Nevertheless this coming is not a coming to destroy the visible

53

heaven and the habitable earth as generally believed; it is a spiritual coming for the sake of separating the evil from the good and that there may be formed from believers a new angelic heaven and a new Church on earth. Then follows the important declaration:

The last judgement took place in the spiritual world in the year 1757. . . . This I solemnly attest, because I saw it with my own eyes, when I was broad awake.

The Lord's sending of His angels to gather together His elect from one end of heaven to the other was fulfilled a few years later when 'the Lord called together His twelve disciples, who followed Him in the world, and the next day He sent them throughout the whole spiritual world to preach the Gospel'; 'this was done on the 19th day of June, in the year 1770'.

Thus the Second Coming of the Lord is a coming not in person but in the word, which is from Him, and is Himself; it is effected by the instrumentality of a man, i.e. Swedenborg himself.

That the Lord manifested Himself before me His servant, that He sent me on this office, and afterward opened the sight of my spirit, and so let me into the spiritual world, permitting me to see the heavens and the hells, and also to converse with angels and spirits and this now continually for many years, I attest in truth.

The prophecy of the new heaven and earth, and the New Jerusalem (Revelation 21), is fulfilled in the New Church. This is the crown of all the Churches which have been until this time on the terrestrial globe. It is the fulfilment of the smiting stone which destroys the image in Daniel 2 and of the Son of man's coming with clouds in Daniel 7. 'This Church is to succeed the Churches which have been extant from the beginning of the world . . . it will endure for ages of ages, and is thus to be the crown of all the Churches that have been before it.'

Swedenborg did not attempt to found a Church himself, but his teaching was spread in this country by two clergymen, T. Hartley and J. Clowes. The first organized congregation met in 1788 and at the present time there are about seventy societies and over 6,000 members. God is identified with 'the Lord and Saviour Jesus Christ in whom is the Divine Trinity of Father, Son, and Holy Spirit'.

The equation of the Advent with spiritual movements is a notable idea and one that we shall encounter again. But it is difficult to take seriously the view that the Last Judgement took place in 1757 and that the New Church is the crown of all the Churches and is the New Jerusalem foretold in scripture. One may admire Swedenborg's work, agree with much of his teaching and accept his sincerity, and at the same time regard this part of his doctrine as mistaken. The sweep of his thought and value of his teaching appear elsewhere than in this particular prophetic announcement. (This, I think, would be the line of my reply to an appreciative discussion of my former book in the *New-Church Magazine*, July–September 1947, and to the question: 'Has Dr Glasson, we wonder, ever heard of the eschatological teachings of Emanuel Swedenborg, or of his claim, that in the truths of which he was the Divinely commissioned revelator, contained in and unfolded in his writings, the predicted Second Coming is an accomplished fact?')

J. N. DARBY AND HIS TEACHING

One form of adventism which is of great importance originated last century with the teaching of J. N. Darby (1800–82), virtually the founder of the Plymouth Brethren. He left the Anglican communion after a curacy at Wicklow in Ireland, and the 'Brethren' associated with him in the south-west of England later gained the adherence of Tregelles the biblical scholar and George Muller, founder of the famous Orphanage. Darby propounded a chiliastic and 'dispensational' scheme which has had an enormous influence outside the Brethren movement as well as within, and is today held by millions of Christians, more particularly in America.

Darby was apparently the first to put forward the conception of 'the Rapture' as an event distinct from Christ's coming to reign. The Second Advent, he taught, is to take place in two stages; first will come the advent described in 1 Thessalonians 4_{14-18}, an event which may take place at any moment and consists in the removal of Christians from the earth together with the resurrected saints of past ages, both groups being 'caught up in the clouds, to meet the Lord in the air'—hence the term Rapture. They will be absent from the earth for at least seven years, and during this period terrible developments will take place on the earth culminating in the battle of

Armageddon. Then Christ will come *with* all His saints (not *for* them as on the former occasion) and after the destruction of His enemies will reign on the earth with His people for a thousand years, just as ordinary Chiliasm has always maintained.

The last seven years of the present age are equivalent to the seventieth week of Daniel 9$_{27}$ and it is at some point previous to this that Christ is to descend, not to the earth, but to the air and all believers, living and departed (including those of the Old Testament), are to be caught up to meet the Lord in the air. The life of humanity meanwhile continues, as already mentioned, and the world becomes increasingly evil now that all the Christians have been taken away. Antichrist moves to complete control over the world and during the last three and a half years of this period the great tribulation takes place leading up to the climax of Armageddon. 'Immediately after the tribulation' (Matthew 24$_{29}$) Christ returns with His saints, defeats Antichrist, and sets up the millennial kingdom. All the promises of God in the Old Testament about the Jewish people will then be fulfilled. In fact it is thought that during the great tribulation some of the Jews will be God's messengers and the Jewish nation as a body will welcome Christ as their Messiah when He returns to reign over them and the whole world from Jerusalem. The Old Testament promises of the Messianic time still await fulfilment. They are not to be spiritualized and applied to the Church; they will be literally fulfilled during the Millennium. In fact, the Church period is regarded as a kind of interlude and is nowhere foretold in the Old Testament; it is a parenthesis lying between the sixty-ninth and seventieth weeks of Daniel 9.

Darby travelled widely for forty years visiting several European countries and crossing America from the Atlantic to the Pacific again and again; Canada and New Zealand also figured in these journeys. The prophetic scheme he advocated has had an enormous influence in the U.S.A. particularly among Fundamentalists. Through such books as W. E. Blackstone's *Jesus is Coming* (of which hundreds of thousands of copies were given away) the new dispensational scheme was widely disseminated. It is adopted in detail in the Scofield Bible and over two million copies of this have been sold; it still commands a vast circulation and is constantly reprinted (published 1909; revised 1917). Scores of Bible Schools and Institutes in the U.S.A. and Canada adhere to Dispensationalism and use the Scofield Bible practically as a text-book. In this country Darby's prophetic scheme has found acceptance among adherents of a number of Churches, including certain Baptists and Evangelical Anglicans. A number of speakers at the Keswick Convention have been Darbyites in their prophetic views. For example, Canon F. J. Horsefield (Hon. Canon of Bristol) in his book *The Return of the King* gives in its main outline the advent doctrine promulgated by Darby and later set forth in the Scofield Bible, which he quotes more than once. 'There is to be an interval', he writes (p. 59), 'between the coming of Christ for His saints, when they will rise to meet Him in the air, and His final return to the earth with them to establish His kingdom.'

J. N. Darby was of course not exclusively concerned with eschatology. His main emphasis and aim were those of evangelical Christianity. But our concern at the moment is with the prophetic views which he originated. It may be said here that the Plymouth Brethren are reputed to number about 80,000 in this country, more than half of them belonging to the Open Brethren; the remainder, the Exclusive Brethren, allow only baptized believers to break bread with them. Baptism by immersion upon profession of faith is the general rule. The movement has no separated ministry. For the various divisions see *History of the Brethren* (N. Noel, 1936). They have done some fine evangelistic and missionary work and are keen readers of the Bible. But as already shown, the influence of Darby's 'Dispensationalism' has extended far beyond the borders of the Brethren. It is only fair to mention that George Muller disagreed with Darby on the matter of the Rapture as did Tregelles also; but most Brethren today follow Darby's scheme of an advent in two stages. Within the general framework, certain variations have appeared; thus some hold that luke-warm Christians will have to remain on the earth for the great tribulation—only the faithful and watchful will 'escape all these things that shall come to pass' and 'stand before the Son of man'.

According to Darby's own account it was 2 Thessalonians 2_{1-2} which about the year 1830 'made me understand the Rapture of the saints before—perhaps a considerable time before—the Day of the Lord (that is, before the judgement of the living)'.

Few people, however, reading the New Testament would imagine that the Second Advent was to take place in two stages, and the idea does not seem to have occurred to anyone during the first eighteen centuries of Christianity.

Dr O. T. Allis in his book *Prophecy and the Church* (1945) has subjected the Darbyite scheme to a searching examination and has given a careful account of its astonishing spread during the past hundred years. The Rev. A. Reese has done the same in *The Approaching Advent of Christ* (1937; a critique written from the pre-millennial standpoint). Both these writers hold very conservative views of biblical inspiration. Allis quotes on his title page the words of Acts 3_{24} and it is difficult to see how the case which he builds up can be answered: 'Yea and all the prophets from Samuel and them that followed after, as many as have spoken, they also told of these days.' Such passages show clearly how opposed to the New Testament is the view that the Church is an interlude and the present age is not foretold in the Old Testament. The New Testament teaches plainly that the Church is now the Israel of God, the representative of 'the people of God'. Hebrews 8 takes Jeremiah's prophecy of the New Covenant (made with Israel) and applies it to the Christian Church; it is now in operation. Surely this indicates the line which should be taken with this whole class of prophecy. The new age which Ezekiel prophesies includes a system of animal sacrifice; the Scofield Bible does not scruple to say that this whole prophecy will be literally fulfilled in the future! To the New Testament writers and to most Christians today the idea of a return to animal sacrifice would be unthinkable. Yet this is to take place, we are told, during the Millennium. This is the kind of insuperable difficulty which arises when we insist on a literal fulfillment of the promises made to the Jews. Paul's teaching is that the distinction between Jew and Gentile is now obsolete and that 'if ye are Christ's, then are ye Abraham's seed, heirs according to promise'.

IRVING AND THE CATHOLIC APOSTOLIC CHURCH

The 'Catholic Apostolic Church' began about the same time as the Plymouth Brethren movement. It grew out of the work of Edward Irving (1792–1834), who before his deposition was a minister of the Church of Scotland. He was a friend of Carlyle and had been Jane Welsh's tutor. His eloquent preaching made a great sensation in London, and in the crowds which flocked to Hatton Garden were many 'society' and 'fashionable' people. Hazlitt devoted a chapter to him in his *Spirit of the Age*. Irving got into trouble for asserting that in the Incarnation our Lord took upon Him 'fallen' human nature, though personally He was a sinless man. (A similar view is apparently advocated by Karl Barth.)

But our interest is with his prophetic teaching. In his book *Babylon and Infidelity Foredoomed* he maintained that 1,260 years is given in scripture as the period of the anti-Christian power. This period began in A.D. 533 when the emperor Justinian in the Pandects gave the Bishop of Rome authority over the Churches, acknowledging the Pope as head of the Church. Since a day in scripture stands for a year, the period of 1,260 days there mentioned brings us to 1793, the year of the French Revolution. It was then that the judgement on Babylon commenced, the first six vials being poured on the Beast during the thirty years, 1793-1823. A second period is now opening, said Irving, to last forty-five years and the seventh vial is about to be poured out. The battle of Armageddon will occur in 1868, Christ will come and the Millennium will begin.

An outbreak of glossolalia, speaking with tongues, became associated with Irving's work and estranged many of his hearers. He did not live many years after his deposition in 1831, and the development of his teaching and the founding of the Catholic Apostolic Church were really the work of his followers. He was related to the movement as a kind of John the Baptist.

A careful and well-documented account may be found in P. E. Shaw's *Catholic Apostolic Church* (1946, New York) from which most of the following details are taken. The followers of Irving appointed new 'apostles', beginning with J. B. Cardale in 1832. Irving himself was not an apostle and it seems that these appointments and developments were taken out of his hands by his enthusiastic disciples. The full college of twelve apostles was not completed until 1835, by which time Irving had died. Among the twelve were S. Perceval, son of a Prime Minister; Dalton and Armstrong, two Church of England clergymen; and Woodhouse, son of the Dean of Lichfield. Various areas of the world were allocated to the apostles for their supervision; thus T. Carlyle (not the famous

Carlyle mentioned above) was connected with the tribe of Simeon, which represented North Germany.

Other ministers were ordained by the apostles, and each local church had an angel or bishop, with elders and deacons. An elaborate ceremonial came into use, with a liturgy compiled from Anglican, Roman, and Greek sources. The fine church in Gordon Square, London, still serves as the headquarters of the movement; and the present membership of the Catholic Apostolic Church is said to be in the region of 15,000.

Irving's expectation of an early end of the age was sustained by his followers. Thus in April 1858, the American Angel's Testimony declared: 'All things indicate that the end of this Dispensation is now nigh at hand. On every side we see the tokens of the breaking-up of all social, political, and ecclesiastical institution.' Apostasy would increase, Antichrist would come; and then would follow 'the hour of temptation which is to come upon all the world to try them that dwell upon the earth'.

Some adjustment of the original prophetic scheme became necessary, particularly when Irving's date for Armageddon, 1868, passed. While the adjustment of dates was not difficult, the rules governing ordination proved more intractable. The last of the twelve Apostles died in 1901, and without Apostles no further ministers can be created. According to Shaw (op. cit., p. 235): 'To all appearances the Church is dying out, and the people are content that it should be so.'

The Catholic Apostolic Church now awaits dissolution within ten years, not because it has no funds . . . nor from lack of devotees, but simply because the belief on which the Church was founded was that the Second Advent was at hand. Twelve Apostles were appointed who alone had the power to ordain, and as the last Apostle died in 1901 all the surviving ministers are either elderly or aged. The youngest in London is 65. The one in charge of the Paddington Catholic Apostolic Church is 89, and one who conducted services in Gordon Square last week—there are still services every day—was 90.

(*Manchester Guardian*, 12th December 1934.)

It may be recalled that the parents of C. F. Andrews, the famous missionary and friend of Gandhi and Tagore, were Irvingites. He gives a vivid sketch of their religious life in the early part of his fine book, *What I owe to Christ.*

BRITISH ISRAELITISM

The British Israelites do not form a separate denomination but consist of members of the main Churches who individually hold the particular views concerned. They maintain that the Anglo-Saxon races are descended from the lost ten tribes of Israel. Like other pre-millenarians they believe in the imminence of Christ's return to reign over the earth for a thousand years. But whereas Plymouth Brethren and others believe in the restoration of the Jewish kingdom, British Israelites hold that Israel is now represented by the British Commonwealth and the United States of America. Our Royal Family is descended from the House of David. God's promises of conquest and expansion for Israel are said to be fulfilled in the British Empire, England being 'the isle beyond the sea' (Jeremiah 25_{22}). This contention is supported by some strange etymology. The word 'Saxons' is derived from 'Isaac's sons'. It has been seriously suggested that the word 'Britain' comes from the Hebrew 'B'rith' (covenant), and Cymru from Omri, the king of Israel.

Jeremiah and Baruch, it is said, went to Egypt taking with them the daughter of Zedekiah, the last Davidic king in Palestine, and the stone on which Jacob slept at Bethel. This is connected with the Irish tradition that a learned prophet, with a princess and a scribe named Brug (=Baruch) arrived in Ireland before 500 B.C. Thence the descent is traced to our royal family. Jacob's stone eventually became the coronation stone and is now in Westminster Abbey. It used to be maintained that Edward the Eighth (one of whose names was David) would be the last British king; no doubt his abdication necessitated some revision in this prophecy—the Advent was evidently not as near as was confidently expected.

The curious thing is that current writings of British Israelites still tell us we are very near the end of the present age. A leaflet now before me, which maintains that 'the origin, growth, destiny, and indestructibility of the Anglo-Saxon-Celtic race has been foretold in innumerable Scriptures', affirms that 'we have now (1949) almost reached the end of this present evil Age, leading on into a new and glorious Age of unbroken peace, known as the "Millennium" embracing Christ's earthly reign, after "Armageddon".'

British Israelites are said to number tens of thousands. The headquarters for this country is the British Israel World Federation, London; and there are also autonomous bodies in the Dominions and the United States.

JEHOVAH'S WITNESSES

This movement, which is also known as Watch Tower Bible and Tract Society, and as International Bible Students' Association, originated in 1872 when a group of 'a few Christian persons' were called together by a Pittsburg draper named C. T. Russell—hence their original name 'Russellites'. A little later he maintained that the Second Advent had occurred in 1874; it was an invisible Advent. The Kingdom of God would be set up on earth in 1914: 'We consider it an established truth that the final end of the kingdoms of this world and the full establishment of the Kingdom of God will be accomplished at the close of A.D. 1914.'

In 1916, two years after the discrediting of his prophecy, Russell died and his place was taken by a lawyer, J. F. Rutherford. 'Judge' Rutherford's attempts at prophecy seem to have been no more successful than his predecessor's. Thus in 1938 in the Albert Hall, London, he foretold the destruction of the British Empire by the Nazis and Fascists. He did not commit himself to explicit dates but popularized the slogan, 'Millions now living will never die', and affirmed that soon God would interpose after a fearful Armageddon and would set up His Kingdom on earth.

The following details are taken from Russell's book *The Divine Plan of the Ages*. The copyright is dated 1889; the particular edition I am using was printed in 1915, completing four and a half million copies. Russell's interpretation of the millennium is of particular interest. All the human beings who have ever lived will rise at the beginning of the millennium. There will be plenty of room for them on the earth. Ireland alone would provide standing room for far more than twice the number of people who have ever lived on the earth. Moreover the desert will then blossom as the rose, so that food supply will be sufficient. (It is worth noting that in Jewish teaching *no* resurrection is associated with the temporary Messianic kingdom; in Revelation 20 *martyrs* rise at the beginning of the millennium; in Christian Chiliasm *all the saints* rise to share in it; Russell widens the circle still further and teaches that all who have ever lived will rise again at the beginning of the millennium.) The millennium will provide a further and final test for men; it was to secure this that Christ died, thus reversing the effect of Adam's sin which brought death upon the world. Those who fail in this second test will die the second death of complete extinction. The rest will pass to heaven at the close of the millennium. This earthly reign of Christ is in effect the Judgement Day; no literal assize is to be expected—Judgement Day is this extended test. This does not mean that everyone will live right through the thousand years. All will have at least one hundred years of trial, but those who by the end of the first century reveal no progress toward perfection will be cut off, in accordance with the prophecy of Isaiah 65_{20}. The trial of the rest will continue for the remaining nine hundred years. The parable of the sheep and the goats (Matthew 25) refers to a Final Judgement at the close of the millennium, by which time two classes will have completely separated, the obedient and the disobedient. The former will receive eternal life and the latter will die the second death of extinction.

The two classes of Old Testament saints and true Christians will have a special position during the millennium. Their first earthly life was a sufficient Judgement Day for them, and they are no longer on trial. They will serve as God's agents in the blessing of the world, giving men instruction and training for their final testing (1 Corinthians 6_2).

The Russellite view of Christ appears to be Arian, and emphasis is given to the description of Christ as 'the beginning of the creation of God' (Revelation 3_{14}, where actually the word means 'origin' and does not imply that Christ is a creature, as the Russellites maintain).

OTHER MOVEMENTS

No attempt at completeness is made in this chapter, but one or two other groups may be mentioned briefly. It will be noticed that in spite of their differences they include, like most of the foregoing, the conception of the millennial reign of Christ.

The *Assemblies of God* originated toward the close of the nineteenth century. The adherents are fundamentalist and hold to the pre-millennial return of Christ; they claim a following of five millions throughout the world.

The *Christadelphians* began in America last century and were originated by John Thomas (1805–71) who had formerly been a Campbellite. The restoration of the Kingdom of Israel in Palestine is looked for, the rebuilding of Jerusalem, and the personal reign of Christ for a thousand years over this restored Kingdom.

The *Four Square Gospel Alliance* began in Ireland in 1915; it is a fundamentalist body, which combines religious healing with its evangelistic work. Again the pre-millennial return of Christ is made prominent. The movement has four hundred branches in the British Isles.

The riot of thought and speculation suggested by the foregoing shows the need for some restatement. It would of course be a mistake to imagine that we can ever again give the detailed answers which Aquinas gave, with all the definiteness of a railway time-table. But we ought to attempt an answer to the plain man who wants to know what a Christian may believe about the course of future history and its climax. It is hardly sufficient merely to state that the Second Advent is a symbol. We should be able to say what it symbolizes. If 1960 is to be succeeded by 1961 and that by 1962, how long is the process to last and how will it all end? Are we simply to go to scientists for the answer they derive from physical studies, or is there some sure guidance from Christian thought?

Before we consider the future course and consummation of history, something must be said on the subject of the Judgement.

F

I cannot dream that there should be at the last day any such Judicial proceeding, or calling to the Bar, as indeed the Scripture seems to imply, and the literal Commentators do conceive; for unspeakable mysteries in the Scriptures are often delivered in a vulgar and illustrative way; and, being written unto man, are delivered, not as they truly are, but as they may be understood; wherein, notwithstanding, the different interpretations according to different capacities may stand firm with our devotion, nor be any way prejudiced to each single edification.

SIR THOMAS BROWNE, Religio Medici

The Last Judgement is not Fable or Allegory, but Vision. Fable or Allegory are a totally distinct and inferior kind of Poetry. Vision or Imagination is a Representation of what Eternally Exists, Really and Unchangeably. Fable or Allegory is Form'd by the daughters of Memory. Imagination is surrounded by the daughters of Inspiration, who in the aggregate are call'd Jerusalem. Fable is allegory, but what Critics call The Fable, is Vision itself. The Hebrew Bible and the Gospel of Jesus are not Allegory, but Eternal Vision or Imagination of All that Exists.

WILLIAM BLAKE

Section B—Judgement and Resurrection

From thence He shall come to judge the quick and the dead

CHAPTER 7

THE TRADITIONAL PICTURE OF JUDGEMENT

THE SISTINE CHAPEL

A GOOD example of the traditional picture is provided by the great fresco, *The Last Judgement*, on the west wall of the Sistine Chapel at Rome. Here Michelangelo has shown Christ as a stern, highly muscular figure, at the very moment of banishing the lost from His presence. Above Him are angels with the instruments of the Passion, the Cross, the column, the crown of thorns, the sponge, and the nails. At the judge's side is the Virgin Mary with averted head; and around Him are the great martyrs, Sebastian with his arrows, Bartholomew with his skin and the knife which flayed him, Lawrence with his gridiron, Catherine with her wheel, and Blaise with his carding-comb. It is as though they are reminding Him to redress their wrongs with a fitting sentence on their torturers. On the left is the line of ascent from the grave, where risen men and women approach to receive their awards of pain or bliss. On the right a confused mass of figures in every conceivable condition of fear and horror descend to Hell. Below, Minos the judge of the underworld awaits them, complete with asses' ears and the features of Messer Biagio da Cesena, the Pope's Chamberlain and the artist's critic. The angels sound their trump of doom and Charon ferries the lost over the stream from which there is no return. With his oar he beats forward the laggards, just as Dante had described him in the *Inferno* (iii):

> Charon, demoniac form,
> With eyes of burning coal collects them all,
> Beckoning, and each that lingers, with his oar
> Strikes.

67

One cannot help agreeing with J. A. Symonds's words on this
great picture: 'We do not hear the still small voice of pathos
and of human hope which thrills through Thomas a Celano's
hymn. . . . The note is one of sustained menace and terror'
(*Life of Michelangelo*, II. 65). True, a cloud of the redeemed
float upward to Paradise, but the whole interest of the work
is centred in the doom of the lost, whose emotions are portrayed
so vividly. It is not likely that the great artist meant us to
accept everything he represented in a literal fashion, any more
than Dante did, the seer and poet whom he followed. But the
actual event was to be something like this, only far more
sublime and terrifying. Earlier masters who had dealt with the
same subject were, like Michelangelo, but following the main
lines of Christian tradition—Giotto, Orcagna, Fra Angelico,
and Signorelli.

THE GREAT ASSIZE

The traditional conception is that all the people who have ever
lived since the days of Adam will rise from their graves and be
assembled in a vast concourse before the Judge; after the
Judgement they will pass to their eternal destiny in Heaven or
Hell. One of the most impressive pictures is to be found in the
Book of Revelation (20_{11-15}), the passage concerning the
Great White Throne. A somewhat similar but more extended
description may be found in 2 Esdras 7:

And the earth shall restore those that are asleep in her, and so shall
the dust those that dwell therein in silence, and the secret places
shall deliver those souls that were committed unto them. And the
Most High shall be revealed upon the seat of judgement, and com-
passion shall pass away, and longsuffering shall be withdrawn:
but judgement only shall remain, truth shall stand, and faith shall
wax strong: and the work shall follow, and the reward shall be
showed, and good deeds shall awake, and wicked deeds shall not
sleep. And the pit of torment shall appear, and over against it shall
be the place of rest: and the furnace of hell shall be showed, and
over against it the paradise of delight. And then shall the Most High
say to the nations that are raised from the dead, See ye and understand whom ye have denied, or whom ye have not served, or whose
commandments ye have despised. Look on this side and on that:
here is delight and rest, and there fire and torments. Thus shall he
speak unto them in the day of judgement: This is a day that hath
neither sun, nor moon, nor stars, neither cloud, nor thunder, nor

lightning, neither wind, nor water, nor air, neither darkness, nor evening, nor morning, neither summer, nor spring, nor heat, nor winter, neither frost, nor cold, nor hail, nor rain, nor dew, neither noon, nor night, nor dawn, neither shining, nor brightness, nor light, save only the splendour of the glory of the Most High, whereby all shall see the things that are set before them: for it shall endure as it were a week of years.

Apart from Revelation 20 the only extended description of the Judgement in the New Testament is Matthew 25_{31-46}. It is not certain that this is a judgement of individuals at the end of time, and there is no conclusive evidence to show that our Lord taught this doctrine of a Great Assize at the world's end. (Even the Scofield Bible describes Matthew 25 as a judgement of nations: 'This judgement is to be distinguished from the judgement of the Great White Throne. Here there is no resurrection; the persons judged are living nations. . . .') Our Lord certainly taught that men were accountable to God; but that His teaching on this subject took the particular form of an assembly of all humanity, quick and dead, before a Great White Throne, has little evidence to support it. He certainly did not hold that men's fates were undecided until the Last Judgement.

The Babylonian Talmud has a judgement scene near the beginning of the tractate Abodah Zarah. It is noteworthy that this is in a sense a judgement of nations. Rome and Persia first claim that they have served Israel, but are condemned; these two are singled out 'because their reign will last till the coming of the Messiah'. Other nations follow making the claim that they have not oppressed Israel. As in 2 Esdras, the Judgement is conducted by God Himself, who takes a scroll of the Law saying: 'Let him who has occupied himself herewith, come and take his reward.'

Attempts have been made to locate the exact spot where the Last Judgement will be held; Jews and Moslems as well as Christians have fixed upon 'the valley of Jehoshaphat' (see Joel 3_2). Without adequate evidence this has been indentified with the valley east of Jerusalem, between the temple mount and the Mount of Olives. The slopes of this valley are covered with thousands of Jewish and Moslem tombs, and burial there is still coveted. According to one account, devout Moslems believe that a pillar already in position on the east of the Haram ash-Sherif at Jerusalem is to be the beginning of the bridge over which all men must pass; it will lead the righteous to Paradise, but the lost will find it so narrow that they will fall off into the fire. It is said that Moslems may be seen early in the morning practising the first steps to Paradise as they stand upon this piece of masonry.

Support for this view was sometimes found in the prophecy of Zechariah 14 $_{3ff}$: 'His feet shall stand in that day upon the Mount of Olives . . . and the Mount of Olives shall cleave in the midst thereof.' Certain Rabbis took this to mean 'that the Resurrection would take place through the cleft in the Mount of Olives, and that the righteous dead who had died outside of Palestine would be moved along underground, and so be able to come up in the proper place' (so K. Lake, *Beginnings of Christianity*, V. 22). This curious idea is referred to in the Babylonian Talmud where the discussion of certain Rabbis is reported as to whether the resurrection would apply to any outside the land of Israel. Jacob, it is said, wished to be buried in Canaan 'because he might possibly be unworthy to roll through the cavities' (*Kethuboth*, 111a).

It is clear that Jewish and Christian doctrines of these subjects are closely interrelated. One or two other accounts of the Great Assize from Christian writers may be mentioned at this point in order to show how the traditional conception has been envisaged. A fairly full description of the Last Judgement may be found in John Bunyan's treatise, *Of the Resurrection of the Dead* (1665). According to his interpretation the good rise and are judged first, then follows the resurrection and judgement of the evil. The saved are assessors during the judgement of the lost. Books and witnesses are referred to at some length, but how far Bunyan accepted the view that each one would be judged in isolation before the assembly is not clear. One eloquent passage from this deeply moving study may be quoted:

Ah, Lord, what a condition will a Christless soul be in at this day! . . . With what shame will that man stand before the judgement-seat of Christ who must have all things he hath done against God, to provoke the eyes of His glory to jealousy, laid open before the whole host of the heavenly train! It would make a man blush to have his pockets searched, for things that are stolen in the midst of a market, especially if he stand upon his reputation and his honour. But thou must have thy heart searched, the bottom of thy heart searched; and that, I say, before thy neighbour whom thou hast wronged, and before the devils whom thou hast served; yea, before God whom thou hast despised, and before the angels, those holy and delicate creatures, whose holy and chaste faces will scarce forbear blushing, while God is making thee vomit up all thou hast swallowed; for God shall bring it out of thy belly (Job 20_{12-15}).

Another treatment of the Last Judgement, almost of the same date as Bunyan's, may be found in the famous *Exposition of the Creed* (1659) by the learned Bishop Pearson of Chester. Under Article 7 ('From thence He shall come to judge the quick and the dead') he asks: 'What may the nature of this judgement be; in what that judicial action doth consist; what he shall then do, when "he cometh to judge".'

While 'the reality of this act doth certainly consist in the final determination and actual disposing of all persons in soul and body to their eternal condition', the admission is made that 'in what manner this shall particularly be performed is not so certain unto us; but, that which is sufficient for us, it is represented under a formal judiciary process.' Five particulars are set out with scriptural proofs:

1. There will be a throne, a tribunal, a judgement-seat. 'In respect then of the Son of man, he shall appear in the proper form and condition of a Judge, sitting upon a throne of judicature.'

2. There is to be a personal appearance of all men before that seat of judicature.

3. When those which are to be judged are brought before the judgement-seat of Christ, all their actions shall appear; he 'will bring to light the hidden things of darkness, and will make manifest the counsels of the hearts' (1 Corinthians 4_5).

4. After the manifestation of all their actions, there followeth a definitive sentence passed upon all their persons, according to those actions, which is the fundamental and essential consideration of this judgement.

5. Lastly, after the promulgation of the sentence, followeth the execution; as it is written, And these shall go away into everlasting punishment; but the righteous into life eternal.

Thus appeareth Christ's majesty, by sitting on the throne; His authority, by convening all before Him; His knowledge and wisdom, by opening all secrets, revealing all actions, discerning all inclinations; His justice, in condemning sinners; His mercy, in absolving believers; His power, in His execution of the sentence.

DIFFICULTIES

Numerous difficulties arise if we attempt to accept with literal exactness this conception of a Great Assize. The question of men's immediate fate after death is involved at the outset. Let us consider this. The purpose of a trial is to elicit the facts, decide upon the measure of guilt or otherwise and pronounce the sentence. If this is the purpose of the Last Judgement it would seem to follow that every man's eternal destiny is undecided until that time.

It can hardly be maintained that everyone is in a state of unconsciousness between his death and the Judgement. This view has been held in some quarters. There is a passage in the Koran which perhaps points in this direction: 'On the day when they shall see it (i.e. the Hour) it shall seem to them as though they had not tarried in the tomb, longer than its evening or its morn' (Sura 79). This seems to imply a state of unconsciousness after death, which shall seem of short duration. The references to 'sleep' in the New Testament are sometimes interpreted in a similar way; and the Last Trump has been associated with the awakening of the dead. But the clear statements of the New Testament are quite inconsistent with the view that the departed are in a state of unconsciousness or that their fate remains undecided until the Last Judgement. Where, we may ask; is St Paul at this moment? Not in unconsciousness awaiting trial. His own hope was that he might depart and be with Christ. Stephen prayed in his dying moments: 'Lord Jesus, receive my spirit.' Surely his prayer was answered. Thousands of others have died in the same confidence. Is it credible that these multitudes who have been with Christ in the beyond, who see no longer as in a mirror, but face to face, are at the end of time to be placed in the dock for their eternal destiny to be decided? Jesus said to the dying thief: 'This day shalt thou be with me in Paradise.' Is this penitent thief, who has already been nineteen centuries in Paradise, to be placed on trial for all his past to be raked over?

The inconsistency we have noted has of course not escaped attention and yet none of the attempts made to smooth over the difficulty can be called successful. In the completed Catholic scheme the problem was solved by postulating two judgements, the Particular Judgement immediately after death and the Last Judgement. This appears to rob the latter entirely of its original meaning, since before it opens everyone's fate is already settled. Dante's carefully graduated realms of Hell, Purgatory, and Heaven, leave no real room for a Final Judgement. Every soul at death goes to its own place, the various terraces and abodes being portioned out with exact discrimination; the temporary pains of Purgatory are adjusted to the precise condition of each soul sent thither. In the *Inferno* Dante employs the classical figure of Minos to act as judge; the number of twists in his tail indicate the particular terrace of Hell to which the soul appearing before him is assigned. In the *Odyssey*, Minos, who is described as the 'glorious son of Zeus wielding golden sceptre, giving sentence from his throne to the dead while they sat and stood around the prince' (Book XI), is regarded as continuing in the beyond his earthly occupation as lawgiver; but later he becomes judge of the underworld, as in Plato and Virgil. Dante borrows this imagery to express the idea of the Particular Judgement at death; but he still retains at the same time the conception of the Last Judgement:

> When shall approach the Hostile Potentate
> Each one shall find again his dismal tomb,
> Shall re-assume his flesh and his own figure,
> Shall hear what through eternity re-echoes.
>
> (*Inferno*, VI.)

The Judgement is important as the time of the resurrection, as a result of which both bliss and pain will be increased. Dante agrees with Augustine's dictum that when the resurrection of the flesh has taken place, both the joys of the good and the torments of the evil will be greater, since the body as well as the soul is now affected. But the Judgement appears to have lost its original meaning as an inquisition into the deeds of individual men. This function is fulfilled by the Particular Judgement, and the two conceptions do not hang well together.

This inconsistency may be illustrated from Shakespeare. Othello says of the dead Desdemona whom he has just strangled: 'She's like a liar gone to burning hell.' If that was so, a Final Judgement to decide her fate would be entirely useless. Yet this same Moor of Venice a little later in the same scene declares, after realizing his wife's innocence:

O ill-starr'd wench,
Pale as thy smock! when we shall meet at compt,
This look of thine will hurl my soul from heaven
And fiends will snatch at it.

Othello expects that he himself will be washed in gulfs of liquid fire, but this apparently is to be the sequel of the Last Judgement—'when we shall meet at compt'—it is then that his fate is to be decided. This is the kind of confusion that runs through Christian language on these subjects.

An old eighteenth-century letter has come to my notice, written by a Mrs Howe to her mother, just before the writer's death. The letter begins, 'I am now taking my final adieu of this world', and ends: 'But in the merits and perfect righteousness of God my Saviour, I hope to appear justified at the supreme tribunal, where I must shortly stand to be judged.' It is clear that the religious consciousness is continually reverting to the conception of a Personal Judgement following death.

PATRISTIC UNCERTAINTY

Although the fully developed Catholic scheme (to which we shall return at a later stage) envisaged two judgements, particular and general, it was some time before this solution was reached. Some of the Fathers denied that the souls of departed Christians were in heaven. The teaching of Tertullian on this point is well summarized by Dr R. E. Roberts in his *Theology of Tertullian*, where it is pointed out that this Father denies that the souls of the faithful mount immediately to heaven at death. This would be to anticipate the resurrection and the day of the Lord. The souls of all pass into the 'lower world' where they remain until the resurrection. But within the lower world there are two sections, one of punishment and one of consolation. Here the soul undergoes some compensatory discipline, thus atoning in some measure for its sins before the resurrection, but without prejudice to the Final Judgement of the resurrection. There is however one exception. The souls of the martyrs pass immediately into Paradise, into the presence of the Lord. 'For no one, on becoming absent from the body, is at once a dweller in the presence of the Lord, except by the prerogative of martyrdom, whereby (the saint) gets at once a lodging in Paradise, not in the lower world' (*De Resurrectione Carnis*, 43).

This explains why St John the Divine saw the souls of the martyrs underneath the altar (Revelation 6₉), and why Perpetua saw only her fellow-martyrs in her vision of Paradise.

Tertullian refers to a lost work, *De Paradiso*, in which he had shown 'that every soul is detained in safe keeping among the inhabitants of the lower world until the day of the Lord'. This lower world is 'a vast deep space in the interior of the earth, and a concealed recess in its very bowels'.

Lactantius, another Latin Father (born about A.D. 250), writes in his *Divine Institutes* (vii): 'Nor, however, let anyone imagine that souls are immediately judged after death. For all are detained in one and a common place of confinement, until the arrival of the time in which the great Judge shall make an investigation of their deserts.'

Later on as we have seen, the view of a Particular Judgement at death became usual. At the same time the conception of a literal 'great assize' was not abandoned, but a new reason for it had to be put forward, different from the original one. It was now a public vindication of the ways of God rather than an investigation of men's deserts. This compromise has never been entirely successful. The same people will at one time refer to the Last Judgement as the time when men's fates are to be decided; at another time they will refer to their departed friends as 'in heaven'. The real trouble behind these uneasy adjustments is that religious thought is habitually so conservative that it abandons outworn views with very great reluctance; and in its acceptance of new truth always tries to find ways of leaving the former framework undisturbed. Even the invention of quite new developments is resorted to if by that means a compromise embracing new and old can be contrived.

CHAPTER 8

HOW THE CONFUSION BEGAN

OLD TESTAMENT ORIGINS

THE IDEA of the 'great assize' has come from the Old Testament 'Day of the Lord', which was originally part of the *national* eschatology before *individual* eschatology emerged.

The Hebrews, as is well known, had for many years no doctrine of a happy future life. Like the Assyrians they believed that the realm of Sheol was under the ground and that when men died, whether they were good or bad, they went to this subterranean cavern where they lived a shadowy life repeating for the most part the kind of activity they had followed on the earth. One of the best descriptions of Sheol is in Isaiah 14$_{9-20}$.

But there was a national eschatology in Israel before a personal one was developed. The Day of the Lord was to be a judgement of the hostile nations and was to inaugurate the reign of God. The enemies of Israel would be destroyed by the power of God and then would follow the Kingdom, God reigning (visibly or otherwise) over His people. This advent of God for judgement was one of the great themes of the prophets.

When the doctrine of personal immortality was developed, this new faith had somehow to be accommodated to the old framework, to the old conceptions of a Judgement Day and its sequel, the kingdom. The result was that the Judgement Day became a judgement of individual men. The righteous dead were to share in the blessings of the eternal kingdom on the renewed earth, and in order to do so they must return to the earth in bodily form—hence the resurrection of the dead. How the Jews arrived at their faith in a blessed immortality is not our immediate concern. Some authorities emphasize the element of personal communion with God; one or two of the Psalmists (49, 73) almost tremble on the verge of this faith that death cannot sever their fellowship with God. Others would derive the new Jewish belief from Zoroastrianism whose eschatology already contained the conceptions of judgement and resurrection. Whatever our choice may be between these

76

and other suggestions, the fact remains that almost from the outset faith in personal immortality was tied up with the earlier belief in the Day of the Lord. In the prophets the divine advent is for the purpose of destroying evil and vindicating righteousness; but in the apocalypses it becomes the Last Judgement, a settling of fate for individuals, not nations—a passing of sentences upon the souls of men, a judgement of quick and dead.

One advantage of this attachment was the merging into one of the corporate hope and the individual hope: the social element in the doctrine of immortality was thus preserved. But there were certain problems left unsolved by this synthesis, indeed provoked by it. What was to happen to the souls of men before the Judgement? The answer was that they were in 'the intermediate state'. Was this then to be the same for all men? It was decided that even there there was a difference between the experiences of the righteous and the evil. But if this were so, it inevitably followed that there must be a judgement or discrimination of some kind to decide upon the character of this intermediate fate. And if there was a judgement of the individual immediately after death, what was the purpose of the Last Judgement? According to Oesterley and Robinson, this inconsistency was present in Zoroastrian teaching. Following Bousset they point out that

in Jewish Eschatology we have two incongruous ideas side by side; there is, *in addition* to the Judgement and the general Resurrection of the dead at the last day, retribution on the individual immediately after death, and therefore before the Resurrection. The idea of a twofold retribution in the Hereafter occurs nowhere else but in Iranian Eschatology.

(*Hebrew Religion*, p. 350.)

There is some uncertainty about the exact details of Zoroastrian eschatology at the period when it may have affected Jewish thought, an uncertainty arising from the dates of the relevant documents. But there is no doubt about the presence of this incongruous element in Jewish teaching. From Judaism it has passed into Christianity and also to Islam.

THE INTERMEDIATE STATE

It will be a help if at this point we look more closely at the subject of the intermediate state. It seems that this whole department of eschatology has come into existence because of the attempt to harmonize two inconsistent ideas. One of the fullest descriptions we have comes from the apocalypse, 2 Esdras (usually included in English editions of the Apocrypha), and the relevant part of Chapter 7 is of such interest that it should by all means be consulted. It begins as follows:

And I answered and said, If I have found grace in thy sight, O Lord, show this also unto thy servant, whether after death, even now when every one of us giveth up his soul, we shall be kept in rest until those times come, in which thou shalt renew the creation, or whether we shall be tormented forthwith.

And he answered me, and said, I will show thee this also; but join not thyself with them that are scorners, nor number thyself with them that are tormented. For thou hast a treasure of good works laid up with the Most High, but it shall not be showed thee until the last times. For concerning death the teaching is: When the determinate sentence hath gone forth from the Most High that a man should die, as the spirit leaveth the body to return again to him who gave it, it adoreth the glory of the Most High first of all. And if it be one of those that have been scorners and have not kept the way of the Most High and that have despised his law, and that hate them that fear God, these spirits shall not enter into habitations, but shall wander and be in torments forthwith, ever grieving and sad, in seven ways. [These seven ways are then described.] . . .

Now this is the order of those who have kept the ways of the Most High, when they shall be separated from the corruptible vessel. . . . First of all they shall see with great joy the glory of him who taketh them up, for they shall have rest in seven orders. [Seven orders are described.]

And I answered and said, Shall time therefore be given unto the souls after they are separated from the bodies, that they may see that whereof thou hast spoken unto me? And he said, Their freedom shall be for seven days, that for seven days they may see the things whereof thou hast been told, and afterwards they shall be gathered together in their habitations.

It is clear from this passage that the intermediate conditions of the lost and the saved were regarded as vastly different; a kind of judgement was the immediate sequel of death and souls knew long before the Last Day on which side of the great divide they stood. The souls of the righteous are here considered as preserved in chambers or habitations until the Judgement. The description of the Judgement in 2 Esdras has been quoted in an earlier chapter. The total impression given is that the soul knows its final destiny soon after death. The lost are virtually in the position of condemned felons awaiting definitive sentence.

The Christian Church did not remain satisfied with the view that all the departed were in Hades until the Judgement. Some have maintained that Paradise (in the promise to the dying thief, Luke 23$_{43}$) and Abraham's bosom (the abode of Lazarus in Luke 16$_{22}$) were actually in Hades, these names referring to one division of the great realm of the dead. According to this view Hades (or Sheol as the Hebrews called it) is divided into two sections, one for the good and the other for the evil. Finally however the Church decided that the saints were already in Heaven, though disembodied. It was intolerable to imagine that the blessed dead were in the shadowy underworld, away from the light and glory of God's presence. Such a belief was indeed difficult to harmonize with the conviction that neither life nor death can sever one's fellowship with God, the very conviction upon which the assurance of immortality is partly based. One statement of the view which finally prevailed is to be found in the words of the Westminster Confession:

The bodies of men after death return to dust, and see corruption; but their souls . . . immediately return to God who gave them. The souls of the righteous, being then made perfect in holiness, are received unto the highest heavens, where they behold the face of God in light and glory, waiting for the full redemption of their bodies.

Roman Catholics would of course modify the phrase 'being then made perfect in holiness', and would interpose the temporary discipline of Purgatory before the actual passage to Heaven, few being ready for the immediate experience of the Beatific Vision. The Catholic scheme can be seen in Dante's *Commedia*, where the lost are already in Hell, and the rest are either in Heaven or else being made fit to enter by means of a temporary sojourn in Purgatory. As souls pass from Purgatory to Heaven they hear the words, 'Come, ye blessed of my Father', from the Judgement passage of Matthew 25.

RESOLVING THE ELEMENTS

Discussion of the Intermediate State has taken us into some strange by-paths. But in the early part of this chapter it was shown that the association of Personal Judgement with the Day of the Lord was originally due to historical circumstances.

The two things have no necessary connexion; and the attempt to hold them together has aroused problems which have never been successfully solved. The idea of combining the Final Judgement of all human souls with the Old Testament Day of the Lord and the divine advent was from the first involved in serious inconsistencies. All the elements which went to the making of this composite picture are true and of permanent value: it is their association together that has not been happily contrived. These elements can still be separated, disentangled. Let us consider these elements. The Day of the Lord included both judgement and deliverance; some prophets emphasized the former and others the latter. The judgement of human souls is really a different subject from the judgement of the nations, as is the resurrection. Then there is also the concept of an end of human history, another factor which the Last Judgement has embraced. There are at least five elements here, and instead of the original synthesis which tended to unite them in an uneasy association we now need a process of analysis. All these conceptions which became linked together, partly by a historical accident, can be preserved to an independent and more developed life.

(1) The original message of a divine judgement upon nations and communities is a profound truth which has no necessary connexion with the others. Was it not Schiller who affirmed that world-history was world-judgement? (*Die Weltgeschichte ist das Weltgericht*). Here is a thoroughly biblical doctrine, the divine judgement which runs through history.

(2) Then there is the judgement of human souls, which logically belongs to the close of each earthly life; and this is where the Catholic doctrine of the Particular Judgement places it. This together with (3) the Resurrection, and (4) the end of human history, will be considered in later chapters.

(5) The Day of the Lord was not only a judgement upon the nations, it was also a deliverance, a divine intervention to establish the rule of righteousness. There are a number of indications in the New Testament that the coming and ministry of our Lord were regarded as initiating this Day of the Lord. Sir George Adam Smith is surely right in linking the prophecies of the advent of God with the Incarnation. He refers to these premonitions of the fact that a Divine Being shall some day dwell among men, and in an interesting passage (*Isaiah*, I. 144) draws out the relation of the anthropomorphism of the Old Testament to the Incarnation. It was in Christ that fulfilment

was found for the instinctive premonition and desire that the Divine should take human form and tabernacle amongst men. Smith is not thinking primarily of our present subject; he is as it were beginning at the other end, but his words are nevertheless relevant for our immediate purpose. (See also II. VIII, 'The Passion of God'.)

According to Luke 4 our Lord Himself read in the synagogue at Nazareth an Old Testament description of the Day of the Lord. It originally spoke of the acceptable year and the day of vengeance (Isaiah 61_{1-2}). Though Jesus omitted the reference to vengeance, He made the claim: 'Today hath this scripture been fulfilled in your ears.' Similarly the healing miracles of Jesus appear to be presented as a fulfilment of Isaiah 35, part of another description of the great divine advent (34–5), whose keynote is given in the words: 'He will come and save you.' The significance of the references to this chapter are well brought out in Hoskyns and Davey's *Riddle of the New Testament.*

'The Lord God will come as a mighty one,' declares Isaiah 40_{10}; but first His way will be prepared by a forerunner spoken of in verse 3, a verse which is quoted in all four Gospels, the forerunner being equated with John the Baptist. The imagery of the Mighty One, here and in Isaiah 49_{24-6}, reappears in the claim of Jesus that the strong man had been bound and therefore his spoils could be divided (Luke 11_{20-2}). Already Satan had fallen from heaven (Luke 10_{18}).

These and similar passages show that in the New Testament the work of Christ is presented as at least one fulfilment of the great Day of the Lord prophecies. This Day had two sides, on the one hand there was the negative element of the overthrow of evil, on the other hand the positive element of superlative blessing. The judgement of God's enemies and the gathering and saving of His people had long been linked together and so in the New Testament we have the great declaration: 'Now is the judgement of this world: now shall the prince of this world be cast out. And I, if I be lifted up from the earth, will draw all men unto myself' (John 12_{31-2}).

> For the end of the world was long ago,
> And all we dwell today
> As children of some second birth,
> Like a strange people left on earth
> After a judgement day.

C. H. Dodd aptly quotes this verse (from Chesterton's *Ballad of the White Horse*) in his *Apostolic Preaching.*

G

This of course does not provide the complete fulfilment. In a sense the Day of the Lord itself has been broken up by the coming of Christ; His advent was the answer to the hope, 'He will come and save you'; but this began a process which is to move forward to final victory, when all things in heaven and earth are reconciled and summed up in Him. During the last war, the occupied nations of Europe looked forward to their deliverance as to a single event; they said in effect: 'The Allies will come and save us.' But D-day came first, and although the leaders were confident of victory from the start, it was a long time before V-day came. The Church today is living between D-day and V-day; we are to look for the growing victory of Christ, or rather the outworking on the earth of a victory already achieved. The Incarnation was God's D-day, His redemptive invasion of the world; and though Christ assures us, 'I have overcome the world'—'the kingdom of God is come upon you' 'I beheld Satan fallen as lightning from heaven', we have not yet reached V-day. Though we see Jesus crowned, 'we see not yet all things subjected to him'; He 'sat down on the right hand of God, from henceforth expecting till his enemies be made the footstool of his feet'. That must be our attitude too, 'henceforth expecting', until 'the kingdom of the world is become the kingdom of our Lord, and of his Christ'. Then the Day of the Lord will be consummated by Christ's final victory.

In regarding the Day of the Lord in this way, and in separating it from the judgement of individual souls, we shall virtually be returning to its original reference in the Old Testament to a victory of righteousness upon the earth. As is pointed out in Hastings's *Dictionary of the Bible* (I. 751) the Old Testament has a Final Judgement, for Israel, or the nations, or the world, 'but for the most part it is a world-judgement which has its scene in this world, a triumph of the kingdom of God in the form of an overthrow of its living adversaries on earth' (S. D. F. Salmond). We shall return to the conception of God's reign on the earth when we consider the Kingdom of Christ in Part Two. Our next concern is to examine more closely the judgement of the souls of men, disengaged from its traditional context. It will transpire that if we place this at the close of each earthly life we shall not be out of harmony with the teaching of our Lord or with Catholic doctrine.

CHAPTER 9

INDIVIDUAL JUDGEMENT

BEFORE we consider the Christian doctrine of the Particular Judgement, it will be of interest to notice that the oldest form which the conception of judgement has taken is that of a judgement after death for the individual. The words of Pascal connect with a very ancient conviction:

I know, O Lord, that at the instant of my death I shall find myself entirely separated from the world, stripped naked of all things, standing alone before Thee, to answer to Thy justice concerning all the motions of my thoughts and spirit. . . .

ANCIENT EGYPT

If we go back to the beliefs of the Egyptians we find there a developed doctrine of Individual Judgement. The involved ritual of the funeral included the placing of a book of instructions in the coffin giving full information to help the soul in its journey and to supply it with the correct answers, a complete word and phrase book, as it were, for use in the new territory. Unfortunately some of the undertakers were dishonest and defective copies of the Book of the Dead with sections missing were not unusual; the purchasers would be taken in by the outward appearance and would be unaware of the fraud practised upon them.

The funeral itself included the embalming process and the details are known with some completeness. A brief description of three processes of varying price is given by Herodotus, Book II. 86ff., written in the fifth century B.C. An excellent modern account may be found in A. W. Shorter's *Everyday Life in Ancient Egypt*. A chisel was forced up the nose and the brains were raked out with a crooked piece of iron, the skull then being rinsed out with drugs. An incision was made in the left flank of the body and another in the diaphragm and the viscera were removed, the heart being left in position. The viscera were placed in four alabaster jars. The body was soaked in a salt

83

bath for several weeks (seventy days, says Herodotus) and all the fat dissolved away. The corpse was then straightened out again and thoroughly dried either by means of a slow fire or the heat of the sun. Next a mixture of resin and natron and animal fat were applied to the body and the cavity was filled with wads of linen. The cranium too was packed with resin-soaked linen and the nostrils plugged. After elaborate bandaging the body was placed in its coffin and provided with a long papyrus roll containing the Book of the Dead already referred to. This included appropriate words to be addressed to Osiris the Judge of the underworld, and the other judges:

Hail to thee! Great god, lord of the Two Truths! . . . I know thee and I know thy name and I know the names of the forty-two gods who are with thee in this Hall. . . . I have brought unto thee righteousness and have driven out evil for thee. I have not done evil to mankind. I have not oppressed my relations. I have not blasphemed a god. I have not defrauded the orphan of his possessions. I have not maligned a servant to his superiors. I have not caused pain . . . hunger . . . weeping. I have done no murder. I am pure!

The soul, it was thought, passed beneath the earth and after going through a number of different portals and chambers came at length to the great Judgement Hall of Osiris, where the judge and his forty-two assessors are to determine the destiny of the dead person. Also present are the jackal-headed god Anubis, and the ibis-headed scribe of the gods, Thoth. The decisive part of the ordeal is the weighing of the heart in the scales, the heart being in one pan and the symbol of Truth, a feather, in the other. If 'weighed in the balances and found wanting', the condemned soul is devoured by the fierce monster Ammut, who is waiting for his prey. If acquitted, the defendant is led to the throne of Osiris by Horus, his son, and rewarded with final bliss. It will be noticed that there appear to be only two destinies, vastly different: no intermediate stages are provided for those who are neither desperately wicked nor completely good. Illustrations of the various stages and scenes of the soul's journey may be conveniently examined in the Egyptian Room at the British Museum.

The main point we note here is that judgement does not take the form of a great assize but is an individual affair, a much more searching experience, immediately following death.

PLATO

For another illustration we turn to the dialogues of the Greek philosopher Plato. In his splendid dialogue the *Gorgias* he draws upon Orphic teaching in building up the myth of judgement with which the dialogue closes, a passage which it is difficult ever to forget once it has been read.

The main thought of the myth, writes A. E. Taylor (*Plato*, 128),

is the impossibility of escaping the scrutiny of the eye of the divine judge. In the old days, men were judged while still in the body, and the stains and sores of the soul often escaped notice, especially when the party to be judged was a great man, who appeared with all the splendours of external pomp and circumstance. To prevent such mistakes, the judgement has now been placed after death, that the soul may appear at the tribunal naked, without the 'tunic' of the body. This ensures that its destiny shall be decided by its worth, not by the station it has held on earth.

We continue with Plato's own words, as placed in the mouth, of Socrates:

Death, as it seems to me, is actually nothing but the disconnexion of two things, the soul and the body, from each other. And so when they are disconnected from one another, each of them keeps its own condition very much as it was when the man was alive, the body having its own nature, with its treatments and experiences all manifest upon it.

If the man had long hair, or broken limbs, stripes and scars, these are all to be seen on his body when he is dead. So it is with the soul.

When a man's soul is stripped bare of the body, all its natural gifts, and the experiences added to that soul as the result of his various pursuits, are manifest in it. So when they have arrived in presence of their judge, they of Asia before Rhadamanthus, these Rhadamanthus sets before him and surveys the soul of each, not knowing whose it is; nay, often when he has laid hold of the Great King or some other prince or potentate, he perceives the utter unhealthiness of his soul, striped all over with the scourge, and a mass of wounds, the work of perjuries and injustice; where every act has left its smirch upon his soul, where all is awry through falsehood and imposture, and nothing straight because of a nurture that knew not truth; or, as the result of an unbridled course of fastidiousness,

insolence, and incontinence, he finds the soul full fraught with dis-
proportion and ugliness. Beholding this he sends it away in dis-
honour straight to the place of custody, where on its arrival it is to
endure the sufferings that are fitting. And it is fitting that every
one under punishment rightly inflicted on him by another, should
either be made better and profit thereby, or serve as an example to
the rest, that others seeing the sufferings he endures may in fear
amend themselves. . . . Now for my part, Callicles, I am convinced
by these accounts, and I consider how I may be able to show my
judge that my soul is in the best of health. So giving the go-by to the
honours that most men seek I shall try, by inquiry into the truth,
to be really good in as high a degree as I am able, both in my life
and, when I come to die, in my death. And I invite all other men
likewise, to the best of my power, and you particularly I invite, to
this life and this contest, which I say is worth all other contests on
this earth. (Jowett's translation.)

Plato did not intend that this and his other 'myths' should be
taken literally; but they did stand for something real, some
thing which could best be expressed in pictorial form.

Similar teaching might be adduced from Zoroastrianism,
Islam, and Judaism; and this, coupled with the extracts
just given from Ancient Egypt and Greece, shows how widespread is the conviction that the human soul is subjected to
some kind of judgement or discrimination immediately after
death. It is not surprising to find that the doctrine of Individual
Judgement has been explicity adopted by Christianity.

CHRISTIAN TEACHING

Catholic doctrine declares that there are two judgements, the
Particular Judgement immediately following the death of the
individual, and the General Judgement at the last day. Pascal
is quite orthodox in the words of his prayer: 'O God, before
whom I shall be obliged to give an exact account of my actions
at the end of my life, and the end of the world. . . .'

St Thomas Aquinas discusses the question, Whether there
will be a General Judgement (Pt. III, Qu. 88. Art. 1), and
mentions these two judgements:

Each man is both an individual person and a part of the whole
human race: wherefore a two-fold judgement is due to him. One,
the Particular Judgement, is that to which he will be subjected after
death, when he will receive according as he hath done in the body,

not indeed entirely, but only in part, since he will receive not in the body but only in the soul. The other judgement will be passed on him as a part of the human race.

This Final Judgement is the time of 'the general separation of the good from the wicked'. Aquinas deals with the objection that the sentence is carried out before judgement is pronounced and replies:

The sentence proper to this General Judgement is the general separation of the good from the wicked, which will not precede this judgement. Yet even now, as regards the particular sentence on each individual, the judgement does not at once take full effect, since even the good will receive an increase of reward after the judgement, both from the added glory of the body and from the completion of the number of the saints.

Another objection points out that 'the reason why certain things are submitted to judgement is that we may come to a decision about them', but according to the Catholic scheme men know their fates before the Last Judgement. To this Aquinas replies:

The General Judgement will regard more directly the generality of men than each individual to be judged. . . . Wherefore although before that judgement each one will be certain of his condemnation or reward, he will not be cognizant of the condemnation or reward of everyone else. Hence the necessity of the General Judgement.

This reply can hardly be regarded as adequate, especially as elsewhere Aquinas teaches that everyone will receive supernatural enlightenment respecting the details of judgement. The real fact of the matter is that the Particular Judgement makes the General Judgement redundant and the retention of the latter seems to be due in part to religious conservatism and also to a desire to accept faithfully every part of scripture in its literal sense. The concept of the Last Judgement has been defended on the ground that it is the time of the Resurrection, and also the time when the righteous judgements of God are made manifest to all. We shall return to these two points later; at the moment we are calling attention to the fact that the Particular Judgement has for centuries been accepted as part of orthodox Christian teaching. According to one tradition it was the office of the archangel Michael to lead each soul from earth to the judgement-seat of Christ.

The conception of an Individual Judgement after death is in harmony with the teaching of our Lord. (1) Mark 12$_{26-7}$ implies that the patriarchs are even now with God; 'for all live unto him' (Luke 20$_{38}$). (2) The rather puzzling passage, Luke 16$_9$, also implies that men pass to their 'dwelling' at death: 'that . . . they may receive you into the eternal habitations' (verse 9). (3) Then in the same chapter there is the parable of Lazarus and Dives which assumes a judgement and separation long before the Last Day (Luke 16$_{19-31}$). (4) There is also the promise to the dying thief: 'Today shalt thou be with me in Paradise' (Luke 23$_{43}$). These passages all assume that men pass to bliss or loss after death.

In the Synoptic Gospels the references to a 'day of judgement' and to Christ as judge appear to be confined to Matthew, and comparison with the other Gospels shows that this evangelist heightened the eschatological element in the teaching of Jesus. This tendency appears also in some of the manuscripts and versions of the Gospels. Thus in Mark 6$_{11}$ the Authorized Version has the words: 'It shall be more tolerable for Sodom and Gomorrha in the day of judgement, than for that city.' These words do not appear in our best manuscripts, and they are omitted in the Revised Version. They do not appear in Wyclif's version or the Rheims version, or the Latin Vulgate which they followed. (The same applies to the phrase 'when the Son of man shall come', in Matthew 25$_{13}$, which is in the Authorized Version, but missing from the Revised, Vulgate, Wyclif, Rheims and the best manuscripts.) Another interesting passage is Matthew 12$_{41-2}$, which speaks of the men of Nineveh and the queen of Sheba rising up in the judgement with that generation. It is said by some authorities that the phrase, 'to rise in judgement', simply means 'to accuse' as in Isaiah 54$_{17}$: 'No weapon that is formed against thee shall prosper; and every tongue that shall rise against thee in judgement thou shalt condemn.' The original meaning may have been somewhat as follows: The men of Nineveh are your accusers; their ready response to Jonah is an indictment of your indifference; the contrast accuses and condemns you. No 'day' is mentioned in the Greek, but Tyndale translated the passage: 'shall rise at the day of judgement'. The French version of Ostervald also had 'at the day of judgement' and Luther's German 'at the Last Judgement'. In view of these examples, it is not surprising that in the Gospels themselves there are passages which show the same tendency to give greater definition to our Lord's eschatological teaching.

It is important to notice that Matthew often modifies the language of Mark in the direction of his own apocalyptic interests. This should lead us to examine with great care matter peculiar to the first Gospel. Dr T. W. Manson, one of our leading New Testament scholars and a writer of sober judgement, in his book *The Teaching of Jesus* declares that M (i.e. the supposed source of matter peculiar to Matthew) 'is a source which must be used with the utmost caution' (p. 37). It is inconceivable, he says, that the same person could say both Mark 7_9 and Matthew 23_{2-3}. 'On the whole, the testimony of M must be regarded as inferior in value to that of Mark and Q and can only be admitted after the strictest examination.'

Quite apart from this, the interpretation of our Lord's teaching on judgement must allow for the element of symbolism while holding fast to the undoubted importance He attached to man's accountability to God. The fact of judgement is not in dispute; but whether the teaching of Jesus necessarily carries with it the traditional picture is another question. Karl Adam discusses the matter in his *Spirit of Catholicism*:

But it is a far harder matter to determine from the Gospels His exact conception of the coming of the Last Day. Did He conceive it as an abrupt and catastrophic event, or as the gradual development of divine destructive forces which effected the Judgement in their process? . . . The great separation of spirits, the judgement of the world, had already begun in His Person. . . . He necessarily regarded all the events that depended on His Person as particular moments of the General Judgement which was fundamentally and practically inaugurated with His Person. (Dom J. McCann's translation.)

This thought of a present judgement is one which St John's Gospel emphasizes. Here and there are references to the traditional eschatology of 'the last day' but the main emphasis is on a present judgement. 'He that believeth on him is not judged; he that believeth not hath been judged already . . . this is the judgement that the light is come into the world, and men loved the darkness rather than the light' (3_{18-19}). See also 5_{24}; and 9_{39}: 'For judgement came I into this world.' Men pass judgement upon themselves by their attitude to Him.

THE MODE OF JUDGEMENT

If men virtually pass judgement upon themselves by their response to the divine approach during their lives, does it not follow that at death men continue in that spiritual condition which their lives have created? Those who have lived in fellowship with God continue in that relationship, and those who have turned their backs upon Him continue in that outer darkness they have made for themselves. This has suggested to some that the Particular Judgement is almost an 'automatic' process. Without anything corresponding to a judicial inquiry, the realities of the situation are self-registering: the soul finds its level, as it were, and goes to its own place (cf. Acts 1$_{25}$). This is the kind of judgement that is suggested in Plato's *Laws*, Book X, where it is shown that the regulation of human destiny does not involve endless interference with the machinery of things. 'The result', (as A. E. Taylor summarizes the argument, *Plato*, p. 493) 'is secured from the first by a law of singular simplicity, the law that "like finds its like", souls, like liquids, "find their level". A man "gravitates" toward the society of his mental and moral likes. . . .'

O lad, that think yourself forgotten by the gods, know that as you become more evil, you join the company of more evil souls, and as you become better, the company of better; and that both in life and in all that follows death you will do and suffer exactly as it is meet you should, like going to like. For this is a divine judgement which neither you nor any other luckless lad will ever boast of having escaped.
(Plato's *Laws*, as rendered in J. Baillie's *And the Life Everlasting*.)

It is interesting to find the same conception in St Thomas Aquinas in connexion with the Particular Judgement:

Even as in bodies there is gravity or levity whereby they are borne to their own place which is the end of their movement, so in souls there is merit or demerit whereby they reach their reward or punishment, which are the ends of their deeds. . . . Since a place is assigned to souls in keeping with their reward or punishment, as soon as the soul is set free from the body it is either plunged into hell or soars to heaven, unless it be held back by some debt, for which its flight must needs be delayed until the soul is first of all cleansed.

It may seem irreverent to attempt to pry into the details of the Particular Judgement; but the prevailing Christian belief has not been satisfied merely with a judgement that is automatic and self-registering. The bringing of the soul in some way into the presence of God has also been included as an essential element. G. A. Studdert Kennedy in his poem, *Well?*, gives a helpful interpretation in the form of a soldier's dream. The soldier imagines he has died and he finds himself in the presence of Christ and under His searching scrutiny. 'There ain't no throne, and there ain't no books, It's 'Im you've got to see.' The poem is well worth reading, in spite of the Cockney dialect. Kennedy expressed the same ideas in more normal diction in another poem entitled *Judgement*. Both poems may be found in the volume *The Unutterable Beauty*.

For a classic statement on this subject we should perhaps turn not to the direct prose of theology but to the realm of reverent imagination as expressed in religious verse. Probably the best known presentation of the Particular Judgement occurs in J. H. Newman's *Dream of Gerontius*; and even those who cannot subscribe to a doctrine of Purgatory in its Roman form will nevertheless find themselves in sympathy with the spirit of this great work. In Part I Gerontius dies and Part II gives his experiences immediately after. He finds himself in the company of his guardian angel and says to him:

> I ever had believed
> That on the moment when the struggling soul
> Quitted its mortal case, forthwith it fell
> Under the awful Presence of its God,
> There to be judged and sent to its own place.
> What lets me now from going to my Lord?

ANGEL   Thou art not let; but with extremest speed
> Art hurrying to the Just and Holy Judge.

SOUL   Dear Angel, say,
> Why have I now no fear of meeting Him?
> Along my earthly life, the thought of death
> And judgement was to me most terrible.

ANGEL   It is because
> Then thou didst fear, that now thou dost not fear.
> Thou hast forestalled the agony, and so
> For thee the bitterness of death is passed.
> Also, because already in thy soul
> The judgement is begun.

>   . . . We are now arrived
> Close on the judgement-court; that sullen howl
> Is from the demons who assemble there.
> [The words of the demons follow]

SOUL: I see not those false spirits; shall I see
> My dearest Master, when I reach His throne?

ANGEL: Yes—for one moment thou shalt see thy Lord.
> One moment; but thou knowest not, my child,
> What thou dost ask: that sight of the Most Fair
> Will gladden thee, but it will pierce thee too.

Later, after the singing of the hymn, 'Praise to the holiest in the height', the Angel continues:

> Thy judgement now is near, for we are come
> Into the veiled presence of our God. . . .

SOUL: I go before my Judge. . . .

VOICES ON EARTH: Be merciful, be gracious; spare him, Lord.
>   Be merciful, be gracious; Lord, deliver him.

ANGEL: . . . Praise to His Name!
> O happy, suffering soul! for it is safe,
> Consumed, yet quickened, by the glance of God.

SOUL: Take me away, and in the lowest deep
>   There let me be,
> And there in hope the lone night-watches keep,
>   Told out for me

>   . . . . .

>   Take me away,
> That sooner I may rise, and go above,
> And see Him in the truth of everlasting day.

CHAPTER 10

DIFFICULTIES OF PROCEDURE AND PURPOSE

PROBLEMS OF PROCEDURE

Anyone who thoughtfully examines the traditional picture of the Last Judgement must be conscious of the grave difficulties which the conception involves. It should be noticed that centuries ago Christian thinkers like Augustine and Aquinas saw that a literal trial with witnesses, records, and defence, was impossible and that much of the traditional imagery which popular belief accepted rather unthinkingly as literal must be regarded as symbolic. They nevertheless retained the general idea of a literal resurrection and an assembling together of all who had ever lived. But if we carry further the process which they themselves encouraged, we shall see that this literal gathering of an enormous crowd on some spot on the earth or in the air cannot and need not be retained.

Let us consider one or two of their statements. Augustine in his *City of God* refers to the Book of the Judgement (Revelation 20):

If we should imagine this to be an earthly book, such as ours are, who is he that could imagine how huge a volume it were, or how long the contents of it all would be a-reading? Shall there be as many angels as men, and each one recite his deeds that were committed to his ward? then shall there not be one book for all, but each one shall have one. Aye, but the Scripture here mentions but one in this kind; it is therefore some divine power infused into the consciences of each individual, calling all their works (wonderfully and strangely) unto memory, and so making each man's knowledge accuse or excuse his own conscience; these are all, and singular, judged in themselves. This power divine is called a book, and fitly, for therein is read all the deeds that the doer has committed, by the working of this he remembers all (20_{14}).

This interpretation of the Book of the Judgement was taken up by later writers, and it came to be believed that men would by divine power be able to read not only the record of their own conscience but those of their fellows too. Thus Peter Lombard said in his famous *Sentences* that the books are the consciences of individual men, each of which will then be opened to the others. Aquinas declared that after the resurrection everyone will know what sins he has committed for 'each man's conscience will be as a book containing his deeds on which judgement will be pronounced, even as in the human court of law we make use of records' (*Summa*, III, suppl., Qu. 87). Article 2 under the same question maintains that everyone will read all that is in another's conscience:

As each one will recall his own merits or demerits, so will he be cognizant of those of others. This is the more probable and more common opinion, although the Master (i.e. Peter Lombard) says the contrary, namely that a man's sins blotted out by repentance will not be made known to others at the judgement. But it would follow from this that neither would his repentance for these sins be perfectly known, which would detract considerably from the glory of the saints and the praise due to God for having so mercifully delivered them.

Article 3 discusses 'Whether all merits and demerits, one's own as well as those of others, will be seen by anyone at a single glance?' and reference is made to Augustine's opinion that it is unfitting that at the Judgement a material book should be read. 'The blessed', says Aquinas, 'will see all merits and demerits at the same time in an instant; . . . since they will see all things in the Word.' The damned will not see all instantaneously, 'but in a very short time, the Divine power coming to their aid'.

It is interesting to note how ancient is this way of explaining the Judgement-book; many people regard it as a modern interpretation, as did De Quincey in a passage concerning a relative who was nearly drowned:

She saw in a moment her whole life, in its minutest incidents, arrayed before her simultaneously as in a mirror; and she had a faculty developed as suddenly for comprehending the whole and every part. This, from some opium experiences of mine, I can believe; I have, indeed, seen the same thing asserted twice in modern books, and accompanied by a remark which I am convinced is true—viz. that the dread book of account, which the Scriptures speak of, is, in fact, the mind itself of each individual . . . there is no such thing as forgetting possible to the mind.

Aquinas discusses the question 'whether the judgement will take place by word of mouth' (Qu. 88, Art. 2), and while he does not make a definite pronouncement he thinks it the more probable opinion

that the whole of this judgement, whether as regards the inquiry, or as regards the accusation of the wicked and the approval of the good, or again as regards the sentence on both, will take place mentally. For if the deeds of each individual were to be related by word of mouth, this would require an inconceivable length of time . . . probably we should understand that the details set forth in Matthew 25 will be fulfilled not by word of mouth but mentally.

Anyone who wishes to press the judgement literally and to maintain that everyone will have to stand alone before the throne in the view of all mankind, should note St Thomas's point about the 'inconceivable length of time'. When we recall that many thousands die every day (probably more than 100,000, more than one per second), it will be obvious that a merely summary treatment which allowed only a few minutes to each life would involve a Judgement Day lasting many times longer than the whole span of human history. John Wesley in his sermon on the Great Assize makes the admission that the Judgement may last thousands of years. This is inevitable if we think of each individual standing before the judgement-seat and giving an account of himself to God.

THE PURPOSE OF JUDGEMENT DAY

Aquinas is surely right in saying that the judgement must be conducted mentally and not by word of mouth. But if so much is admitted is not the main purpose of an assembly of humanity surrendered? Men are assembled that they may hear or see simultaneously. If the judgement is a mental process the point of assembling them is lost. If each mind is supernaturally enlightened, either in a moment (as with the blessed) or in a short space of time (as with the lost), this enlightenment could take place without any assembling of the whole race together in physical contiguity—either in the valley of Jehoshaphat or anywhere else. If the facts are imparted mentally there is no need to assemble men to hear an audible pronouncement. Of course Thomas's conception included resurrection as well as judgement; and in a sense the giving of the resurrection body to all men naturally coheres with the idea of a vast assembly before the great divide. And if the bodies of men are to arise from their graves, then naturally they will find themselves standing on the earth. We shall look at the conception of resurrection more closely in the next chapter. What we believe about the character of the resurrection will affect our beliefs concerning the Last Judgement.

Aquinas is quite conscious of the difficulty that men know their fates beforehand; and he quotes the objection (*Summa*, III, Qu. 89) that 'what is certain is not submitted to judgement'; why then are the saved to be judged? He replies:

The merits of the elect will be discussed, not to remove the uncertainty of their beatitude from the hearts of those who are to be judged, but that it may be made manifest to us that their good merits outweigh their evil merits, and thus God's justice be proved.

This reference to God's justice is an important element; and those who recognize that the Particular Judgement appears to make the General Judgement unnecessary have usually defended the latter by saying that then the righteous judgements of God will be made manifest to all. If this is the case, the term 'judgement' would seem to be a misnomer. The purpose of a judgement is to elicit the facts and decide the sentence, and all this is covered by the Particular Judgement. The Last Judgement would then be more in the nature of a public pronouncement. And as we have already seen, if the information about God's judgements is to be conveyed mentally and in a very short time (and in some cases instantaneously) this could be done without any assembling together of the whole race. Again, do we really need to be satisfied not only concerning our own fate, but also that of all our fellow human beings? Is this the only way in which we can be assured that the Judge of all the earth will do right? Is it conceivable or likely that we shall in an instant not only read our own conscience as a book but also those of all the billions of saints and sinners who have ever lived?

For many years Christian thinkers have been conscious of these and similar difficulties and it is not an innovation to suggest that the whole conception of the Final Judgement should be regarded as an important symbol and not as a literal event at the close of history. Professor W. Newton Clarke, the American theologian, was by no means an extremist or a heretic and his *Outline of Christian Theology* written in 1894 was highly esteemed on both sides of the Atlantic. Some words of his on this subject are worth recalling at this point. After referring to the Particular Judgement he continues (p. 463):

No one can doubt that in this judgement at death the immediate and principal end in view in judgement is accomplished.

It is commonly held by Christians that another judgement will occur at the end of the earthly career of the human race; that all who have ever lived will then be assembled, that the entire life of each with all its secrets will be made known to all, and that each will then receive the final sentence, which the revelations of that day will justify in the eyes of all as perfectly righteous. To all but the latest generation this will of course be virtually a repetition of the divine judgement by which destiny was assigned at death; but it will be followed by the completing of the destiny of good or evil that was then entered upon. The special end in view in this universal and simultaneous judgement is held to be the exhibition of God's righteousness, and the vindication of his government as just. God's providential government has been mysterious to men— visible justice has not always been done, and the natural questions of men have been left unanswered; but now at the end God will assemble all his human creatures, and exhibit to them the grounds of all his judgements, in order to vindicate himself as the righteous Lord.

No Scripture is quoted in support of this view of the purpose of Final Judgement. The coming Judgement that is known to Scripture is intended for the assignment of destiny to men; there is no hint that it is intended for vindication of God. . . . God's ordinary method is to allow his action to vindicate its own rightness, and meanwhile to expect his creatures to trust him. This method of faith is the spiritual method, and is morally superior to the method of sight, or definite explanation.

In recent years it has become fairly widely recognized that the traditional conception of the Last Judgement cannot be sustained in its literal sense. Even so anti-liberal a writer as R. Niebuhr, in his *Nature and Destiny of Man* (II. 52) declares that in reinterpreting the New Testament ideas of the Advent, the Resurrection, the Judgement, 'it is important to take biblical symbols seriously but not literally'. A conclusion of this kind is really carrying further the process which Augustine and Aquinas encouraged and the tendencies they followed. We have seen how, in the *Summa*, the various elements of the Great Assize are spiritualized and the Judgement itself is

H

regarded as conducted mentally and in a short space of time—the minds of all men being assisted by divine power to apprehend all the relevant facts concerning themselves and their fellows. It was Aquinas' attitude to the Bible which in part compelled him to retain the conception of a General Judgement, even when on account of the Particular Judgement and the other matters mentioned he was unable to give an adequate account of its purpose. Our attitude to the Bible today does not place us under the same compulsion. It must also be remembered that the Last Judgement was regarded as essential because of its close connexion with the Resurrection and the end of human history, two matters to which we still have to turn.

OTHER DIFFICULTIES

The traditional conception of the judgement makes an enormous cleavage between the saved and the lost. In some interpretations the contrast is so depicted that human life resembles a kind of fantastic Oriental fairy-story in which the central figure either marries a beautiful and wealthy princess or is condemned to fearful penalties and mutilations. It has often been felt that men as we know them do not readily fall into two categories so different as to make such violently contrasted fates appropriate. It is true that the Particular Judgement in its usual form retains this dichotomy and something further must be said on this point.

This fearful and irrevocable alternative facing the soul has fostered terror rather than penitence and an over-emphasis of the Judgement has at times encouraged sub-Christian conceptions of God presenting Him not as our Father but as the super-inquisitor. There was some warrant for Gibbon's scornful words about those who regard God as a jailor and men as convicts. The more spiritual interpretation of judgement traced in earlier pages does suggest an answer to these problems. We are not to think of God passing sentences as though He resembled some assize judge with his carefully calculated list of appropriate penalties, but rather of the actual condition of the soul, the sentence we have as it were passed upon ourselves by our attitude and response to Him. As Origen said, 'each sinner himself lights the flame of his own fire.' No divine interposition is needed to set in operation the law that a man reaps what he has sown. The emphasis of the New Testament is upon the divine grace which breaks in upon this hopeless sequence of cause and effect.

To inquire if and how the divine grace operates in the beyond would take us outside the limits of our present subject. But it may be said here that if God desires the salvation of every soul He has made, it is scarcely credible that the accident of death changes His attitude to His children. Does the Good Shepherd abandon His search for the lost sheep as soon as the border of earthly life is crossed, or will He ever cease to 'go after that which is lost until he find it?' 'If I make my bed in Hell, behold, thou art there.'

We shall best find our way through these difficulties by thinking of the soul's condition rather than its 'place'. We can hardly believe that finally every soul will attain to the highest beatitude; even among the saints one star differeth from another in glory. There may be an infinite number of grada-tions. Heaven and Hell may be the same 'place', the difference being in ourselves.

Canon Streeter in a very helpful contribution to the sympo-sium *Immortality* which he edited pointed out (p. 137) that so long as Heaven, Purgatory and Hell are thought of mainly in terms of place, they must necessarily be thought of as entirely separate one from the other, so that a person who is in one could have little or no communication with a person in the other; but 'if we think of the future in terms of quality of life we should naturally suppose that there would be an infinite number of degrees in quality, shading off into one another, and that this would mean a possibility of progress.'

CHAPTER 11

THE RESURRECTION

THE RESURRECTION of the body has in Christian thought been closely associated with the Judgement and the Final Advent. There are signs that the former crassly material views are being replaced by something nearer to New Testament teaching.

JEWISH AND GREEK VIEWS

There is a difference between survival and resurrection. Roughly speaking the Greek view of immortality as we find it in Platonism was one of escape from the body, the release of the soul which lived on apart from its former bodily prison. The Jewish view was that man consisted of body, soul, and spirit; and that through the final resurrection these elements would be reunited, and the whole man would live again in the resurrection body. These two conceptions correspond to fundamentally different approaches. The Greek philosopher (like the Hindu) thought of matter as evil and the body as a prison of the soul, the divine and spiritual element. The Hebrew (like the Christian) thought of matter as the creation of God.

Since the question of judgement is fresh in our minds from the previous chapter, the following parable from the Talmud will be appropriate at this point as illustrating the essential connexion which some Jewish teachers saw between the Judgement and the Resurrection. 'A human king had a beautiful garden in which were some fine early figs. He set in it two watchmen, one lame and the other blind. Said the lame man to the blind, I see some fine figs, carry me on your shoulders and we will get the fruit and eat it. After a time the owner of the garden came and asked after his missing figs. The lame man protested that he could not walk, the blind that he could not see. So the master put the lame man on the blind man's back and judged them together. So God brings the soul and casts it in

100

the body (i.e. at the resurrection) and judges them together'
(*Sanhedrin* 91 a–b).

The Jews may have originally derived their doctrine of
Resurrection from the Persians, that is from Zoroastrianism.
Or alternatively they may have worked out their own doctrine
in accordance with their conception of the Messianic kingdom.
When this was regarded as an earthly kingdom destined to
last for ever, it was natural to feel that the righteous dead should
have a share in it. The only way they could do so was by
returning from the dark underworld, Sheol, the abode of the
dead, and receiving back their bodily frames so that they could
live once more on the earth. This doctrine of resurrection is
found only twice in the Old Testament (Daniel 12_{2-3} and
Isaiah 26_{19}).

The Orphic, Platonic, and similar systems of Greek thought
regarded the future life in rather a different way. To them
the soul was of heavenly origin and it had in some way become
involved in its imprisoning material surroundings. The body
was a tomb. Death meant the liberation of the soul from this
confinement, this muddy vesture of decay. To the Hindu also
the material world with its bodily experience is an evil snare in
which the soul has become entangled.

There is evidence that the Greek view of immortality (in the
sense indicated above) influenced some Jewish writers like
Philo and the writer of the Wisdom of Solomon. But in the
main, Jewish thought remained true to the doctrine of resu-
rection. This is in keeping with an eternal kingdom on a
renewed and transformed earth, such as we find in a number
of the apocalypses. In these writings it was customary to
emphasize the new powers and characteristics of the resurrection life. Thus 2 Esdras 7_{97} speaks of the transformation of
the righteous, 'how their face is destined to shine as the sun,
and how they are destined to be made like the light of the stars,
henceforth incorruptible'.

2 Baruch presents rather a curious idea, in 49 and the
succeeding sections. The dead, it is said, will rise again, both
the good and the evil, with their previous appearance, for the
purpose of mutual recognition. Later they will be changed,
the bad for the worse and the righteous for the better. The
teaching of the Talmud is similar in *Sanhedrin* 91b, where it is
said: 'They shall rise with their defects and then be healed.'

Judaism includes interpretations of a more spiritual kind

than this, and it is interesting to notice that Maimonides, who formulated the Thirteen Principles of the Jewish faith in the twelfth century A.D., unreservedly asserted: 'In the world to come there are no bodies, but only the souls of the righteous, without bodies like angels.' This looks like a complete surrender to the Greek view of immortality; but it was evidently regarded as a doctrine of resurrection, for the thirteenth principle of Maimonides declares: 'I believe with perfect faith that there will be a resurrection of the dead at the time when it shall please the Creator.' Not many Jewish teachers have presented the doctrine of resurrection in this way, and as Dr I. Abrahams writes after citing the former statement, the schools of Hillel and Shammai in the first century both believed in a restoration of the material form (*Studies in Pharisaism and the Gospels*, 1st series, p. 168). According to Abrahams, Maimonides rested his statement on *Berachoth* 17a: 'In the world to come there is neither eating nor drinking, no marital relations, no business affairs, no envy, hatred nor quarrelling; but the righteous sit with their garlands on their heads, enjoying the splendid light of the Divine Presence (Shekinah) as it is said, And they beheld God and they ate and drank.'

CHRISTIAN TEACHING

The quotation just given from the Talmud (*Berachoth* tractate) reminds us of some similar words of our Lord on this subject: 'When they shall rise from the dead, they neither marry, nor are given in marriage; but are as angels in heaven' (Mark 12_{25}). The rest of our Lord's reply to the Sadducees suggests that the patriarchs, Abraham, Isaac, and Jacob, are already living the resurrection life.

St Paul in 1 Corinthians 15 develops his doctrine of resurrection in terms of a spiritual body. Unfortunately the Church of later times did not pay sufficient heed to his clear statement that 'flesh and blood cannot inherit the kingdom of God'. In 2 Corinthians 5_1 it almost seems that the 'spiritual body' is received immediately after death; 'we know that if the earthly house of our tabernacle be dissolved, we have a building from God, a house not made with hands, eternal, in the heavens'. Some authorities think that this marks a development in Paul's thought in advance of the position represented by 1 Corinthians 15 where the resurrection body is not given until the Parousia. Others like Deissmann (*Paul*, Ch. 9) suggest that Hellenistic and Pharisaic conceptions existed side by side and unreconciled in his mind; the stream of his thought shows the double colouring due to its two tributaries.

In the early Church period the Gnostic heretics tried to introduce into Christianity the view that matter was evil and the accompanying idea of a mere survival, a release of the soul from the body, such as had been taught, as we have seen, by certain schools of Greek thought. The Church quite rightly rejected the Gnostic view of matter. Christianity by its doctrines of creation and Incarnation claims the whole realm of material things for God, looks upon the body as the temple of the Holy Spirit, and protests against the heresy that matter is essentially evil. But at the same time it does seem that in opposing the Gnostics the Church went too far in connexion with this question of the resurrection, developing it in a way that was far too crude. St Paul's words about flesh and blood were explained away and it was taught that the actual material particles would be collected again and built up by the power of God into the resurrection body.

Even when the position was reached that the eternal abode of the saints would be in heaven, not upon a renovated earth, the doctrine of a resurrection body was retained. It could be argued that resurrection logically coheres with the idea of an eternal life upon the earth, and that if eternal life is to be in heaven the whole conception of resurrection should be dropped. Critics of the Christian faith pointed out the apparent absurdity of bodies being lifted up to heaven, for (they said)'nature will allow an earthly body no place except on the earth' (see Augustine, *City of God*, XXII. 4). But the matter is not quite as simple as that. The Greek thinkers referred to earlier resembled the Hindus in blurring the edges of personal separateness; and at times the thought of losing one's identity in the divine provides the only kind of immortality to be expected. Thus in Stoicism the spark of the human soul is finally reabsorbed into the divine fire. The doctrine of resurrection has preserved through the centuries the elements of personal separateness and recognition. This connexion with the Christian view of personality has received more emphasis in recent years. But in the early centuries it seems that it was the struggle with the Gnostic view of matter which led the Church to formulate its doctrine of the resurrection along crude and materialistic lines, as we can see in the writings of the Fathers. The saying, 'Not a hair of your head shall perish' (Luke 21₁₈), was interpreted as a reference to the resurrection and it meant that every single particle of the body would be restored by divine power.

Agustine discusses the difficulty raised by cannibalism, and suggests that any disputed material should revert to the first owner!

The flesh of the famished man that hunger consumed, is exhaled into air, and thence (as we said before) the Creator can fetch it again. This flesh therefore of the man that was eaten, shall return to the first owner, of whom the famished man does but as it were borrow it, and so must repay it again. And that of his own which famine dried up into air, shall be re-collected, and restored into some convenient place of his body, which were it so consumed that no part thereof remained in nature, yet God could fetch it again in an instant, and when He would Himself.

(*City of God*, XXII, 20.)

Augustine ought not to be blamed for the bizarre nature of some of the problems he discussed in this 22nd book of his great work; he patiently deals with the criticisms which the pagans had put forward. Will a man rise, they asked, with all the hair that ever the barber cut from his head? Will deformities be retained? Augustine maintains that there will be no imperfections in the resurrection body. An image-maker can melt down a statue and remodel it without its former unshapeliness, while at the same time using every particle again. Cannot God do the same? Wherefore the fat and the lean need have no fear. As for the martyrs who have suffered mutilation, their scars may be indicated in some way as a part of their glorification, but any limbs they have lost will be restored. No marks of old age shall reappear; men shall be as though they were about thirty years of age. Ephesians 4₁₃, he says, may mean 'that all should arise neither younger nor older, but just of that age whereat Christ Himself suffered and rose again'. 'Everyone shall arise in that stature which he either had at his full man's state, or should have had, if he had not died before.' This, however, is not put forward dogmatically: 'If anyone say that every man shall rise again in the same stature wherein he died, it is not an opinion that requires much opposition.' As for those who die in infancy: 'I say they shall not rise again with that littleness of body in which they died;

the sudden and strange power of God shall give them a stature of full growth. . . . And as for the means of addition, how can that wondrous workman of the world want fit substance to add where He thinks good?'

The resurrection body, says Augustine, will be a spiritual body in the sense that 'the spiritual flesh shall become subject to the spirit, yet shall it be flesh still, as the carnal spirit before was subject to the flesh, and yet a spirit still'. Every single part of the body, whether it is 'made into powder and dust, by chance or cruelty, or dissolved into air or water so that no part remain undispersed', shall be restored and shall become immortal, spiritual and incorruptible.

LATER DEVELOPMENTS

Protestantism abandoned the conception of Purgatory and taught that the souls of all the blessed were with Christ until the reunion of body and soul at the resurrection. 'That soul that hath been these hundreds or thousands of years in the heavens, soaking in the bosom of Christ, it shall in a moment come spangling in to the body again, and inhabit every member and vein of the body, as it did before its departure' (Bunyan).

But the conception of a reassembling of the actual material components of the body was for the most part retained. Thus Bishop Pearson in his work on the Creed (1659) writes:

He which numbereth the sands of the sea, knoweth all the scattered bones, seeth into all the graves and tombs, searcheth all the repositories and dormitories in the earth, knoweth what dust belongeth to each body, what body to each soul. Again: as his all-seeing eye observeth every particle of dissolved and corrupted man, so doth he also see and know all ways and means by which these scattered parts should be reunited, by which this ruined fabric should be recomposed; he knoweth how every bone should be brought to its old neighbour-bone, how every sinew may be re-embroidered on it; he understandeth what are the proper parts to be conjoined, what is the proper *gluten* by which they may become united . . . though therefore the parts of the body of man be dissolved, yet they perish not. . . . Howsoever they are scattered, or wheresoever lodged, they are within the knowledge and power of God, and can have no repugnancy by their separation to be reunited when and how he pleaseth.

This painfully literal view of the resurrection body as a reassembly of actual fragments is not far removed from some of the beliefs registered in J. G. Frazer's *Golden Bough*, where it is said that the Armenians 'do not throw away their cut hair and nails and extracted teeth, but hide them in places that are esteemed holy, such as a crack in the church wall, a pillar of the house, or a hollow tree. They think that all these severed portions of themselves will be wanted at the resurrection, and that he who has not stowed them away in a safe place will have to hunt about for them on the great day.' 'The Turks never throw away the parings of their nails, but carefully stow them in cracks of the walls or of the boards, in the belief that they will be needed at the resurrection' (p. 236 of the abridged edition).

In cemeteries bodies are still buried as far as possible with the feet to the East; the original reason was that at the Resurrection the dead might rise facing the right direction, as a cemetery superintendent once explained to me. The Advent was expected to take place in the East, as in Wordsworth's lines:

> And who, from out the regions of the morn,
> Issuing in pomp, shall come to judge mankind.

Apart from the question of Purgatory, Protestantism made little change in the conception of future life, resurrection, and judgement. The Augustinian teaching was retained that in the resurrection all would appear as in the flower of age. This may be illustrated from a poem that was well known last century, R. Pollok's *Course of Time*. In Book VII he describes the resurrection of the dead and the change of the living at the final advent, though the living are changed without first being reduced to ashes by the conflagration as in Augustine's scheme. The effects are somewhat startling. Old men ripe for the grave feel new vigour flow through their sluggish veins and withered limbs; wrinkles disappear, and upon bald heads rise bushy locks. Mothers, themselves rejuvenated, see their young sons 'grow up and suddenly put on the form of manhood'. The limbless and deformed beggar arises complete in joint and limb. Meanwhile the newly sheeted corpse arises and stares at those who dress it; and to the bleeding ranks on a recent battle-field returns 'the stream of life in healthy flow'. The anatomist is described at work on a body, cutting his way through bones and muscles, when suddenly the victim arises 'complete in immortality'.

It is worthy of note that Bunyan in his treatise *Of the Resurrection of the Dead* did not explain it as a reassembling of scattered dust, as his contemporary Bishop Pearson did and so many others before and since. He is much nearer to St Paul's teaching in 1 Corinthians 15 and he dwells upon the imagery of the grain of wheat. 'It is sown in its husk; but in its rising it leaveth that husk behind it.' The difficulty of the 'flesh and blood' saying (1 Corinthians 15_{50}) is explained along the lines made familiar by Augustine and Aquinas, but his presentation is, in my opinion, more plausible and cogent in respect to this particular point. A quotation will indicate the general lines of his main interpretation:

The body ariseth, as to the nature of it, the self-same nature; but as to the manner of it, how far transcendent is it! There is a poor, dry, wrinkled kernel cast into the ground, and there it lieth, and swelleth, breaketh, and, one would think, perisheth; but behold, it receiveth life, it chitteth (i.e. sprouts), it putteth forth a blade, and groweth into a stalk, there also appeareth an ear; it also sweetly blossoms, with a full kernel in the ear: it is the same wheat, yet behold how the form and fashion of that which now ariseth, doth differ from that which then was sown; its glory also when 'twas sown, is no glory, when compared with that in which it riseth. And yet it is the same that riseth that was sown, and no other; though the same after a far more glorious manner; not the same with its *husk*, but without it. Our *bran* shall be left behind us when we rise again.

He has much to say about the glorious nature and new powers of the resurrection life; and at one point he remarks that 'the Spirit of God also that took its leave of the body when it went to the grave, shall now in all perfection dwell in this body again; I tell you, the body at this day will shine brighter than the face of Moses or Stephen, even as bright as the sun, the stars, and angels'. In this reference to the Holy Spirit he differs from his Roman Catholic contemporary Pascal: 'The Holy Spirit resides invisibly in the remains of those who are departed in the grace of God till He shall appear visibly in them at the resurrection. And it is hence that the relics of the saints become worthy of regard' (*Pensées*).

In recent years there has been a widespread tendency to abandon the traditional conception of a reassembly of identical bodily parts, and Paul's term 'a spiritual body' has received more attention. The modern view is not of a mere survival to a disembodied life, nor a reassembling of material constituents. It maintains that the soul will have some means of expression suited to its new conditions. Tennyson's lines are sometimes quoted in this connexion:

> Eternal form shall still divide
> Th'immortal soul from all beside
> And I shall know him when we meet.

Some would still retain a connexion of some kind between the earthly and heavenly bodies; but this does not seem essential. We cannot understand the miracle by which our present bodies grow, as they do, from a single cell. We must ultimately rely on the same divine Providence to supply all our needs in the future life. We may even steal one of Walt Whitman's 'leaves of grass': 'Did you think Life was so well provided for, and Death, the purport of all Life, is not well provided for?' It has been suggested that the soul may have some power of weaving, as it were, its own 'spiritual body' in the future. Modern scientific views suggest that mind is the ultimate reality, that the old rigid distinction between matter and mind is out of date. This tendency is thoroughly congenial to Christian thought, and it shows that St Paul's words about 'a spiritual body' are not a contradiction in terms but rather a useful way of combining the ideas of continuity and identity with that of a higher mode of existence.

It is of interest to note that according to the *Jewish Encyclopaedia*, Jewish views on the future life have in certain circles of thought undergone considerable modification in a spiritual direction. One of the pronouncements of the Philadelphia Rabbinic Conference of 1869 was that 'the belief in the bodily resurrection has no religious foundation and the doctrine of immortality refers to the after-existence of the soul only'.

Streeter has a helpful discussion of the resurrection in *Immortality*. He shows that the real point at issue between the Sadducees and the Pharisees was whether the future life was the gloomy shadow-like existence of *Sheol* or the richer, fuller life envisaged by the Pharisees. On this point the Pharisees were right and we can accept their main position without necessarily retaining the particular form in which they expressed it. He also maintains that in the next life we shall not be outside Space and Time, and the personality will require some local centre and organ of expression. Through the resurrection body a relation with the universe may be maintained. This question of the place of the universe in eternity will occupy us at a later stage.

Many would support the view that the resurrection body is given immediately after death. Paul's great saying in 2 Corinthians 5_1 has already been quoted, and while there is disagreement about its interpretation, it admirably suits the belief that the 'building from God, a house not made with hands' is ours as soon as 'the earthly house' is relinquished. The main element, however, in the Christian doctrine of immortality is the continuance of fellowship with God. Our Lord's words to the Pharisees concerning Abraham, Isaac, and Jacob, insist that death has not severed their relationship with God. More important than the conditions or the place is the company. Many questions must be left unsolved, not because there is any doubt about the fact of immortality, but because the things which God has prepared for them that love Him have not entered into the heart of man: they are things which eye has not seen nor ear heard. We must be content to say with Baxter: 'It is enough that Christ knows all, and I shall be with Him.'

The matters discussed in this and the preceding chapters concerning judgement and resurrection have a vital bearing on the question of the Second Advent. The Second Coming means Christ's return to the earth. Those who believe that the bodies of all men will rise from the tomb and that they will be assembled in some such spot as the valley of Jehoshaphat are quite logical in holding that Christ must return to the earth in order to conduct the judgement. Similarly millenarians who believe that He will reign on the earth in the sense that He will be visible and resident in Palestine must necessarily believe that He will descend to the earth in order to do so. But those who do not believe in a literal resurrection from actual graves followed by a Great Assize including all who have ever lived, nor in a literal reign of Christ on the earth in person, are somewhat illogical in maintaining that Christ will return to the earth by a descent in glory. For what purpose will He come? The Advent can scarcely be left as an isolated event.

Each reader must decide whether the literal view of these interlocking questions is the only one consonant with the Christian faith. But the position represented in these pages is in agreement with the emphatic words of Canon Streeter in *Immortality* that the General Resurrection and Judgement, while expressing vital truths, should be surrendered avowedly and completely as literal events.

It is by no means an innovation, as some think, to put forward a symbolic rather than a literal interpretation of the Advent of Christ. Fifty years ago Dr Frank Ballard, a well-known Christian evidence lecturer, used to quote with approval the words which Newton Clarke wrote last century: 'No visible return of Christ to the earth is to be expected.'

It must of course be remembered that the important place which the Second Advent has held in Christian tradition is not only due to its association with the Resurrection and the Judgement: it also marked the term of human history or the end of the world. If Christ is not to descend to judge the quick and the dead after calling the latter out of their tombs, what event will mark the consummation of man's story? The whole question of the course and climax of human history will be looked at more closely in Part Two

Part Two
His Kingdom

In his days shall the righteous flourish; and abundance of peace, till the moon be no more. He shall have dominion also from sea to sea, and from the River unto the ends of the earth.

PSALM 72

And it shall come to pass in the latter days, that the mountain of the Lord's house shall be established in the top of the mountains, and shall be exalted above the hills; and all nations shall flow unto it. . . . And he shall judge between the nations, and shall reprove many peoples: and they shall beat their swords into plowshares, and their spears into pruninghooks: nation shall not lift up sword against nation, neither shall they learn war any more.

ISAIAH 2

They shall not hurt nor destroy in all my holy mountain: for the earth shall be full of the knowledge of the Lord, as the waters cover the sea.

Isaiah 11

The idea of a continuous progress of humanity, whatever perversions that idea may have undergone, is really a creation of the Christian faith . . . belief in a moral and social progress of mankind which at bottom is so intimately associated with the belief of Christian men in the coming triumph of the Church.

CANON H. P. LIDDON's Bampton Lectures (1866)

I hold that, to our Lord, the idea of the Kingdom of Heaven included the corporate regeneration of society on earth as well as a life in the world to come. The evidence is, to my mind, conclusive against the view of some recent scholars that it included the latter only.

B. H. STREETER

CHAPTER 12

HOPES AND HINDRANCES

THE QUESTION of the Last Things is inevitably linked with our beliefs concerning the future course of history. Advent teaching has frequently stressed the imminence of the end of the world and this has prevented any hope of the Gospel's triumph. If we dismiss the doctrines of the adventist sects, and allow for the possibility of a long future for the duration of the earth, what are we to believe about the prospects for Christianity? If Christ is not to reign visibly at Jerusalem for a thousand years, will He establish a world-kingdom in the hearts of men by the power of His Gospel? There are elements in the teaching of our Lord which encourage the hope of the world's conversion. While some Christian leaders and thinkers have cherished this hope, it cannot be said that the Church as a whole has done so. Certain factors of varying importance have hindered the expectation of such a victory: (1) Belief that the present age would end with the reign of Antichrist and (2) with a widespread apostasy—this is obviously difficult to reconcile with the hope of a Christian world: (3) a belief that the world will end as soon as a certain number of elect souls is attained should also be taken into account. (4) A literal millennium is equally incompatible with a spiritual victory, and millenarians have usually stressed the terrible apostasy as heralding the millennial reign. While millenarianism has never been the universal belief of the Church, the other three factors did pass into general Christian thought. In the present chapter we shall look more closely at (1), (2), and (3): then the question of the millennium will be taken up.

But first of all it will be well to remind ourselves that the conception of a victory of righteousness upon the earth is not a purely modern idea. The Lord's Prayer speaks of the coming of God's Kingdom and explains the meaning of the phrase with the words: 'Thy will be done in earth as it is in heaven.' The thought of course goes back to the Messianic Age of Hebrew belief, the age of righteousness and peace on earth described so

113

I

frequently in the Old Testament. Elsewhere in our Lord's
teaching there are hints that He believed in the final victory of
His cause on earth. This is not so much a matter of proof-
texts as that again and again we are led back from the pages of
the Gospels to these Messianic prophecies of the Old Testament.
The entry into Jerusalem inevitably reminds us of Zechariah
9₉, where the king who is just and lowly is to speak peace unto
the nations: 'and his dominion shall be from sea to sea, and
from the River to the ends of the earth'.

At the Last Supper the reference to the New Covenant takes
us back to Jeremiah 31 with its description of a time when 'they
shall teach no more every man his neighbour, and every man
his brother, saying, Know the Lord: for they shall all know
me, from the least of them unto the greatest of them'. Again,
our Lord's words before the High Priest take us back to Daniel's
description of the Son of man coming into God's presence and
receiving 'dominion, and glory, and a kingdom, that all the
peoples, nations, and languages should serve him: his dominion
is an everlasting dominion, which shall not pass away, and his
kingdom that which shall not be destroyed' (7₁₄).

In spite of these and similar indications such as the promise
that the meek shall inherit the earth, it must be admitted that a
very different conception of the future has often dominated the
thinking of the Church. We have already hinted at some of the
reasons for this.

It may be observed that in the earlier letters of Paul mention
is made of Antichrist and the apostasy associated with him:
but in the later letters a more comprehensive vision of the
purpose of God is indicated. Some words from Dr R. H.
Charles's *Between the Old and New Testaments* are worth quoting:

The Apostle's ideas on this subject (i.e. eschatology) were continually advancing. He began with expectations of the future that he
had inherited from Judaism, but under the influence of the great
formative Christian conceptions he parted with these, and entered
on a process of development in the course of which the heterogeneous elements were for the most part silently dropped.
Several distinct stages in the process may be distinguished. Of
these we may mention one. In his earlier epistles, under the
influence of inherited Jewish beliefs, St Paul looked forward to a
great apostasy, and the revelation of the man of sin as the immediate precursor of the Advent. Thus the history of the world was to
close in the culmination of evil and the final impenitence of the

bulk of mankind. In Romans 11, on the other hand, the Apostle proclaims the inner and progressive transformation of mankind through the Gospel, culminating in the conversion of the entire Gentile and Jewish worlds as the immediate prelude of the Advent of Christ (pp. 128-9).

In the early centuries the hope of the world's conversion was not entirely lost sight of, and the following words of Origen (d. A.D. 253) are notable. It is perhaps significant that such a statement comes from the Greek-speaking East rather than from the Western Church:

If all did as I do, then the barbarians also would receive the Divine Word and become the most moral and gentle of men. All other religions would cease from the earth and Christianity alone would be supreme, which indeed is destined one day to have the supremacy, since the divine truth is continually bringing more souls under its sway (*Against Celsus*, VIII. 68).

ANTICHRIST

The Jews believed that the divine intervention for which they were looking would be preceded by a time of widespread apostasy and that this falling away would find expression in a single figure of sinister portent—the Antichrist (i.e. Anti-Messiah). The Book of Daniel gives evidence of these two related beliefs. There is litte doubt that the figure described in Daniel represents Antiochus Epiphanes, the great persecutor of the Jews in the second century B.C. The people were encouraged to remain firm in their trial by recognizing that all these events had been foretold: just such a man as Antiochus had been indicated by prophecy and it was certain that he would be destroyed and his fall would be followed by the triumph of God's kingdom. The Book of Daniel, written at this very time to strengthen the resistance movement and nerve the waverers, served its purpose. But when Antiochus perished no golden age followed. The result was that this prophecy of a man of sin was held to be still unfulfilled—some other figure must be looked for in the future: Antiochus was merely a foreshadowing, the real Antichrist would be a man of his stamp.

This conception passed into Christianity, and as we can see by 2 Thessalonians 2 (where the very phrases of Daniel reappear) the Christians came to expect that the present age would reach its climax in a great apostasy and the appearance of the Man

of Sin. Such a belief of course made it very difficult to envisage
the successful evangelization of the world. The mystery of
iniquity, said Paul, is even now working and in time it will
crystallize in the Man of Sin. Although Paul seems to have
advanced from this position, when his letters were collected
they were not studied in chronological order and everything
in them was regarded as of equal authority.

The ages of persecution further stimulated this belief:
persecutors like Nero and Domitian were suspected of being the
Man of Sin: and even when more peaceful days came the belief
in Antichrist had become a settled dogma of the Church. It
was held that he would reign for three and a half years: this was
based upon the 'time, times and half a time' of Daniel. Augustine lays it down quite definitely that Elijah will return, Antichrist will reign for three and a half years and he will then be
destroyed at the Advent of Christ when He comes to judge the
quick and the dead.

The persistence of the Antichrist doctrine among the Jews
and Christians was not only due to the Book of Daniel. The
full story would have to take into account a widespread belief
in a final struggle between God and His enemies. This belief
probably goes back ultimately to Babylonian mythology. Its
origins and its manifold forms in later developments are well
discussed in Bousset's work *The Antichrist Legend*. (See my
Second Advent, pp. 180ff.)

Our point at the moment is that this Antichrist doctrine in
some of its forms stood in the way of any hopeful attitude
toward the world's future. Events, it was thought, were
inevitably leading to this 'overthrower and destroyer of the
human race' as one of the Latin Fathers called him (Lactantius). The fear that the age was near its end was also linked with
this belief. While in some cases the expectation of the Man of
Sin and the final apostasy coloured the whole picture of the
future, in others it was applied to a brief period immediately
before the Second Advent and thus affected merely the last
three and a half years of the present age. On this showing
room was left for the Church's victory in the world, and Antichrist was only a prophetic counter which had to be fitted into
the scheme. When the millennium was interpreted spiritually
as referring to the Church age, his revolt was equated with the
rebellion of Gog and Magog at the end of the thousand years
(Revelation 20$_{7-9}$). Orosius, the friend of Augustine, in his

famous history speaks of the triumphs of Christianity and affirms that the old beliefs will be dead and gone when the new religion shall reign alone. But he goes on: 'We must, of course, make an exception of those last, remote days at the end of the world when Antichrist shall appear, etc.' Thus on the one hand we have the spacious schemes of Augustine and Aquinas who were not obsessed by thoughts of an imminent apostasy: on the other hand we have the steady stream of those fearful and gloomy souls who through the centuries have announced that the world was so bad that the final doom was at hand. But it was rather depressing, on any showing, to feel that the present age was destined to end with an outburst of persecution and fury. By a curious freak of history it was only when Antichrist was identified with the Roman Catholic Church and the Pope that a way out of this difficulty was found. A view then emerged that when the papacy's fall was complete better days for the Church would follow. This development will be traced in a later chapter. Belief in a personal Antichrist then tended to recede. Even Calvin remarked that people who look for an individual Antichrist are crazy.

THE FINAL APOSTASY

Among the signs which are held to be prior to the advent of Christ the apostasy is included with this definition in the *Catholic Encyclopedia*: 'Fathers and interpreters understand by this revolt a great reduction in the number of the faithful through the abandonment of the Christian religion by many nations.' The depressing effect of such an expectation will be evident. If the Advent is to be expected in the not-too-distant future and is to be preceded by a 'reduction' in the size of the Church, there is little room for a spirit of hopefulness in Christian work. The 'falling away' is associated with the Man of Sin in 2 Thessalonians 2_3. Other passages are held to support this belief, e.g. 1 Timothy 4_1, 2 Timothy 3_1, 2 Peter 3_3. The presence of this teaching in the New Testament is undisputed. But it must be noticed that the writers speak of a development which was already upon them. St Paul said that the mystery of iniquity was already at work (2 Thessalonians 2_7). Similarly, 1 John declares:

. . . even now have there arisen many antichrists; whereby we know that it is the last hour. They went out from us, but they were not of us; for if they had been of us, they would have continued with us. . . . Who is the liar but he that denieth that Jesus is the Christ? This is the antichrist, even he that denieth the Father and the Son (2₁₈₋₂₂).

See also 2 John 7. To take these passages which speak of events of that time and to apply them to a period which still lies in the future all these centuries afterwards, is a strange proceeding.

As shown previously the two related ideas of Antichrist and apostasy did not originate with the Christians, and Jewish antecedents can be traced for both. Later literature gives abundant evidence for the persistence of these ideas within Judaism itself.

Jewish writings show that belief in the apostasy was linked with their Messianic expectations. It well expresses the mood of the apocalypses and their despair of the present. The apostasy which precedes the Judgement is mentioned in the Sibylline Oracles: 'But when the faith of godliness has perished among men, and righteousness is no more seen in the world, etc.' (IV. 152ff.) Similarly v. 74 speaks of 'the last time, when men shall be utterly evil'. This doctrine is sustained in Rabbinic writings as well as in the apocalypses, and in the *Mishnah* we have the following:

With the footprints of the Messiah (i.e. signs which herald his coming) presumption shall increase and dearth reach its height . . . the empire shall fall into heresy and there shall be none to utter reproof. . . . The wisdom of the Scribes shall become insipid and they that shun sin shall be deemed contemptible, and truth shall nowhere be found. (Micah 7₆ is quoted) . . . On whom can we stay ourselves? —on our Father in heaven (Sotah IX. 15).

There is a good deal of material on the Messianic woes in Jewish writings: one passage from the Babylonian Talmud may be referred to in which several pages are devoted to the troubles before Messiah's Advent (*Sanhedrin* 97a—98b):

In the generation when the Son of David will come, scholars will be few in number, and as for the rest, their eyes will fail through sorrow and grief. Multitudes of trouble and evil decrees will be promulgated anew, each new evil coming with haste before the other has ended.

Other factors mentioned in this passage are that 'the Torah will be forgotten by its students', 'God-fearing men will be despised, people will be dog-faced (brazen)'.

The thoroughness with which this kind of teaching was incorporated in the Christian message may be illustrated by some words written by Lactantius (born about A.D. 250) in his *Divine Institutes* (Book VII). He was a millenarian, and he is speaking about the final apostasy which is to end the present age before the return of Christ:

For righteousness will so decrease, and impiety, avarice, desire and lust will so greatly increase, that *if there shall then happen to be any good men* they will be a prey to the wicked. . . . There will be no faith among men, nor peace, nor kindness, nor shame, nor truth; and thus also there will be neither security nor government, nor any rest from evils. For all the earth will be in a state of tumult. . . . And the cause of this desolation and confusion will be this, because the Roman name, by which the world is now ruled . . . will be taken away from the earth, and the government return to Asia.

Pages describing the woes and devastations follow. It is at this time that Antichrist is to arise, and finally he is slain at the Advent of Christ who 'shall descend with a company of angels to the middle of the earth, and the power of the angels shall deliver into the hands of the just that multitude, etc. . . . they shall be slain from the third hour until the evening, and blood shall flow like a torrent.'

The reference of Lactantius to Rome reminds us that the common belief in the early centuries was that 'that which restraineth' in 2 Thessalonians 2₆ meant the Roman empire. Christians prayed for the continuance of the empire believing that its fall would release upon the world all the horrors of the last days. Since Rome was held to be the fourth empire of Daniel's visions it must be the last, and no other world-power could succeed it.

It would be impossible even to outline here the various interpretations which have been held concerning the final apostasy. Some have seen the 'falling away' in the emergence of Islam, or the rise of the papacy and the defection from evangelical truth. Without examining these theories it will suffice for us to point out the depressing effect upon Christian endeavour of a belief that the age must inevitably end in widespread apostasy.

What was said about Antichrist also applies here. When the apostasy was merely regarded as a matter affecting the last three and a half years of the age no great harm was done, but when it became an obsession giving a jaundiced view of the whole development of the Church's life it did tend to cut the nerve of Christian endeavour. Men's actions are affected by their hopes and beliefs, and if our conception of Christ's victory is qualified by such dismal forebodings the spirit of expectant faith is bound to be weakened.

The pagan view that the world was degenerating with the lapse of time also had some influence upon Christian thought and reinforced the tendency produced by the prophecies of Antichrist and the final apostasy.

THE NUMBER OF THE ELECT

Another idea, of less importance than the others, which has played a part in Christian thought and needs mention here, is that a definite number of human souls is needed to fill certain vacancies in the Beyond and as soon as this number is reached the end will come. In the *Book of Common Prayer* the burial service refers to 'the number of thine elect' in the prayer which follows the committal and the Lord's Prayer: 'Almighty God, with whom do live the spirits of them that depart hence in the Lord . . . beseeching thee, that it may please thee, of thy gracious goodness, *shortly to accomplish the number of thine elect*, and to hasten thy kingdom. . . .' These particular words did not occur in the *Prayer Book* of 1549 but were added in the book of 1552 and have held their place ever since. Millions of people during the past four hundred years have heard the words of this prayer, words which appear to preclude any hope of the final triumph of the Gospel and which indeed explicitly ask for the speedy winding-up of human affairs.

Here again we have a belief which passed early into the Christian Church, the belief that the age would end when a certain number of the elect had been reached. It would be interesting to trace this idea through Jewish and Christian writings, from the Apocrypha to Spenser and Milton; but it must suffice at the moment to point out that the doctrine of a fixed number of the elect has put a false boundary to human history and obscured its true goal.

CHAPTER 13

THE MILLENNIUM: UP TO AUGUSTINE

In the last chapter we found that three Jewish doctrines, all having a bearing upon the question of the future course of history, had been incorporated into Christian thought—belief in Antichrist, in the final apostasy, and in a fixed number of the elect whose accomplishment would terminate the present age. We now turn to another Jewish doctrine which has had a great influence upon certain sections of the Church, the doctrine of a temporary Messianic kingdom upon the earth. This is usually known as Millenarianism, the word 'millennium' meaning a thousand years. Another name is Chiliasm, derived from the Greek for 'thousand', 'millennium' being of Latin derivation. Unlike the three doctrines mentioned in the previous chapter, belief in the Millennium has never been universal in the Church but has been restricted, as it is today, to certain sections.

Something has already been said on this subject in connexion with the Book of Revelation, but it demands further attention now. In the Church of the early centuries there was a definite strain of millenarianism on account of the teaching of Revelation 20, where the Jewish doctrine of Messiah's limited reign on earth is given a Christian dress. One way of interpreting the kingdom of Christ is thus indicated; He will rule personally and visibly in Jerusalem for a thousand years after His return to the earth. The prevailing conception of the New Testament is that Christ is already on the throne and the alternative view of a Millennium is Judaistic rather than Christian. According to Hebrew 2_9 we already behold Jesus crowned with glory and honour; the frequent quotation of Psalm 110 in the New Testament also brings out what is usually called His 'mediatorial reign'. It is clear that the New Testament writers regarded Christ as having already begun His reign. We see not yet all things subjected to Him (Hebrew 2_8); but 'He must reign, till he hath put all his enemies under his feet' (1 Corinthians 15_{25}).

The view of a future Millennium harmonizes well with belief in Antichrist and the apostasy. Millenarians of the present time try to show that any conversion of the world by the power of the Gospel is impossible since the present age is destined to close in a great 'falling away' and an outstanding manifestation of evil. It is not in virtue of His first Advent that Christ will achieve His victory and kingship in the world, but in virtue of His Second Advent—only then and through some new divine action will He attain His universal reign. Millenarians usually have a very limited expectation as to what Christ's Gospel and Church can achieve, and some of them do not hesitate to affirm that the world is inevitably getting worse.

In the early centuries, however, it was largely on account of the Book of Revelation that millenarianism flourished in some quarters and although it appears in the writings of a number of the best known Fathers, it was not always brought into organic relation with the rest of their teaching. We shall now give evidence for early chiliasm by means of quotations from a few of these Fathers. We shall then turn to Augustine, for it was mainly due to his influence that this doctrine was largely abandoned, and an interpretation of Revelation 20 was found which brought it into line with the rest of the New Testament. Through Augustine a more scriptural view of the kingdom of Christ prevailed. Although his exposition of Revelation 20 was faulty, he nevertheless rendered the Church a great service in throwing the weight of his influence in the direction of a spiritual interpretation of the reign of Christ.

EARLY CHILIASM

It is sometimes alleged that the early Church was entirely chiliastic but there is no good evidence to support this sweeping statement. Papias, Justin Martyr, Irenaeus, and Tertullian, are impressive names and they show that the doctrine was not negligible or obscure. But the wording of the Apostle's Creed is itself sufficient to prove that the doctrine of the Millennium was never a part of the universal faith. The words 'from thence He shall come to judge the quick and the dead' are strictly inconsistent with any chiliastic scheme, for according to the latter Christ comes in order to reign on the earth and only at the end of this earthly reign does the Last Judgement take place. It is true that chiliasts of the past and present could quite sincerely use this form of words and they would simply point out that the millennial reign is omitted, not denied. But the point is that chiliasts could hardly have been responsible for this form of words in the first place. The phrase occurs in the earliest forms of the Apostles' Creed and is derived from the New Testament itself (see 1 Peter 4$_5$). It is difficult to believe that the early Church at any stage was predominantly chiliastic in its doctrine as has often been alleged.

Years ago Neander, the great Church historian, pointed out that 'wherever we meet with Chiliasm, in Papias, Irenaeus, Justin Martyr, everything goes to indicate that it was diffused from one country and from a single fountain-head'. The area concerned is evidently Asia Minor, precisely the soil from which the Book of Revelation sprang. Papias was bishop of Hierapolis; Justin lived for a time at Ephesus; and Irenaeus spent the early part of his Christian life in Asia Minor. Montanus and his followers made Pepuza their centre, again in the same country. Tertullian was a Montanist and in the fullest description of his chiliastic doctrine (*Against Marcion.* III, 24) refers to Montanism, 'the new prophecy'.

It is therefore reckless to say that Chiliasm was a normal part of Christian belief up to the time of Constantine, when the Church transferred its hopes from the future to the present. There is no trace of a millennium in such early Christian writers as Clement of Rome, Ignatius, Polycarp, and the Epistle to Diognetus. If Justin and Irenaeus were millenarians, Clement of Alexandria and Origen were not. More important still is the evidence of the New Testament itself. No one reading 2 Peter 3, where the coming of the Lord is followed by the general dissolution and the new heaven and earth, would imagine that somewhere an unmentioned period of a thousand years has to be interpolated. Nowhere in the Gospels is a temporary earthly kingdom spoken of. St Paul appears to know nothing of it; and attempts to find a millennium in 1 Corinthians 15 must be pronounced unsuccessful.

JUSTIN AND IRENAEUS

Justin Martyr, who wrote about the year 150, has left us his very interesting *Dialogue with Trypho*. In Chapter 80, Trypho the Jew asks: 'But tell me, do you really admit that this place, Jerusalem, shall be rebuilt; and do you expect your people to

be gathered together, and made joyful with Christ and the
patriarchs, and the prophets, both the men of our nation, and
other proselytes who joined them before your Christ came?'
To this Justin replies: 'I admitted to you formerly, that I and
many others are of this opinion, and believe that such will
take place, as you assuredly are aware; but on the other hand,
I signified to you that many who belong to the pure and pious
faith, and are true Christians, think otherwise.' (This qualifica-
tion should be noticed; Justin, while giving his own opinion, is
careful to point out that 'many' true Christians thought
otherwise.) Justin supports his own chiliastic view by quoting
Isaiah 65$_{17-25}$, whose literal fulfilment he evidently looks for.
'And further, there was a certain man with us, whose name
was John, one of the apostles of Christ, who prophesied by a
revelation that was made to him that those who believed in our
Christ would dwell a thousand years in Jerusalem; and that
thereafter the general, and in short the eternal, resurrection
and judgement of all men would likewise take place.'

A little later than Justin, Irenaeus who wrote toward the
end of the second century set forth a profound interpretation of
the Christian faith in his great work *Against Heresies*. In one
section of this (Book v. 32–5) he deals at length with the
material kingdom on the earth which the saints are to enjoy
after the first resurrection. Christ's promise about drinking
new wine is to be literally fulfilled during this period; creation
is to be restored to its original perfection and the animals will
be at peace as foretold in Isaiah 11. He protests against the
spiritualizing of such passages as Isaiah 65 and other descriptions of material prosperity. This protest is no doubt partly
due to his opposition to the Gnostic disparagement of matter.
Strangely enough he does not mention the actual period of a
thousand years, but makes it quite clear that he is speaking of a
limited period. In addition to risen saints there will be on the
earth survivors from the present age, 'those whom the Lord
shall find in the flesh, awaiting Him from heaven, and who have
suffered tribulation and escaped the hands of Antichrist.
For it is in reference to them that the prophet says: And those
that are left shall multiply upon the earth. And Jeremiah the
prophet has pointed out, that as many believers as God has
prepared for this purpose, to multiply those left upon earth,
should both be under the rule of the saints to minister to this
Jerusalem and that His kingdom shall be in it.' After the

kingdom, he says, will come the general resurrection and the Judgement. The reference to Antichrist should be noticed—Irenaeus deals more fully with this subject in Book v. 25–6, where he says that Antichrist is to appear in the days of the ten kings spoken of by Daniel. The fourth empire in Daniel's visions is Rome and there will not be a further empire upon the earth. 'The empire which now rules the earth shall be partitioned' among ten kings in the last times. Antichrist will arise and will overthrow three kings (Daniel 7₂ₐff.) and will reign over the earth for three and a half years. He will be destroyed by the coming of Christ.

In the times of the kingdom Jerusalem will be rebuilt after the pattern of the Jerusalem above (Book v. 35). Afterwards the latter itself is to descend upon the new earth, i.e. when the temporary kingdom is over. 'Of this Jerusalem the former one is an image—that Jerusalem of the former earth in which the righteous are disciplined beforehand for incorruption and prepared for salvation.' This is an important point in the millennial conception of Irenaeus: the disciplinary effect of the kingdom, preparing the saints for their entry upon the eternal state. The earthly kingdom is the 'commencement of incorruption, by means of which kingdom those who shall be worthy are accustomed gradually to partake of the divine nature'. Again, 'as he rises actually, so also shall he be actually disciplined beforehand for incorruption, and shall go forward and flourish in the times of the kingdom, in order that he may be capable of receiving the glory of the Father. Then, when all things are made new, he shall truly dwell in the city of God.'

OTHER EXAMPLES

No attempt at completeness is being made, but one or two further instances of chiliastic teaching may be given on account of their importance or interest. The great African theologian Tertullian apparently wrote a separate treatise on the subject of the millennial kingdom, but it has been lost. He nevertheless refers to it in his work *Against Marcion* (Book III, ch. 24). 'We do confess that a kingdom is promised to us upon the earth, although before heaven, only in another state of existence; inasmuch as it will be after the resurrection for a thousand years in the divinely built city of Jerusalem, "let down from heaven".'

After its thousand years are over, within which period is completed the resurrection of the saints, who rise sooner or later according to their deserts, there will ensue the destruction of the world and the conflagration of all things at the judgement; we shall then be changed in a moment into the substance of angels, even by the investiture of an incorruptible nature, and so be removed to that kingdom in heaven. . . .

Another African, Lactantius, who was converted through seeing the constancy of Christian martyrs and after the loss of his worldly prospects later became tutor to the son of the Emperor Constantine, refers to the Millennium in his work *Divine Institutes*:

But He, when He shall have destroyed unrighteousness and executed His great judgement, and shall have recalled to life the righteous, who have lived from the beginning, will be engaged among men a thousand years, and will rule them with most just command. . . . Then they who shall be alive in their bodies shall not die, but during those thousand years shall produce an infinite multitude, and their offspring shall be holy, and beloved by God; but they who shall be raised from the dead shall preside over the living as judges. But the nations shall not be entirely extinguished, but some shall be left as a victory for God, that they may be the occasion of triumph to the righteous, and may be subjected to perpetual slavery. . . . Throughout this time beasts shall not be nourished by blood, nor birds by prey; but all things shall be peaceful and tranquil. Lions and calves shall stand together at the manger . . . (Book VII. 24).

One incident from the life of Dionysius, Bishop of Alexandria, may be added before we pass on to Augustine. He was troubled by the presence of millennial teaching in Egypt and it appears that Nepos, Bishop of Arsinoe, had written a work entitled *Refutation of the Allegorists* in which he insisted on a literal interpretation of Revelation 20. After the death of Nepos a party headed by Coracion continued his chiliastic views. Accordingly Dionysius called a conference and by means of patient and friendly discussion succeeded in persuading Coracion and his followers to abandon their belief in a literal Millennium. This encouraging result emboldens me to hope that some of the millions of millenarians in the world today may see this present work and copy the example of Coracion. Dionysius tells the story himself and describes how he 'sat with them for three days, from morning till evening'.

I was greatly pleased to observe the constancy, the sincerity, the

docility, and intelligence of the brethren, as we proceeded to advance
in order, and the moderation of our questions and doubts and
mutual concessions. . . . Nor did we attempt to evade objections,
but endeavoured as far as possible to keep to our subject, and to
confirm these. Nor ashamed, if reason prevailed, to change
opinions, and to acknowledge the truth; but rather received with a
good conscience and sincerity, and with single hearts before God,
whatever was established by the proofs and doctrines of the Holy
Scriptures. At length Coracion, who was the founder and leader of
this doctrine, in the hearing of all the brethren present, confessed
and avowed to us, that he would no longer adhere to it, nor discuss
it, that he would neither mention nor teach it, as he had been fully
convinced by the opposite arguments. The other brethren present
rejoiced also at this conference, and at the conciliatory spirit and
unanimity exhibited by all.

AUGUSTINE

The final collapse of chiliasm, as far as the main Christian
tradition was concerned, was due to St. Augustine the famous
Bishop of Hippo in North Africa, who lived from 354 to 430
(not to be confused with the monk Augustine who came to
England in 597). He was responsible more than anyone else
for popularizing the view that we are now living in the millennium spoken of in Revelation 20; it was at the first Advent of
Christ that Satan was bound. He admits however that
formerly he himself had been a chiliast. In his great work
The City of God (xx. 7), after referring to the opinion that after
6000 years of history the seventh thousand would follow and all
the saints would rise corporeally from the dead to celebrate it,
he goes on:

This opinion might be allowed, if it proposed only spiritual delights
unto saints during this space (we were once of the same opinion
ourselves); but seeing the avouchers hereof affirm that the saints
after this resurrection shall do nothing but revel in fleshly banquets,
where the cheer shall exceed both modesty and measure, this is
gross and fit for none but carnal men to believe. But they that are
really and truly spiritual do call those opinionists Chiliasts; the word
is Greek, and may be interpreted Millennaries or Thousand-year-
ists.

He then quotes Mark 3_{27} as an indication that Satan was
already bound at the time of our Lord's ministry and so this
binding is not to be looked for as a future event.

The phrase of Revelation 20 'until the thousand years be fulfilled', may refer to the remainder of the sixth day, that is the last thousand years of the world's history, or to the whole time that the world was to continue. Augustine had touched upon the duration of the course of history at an earlier point in his work (XVIII. 53): 'It befits us not to know the remainder of the world's years. Some talk how it shall last 400, some 500, some 1,000 years after the Ascension.'

If we are to equate the Millennium with the course of the Church's life, what are we to make of the release of Satan at the end of the thousand years (Revelation 20$_7$) and the advance of Gog and Magog and their war against the holy city? The answer is not difficult to find. Augustine saw here the apostasy spoken of elsewhere in scripture, the final apostasy under the leadership of Antichrist. It would be of brief duration and would last only for the three and a half years immediately preceding the Last Judgement.

In estimating this rather remarkable reinterpretation of the Millennium, which was to hold sway for many centuries, we must remember the victory over pagan forces which had recently been achieved. The long years of persecution appeared to be over, the Emperor Constantine had become a Christian in the early part of the fourth century and although the short pagan reaction under Julian had occurred later, this had been followed by the far-reaching laws of Theodosius, marking the final downfall of the old State religion. The Nicene Creed was triumphant and Prudentius was singing of the new glories of Rome. We can see today how shallow the conversion of the empire was, how mixed the influence of Constantine's patronage. We know too that the Roman empire was a small area compared with the real extent of the habitable earth, that the people of distant China were as numerous as the inhabitants of Europe. But all this was unknown to the men of Augustine's time and to them the world had become Christian, the Gospel had triumphed. True there were bad fish in the net, and tares in the field; but in their view the net and the field were world-wide in their range. What was needed was that the Church should consolidate its position by the suppression of heresy. The fall of Rome in 410 was of course a grievous stumbling-block, but even the Goths were Christians of a kind (Arians) and such calamities were unavoidable in this world. Thus the Millennium as a present fact had its sober colouring and its air of resignation, but the world as then known had come into the Christian fold and this, while it was not Heaven, was at any rate the reign of the saints. Augustine was not reducing the Christian hope to small dimensions; he did believe that the victory of Christ had been achieved and that His Church had come into a position of sovereignty.

It is true that Augustine speaks of the two cities, of God and the devil, both continuing as long as the earth lasts; but he does not mean that two forces equally matched are engaged in perpetual struggle, neither side gaining the ascendancy. To him the known world had become Christian. True, there were heretics like the Donatists—we must expect such tares till the end; but the main stream of orthodox Christianity was secure. The triumph of the faith was thus extensive rather than intensive. Yet it is important to notice that when Augustine speaks of bad fish in the Gospel net, he is thinking of evil men within the visible Church, not of the continuance or revival of paganism. 'Many reprobate live amongst the elect; both come into the Gospel's net, and both swim at random in the sea of mortality' (xviii. 49).

He did not envisage uninterrupted peace—how could he with the Vandals at the gate? Speaking of the promised peace he writes: 'He that looks for this great good in this world, is far wrong' (xvii. 13). The mutability of human estate can never grant any realm an absolute security from all incursions of hostility. The place, therefore, where this promised peace will dwell and abide, is the heavenly Jerusalem.

We shall refer again at a later stage to Augustine's philosophy of history. Our concern at the moment is to note his reinterpretation of the Millennium of Revelation 20. For centuries all orthodox writers followed him in referring this to the present Church-age, and the idea of a literal reign of Christ in the chiliastic sense was finally dismissed from the main trend of Christian thought. Jerome, Augustine's contemporary, took the same line and wrote: 'Let us have done with this fable of a thousand years.' While in one passage Jerome admits he cannot condemn chiliastic views 'because many ecclesiastical men and martyrs have taught the same', elsewhere he describes Millenarians as 'our half-Jews who look for a Jerusalem of gold and precious stones from heaven and a future kingdom of a thousand years'.

CHAPTER 14

JOACHIM AND HIS FOLLOWERS

THE TEACHING of Augustine concerning the Millennium was accepted in the succeeding centuries, and his general view of the course of history has been of great influence up to the present time. But in the twelfth century a very important departure from Augustine's scheme was made by Joachim of Floris (c. 1145–1202).

Before we turn to Joachim's teaching it should be pointed out that the period of Augustine had been followed by the Dark Ages and by the rise of Islam. While his conception of the world's conversion was rather a subdued picture as we have seen, the events of succeeding centuries emphasized even more the darker elements which qualified the Christian hope as far as it concerned this world. Islam with its rapid rise in the seventh century and its wide extent from the middle east to Spain could not be looked upon as a mere Christian heresy and it had to be admitted that the known world was not even nominally Christian. The Crusades helped to bring home to men the limited extent of Christendom; later on it came to be thought that there were many more Moslems in the world than Christians. As we saw in an earlier chapter, from century to century men saw around them the signs of the final apostasy and there were ample grounds for such a view in the latter centuries of the first millennium of our era. In Augustine's scheme, Antichrist and the final apostasy did not appear until the last three and a half years of the present age (see *City of God*, xx. 13); they were retained almost as prophetic counters which had to be included but played no real part in the main development. A few centuries later it was different; and the Augustinian interpretation of history took on a more sombre colouring.

JOACHIM OF FLORIS

Joachim lived in Calabria in the south of Italy and in early life he made a journey to Constantinople and the Holy Land.

According to an early account he spent a long time in solitude in Palestine, amidst visions and meditations in an empty cistern. Some of the thoughts which revolved in the mind of Joachim in this solitary spot were later to emerge as battle-cries which rang through Christendom. On his return from Palestine he became a Cistercian lay-brother and went about as a lay preacher. Later he took Holy Orders and became Abbot of the monastery at Corace in Calabria. Later still he founded under a rule of his own creation the monastery of Floris, also in Calabria; he is thus usually known as Joachim of Floris. He became famous as a prophet and as an interpreter of Scripture, and for some time lived almost as a hermit in prayer, meditation, study, and writing. He was on good terms with the Popes, who encouraged his biblical studies. Among numerous works ascribed to him three are regarded as genuine:(i) a *Commentary on the Apocalypse*, (ii) the *Psaltery of Ten Chords*, and (iii) the *Harmony of the Old and New Testaments*.

His teaching on the Trinity was condemned after his death by the Lateran Council in 1215, but nevertheless he was later beatified by the Roman Church. Incidentally J. H. Newman was in error in speaking of him as a canonized saint; the only Saint Joachim is the father of the Virgin Mary. Even his beatification, it is said, has never been officially ratified. He is referred to with great respect by Dante, who places him in the same circle of Paradise as Nathan, Chrysostom and Anselm and describes him as 'endowed with prophetic spirit' (*Paradiso*, XII. 40).

He has attracted considerable attention in recent years and his doctrine of the three ages is well known: the first age was that of the Old Testament Law, the reign of the Father; the second, that of the Gospel, or the reign of the Son; the third, which was about to dawn, was the reign of the Holy Spirit. It is doubtful how far Joachim himself entered into the details of the third age but his followers took up this conception with great enthusiasm.

It is interesting to note that when the English King Richard the First was at Messina in Sicily in 1190 on his way to Palestine he sent for Joachim. An account of the prophet's interview with the king has survived and it includes an exposition of Revelation 17_{10} ('And they are seven kings; the five are fallen, the one is, the other is not yet come . . .'):

There are seven kings; five are fallen (Herod, Nero, Constantius, Mahomet, Melsemut), one is (Saladin), one is not yet come (Antichrist). Saladin at this time oppresses the Church of God, and keeps possession of it with the sepulchre of our Lord, and the holy city Jerusalem, and the land in which the feet of our Lord stood. But he shall in a short time lose it. Antichrist . . . is already born in the city of Rome, and will be elevated to the Apostolic see. And concerning this Antichrist, the Apostle says, He is exalted, and placed in opposition above all that is called God.

The king's reply shows a surprising knowledge of eschatology and is a revealing comment on the thoughts of that time:

I thought that Antichrist would be born in Antioch, or in Babylon, of the tribe of Dan; and would reign in the temple of the Lord, which is in Jerusalem; and would walk in that land in which Christ walked; and would reign in it for three and a half years; and would dispute against Elijah and Enoch, and would kill them; and would afterwards die; and that after his death God would give sixty days of repentance, in which those might repent who should have erred from the way of truth, and have been seduced by the preaching of Antichrist and his false prophets.

JOACHITE TEACHING

The German scholar Bousset maintained that with Joachim a period arrived in which eschatology, and above all the Antichrist doctrine, 'exercised a great influence on the world's history'. He pointed out that lines of connexion can be traced from the visionary Franciscans influenced by Joachim to Matthias of Janow, Wyclif, and Luther. It will be noticed that in the conversation quoted above Joachim affirmed that Antichrist would be 'elevated to the Apostolic see', and similar ideas are to be found in his writings. This idea that there was a connexion between Antichrist and the Roman see was, as we shall see, taken up with enthusiasm by all who had anti-papal tendencies. He himself may have meant no more than that Antichrist would by diabolical cleverness succeed in usurping the Pope's place. But soon the idea gained ground that the papacy itself was 'the mystery of iniquity' and the Pope was Antichrist—not one particular Pope, but the whole succession provided the fulfilment of Paul's prophecy. The reference to one who should sit in the temple of God (2 Thessalonians 2) appeared to support this interpretation. This, of course, was going far beyond anything Joachim himself had taught and it will be remembered that he was on excellent terms with the Popes of his own life-time.

One part of the Joachite teaching which is noteworthy is the insistence that Antichrist is not to be regarded as appearing just before the end of the world. In his commentary on Revelation he says that the idea that all secular time and things would end with the fall of Antichrist had been overthrown by Remigius; a certain time, of undefined length, would still remain after that event; the last day of Scripture is not the last moment of the world but the last age. It will be evident that this was of some importance from the point of view of a philosophy of history. If the history of man is not to terminate with Antichrist and the apostasy, if some period remains after his destruction, the way is left open for a more hopeful consummation than any which current schemes of thought envisaged.

Joachim quite explicity developed this thought of a final age of triumph. In fact it occupied his attention far more than his Antichrist doctrine, although it was the latter which was mainly taken up in the immediately succeeding centuries and which had some part in bringing about the Reformation. But Joachim himself was far more concerned with the 'third age of the Spirit', a final era of peace and righteousness which would bring to a climax the earlier ages of the Father and the Son.

How Joachim regarded this final era is not entirely clear. But he appears to have equated it with the Millennium of Revelation 20, when Jesus Christ would reign either spiritually or visibly. Some authorities maintain that with Joachim the old form of millenarianism revived, and there is some evidence to this effect. But the main emphasis of his teaching gave rise to the hope of a revival of the spiritual life of the Church. It is most difficult to obtain a clear idea of his precise thoughts on this question. The way in which authorities differ may be illustrated from the following. According to the *Encyclopedia of Religion and Ethics* 'Joachim looked for the return of Christ to inaugurate His millennial reign upon earth in the year 1260'. Diametrically opposed to this is the *Catholic Encyclopedia* article on the Millennium which declares that the apocalyptic writers (Joachim of Floris, the Franciscan Spirituals, the Apostolici) 'referred only to a particular form of spiritual renovation of the Church, but did not include a second advent of Christ'. Some writers attribute to Joachim the revival of millenarianism (so Harnack, R. H. Charles); others make no mention of this whatever but concentrate on his doctrine of the third era of the Spirit.

There are reasons for this confusion. Numerous works were put forward in Joachim's name, developing his teaching in new and extravagant ways. On some points he revised his own judgement. Some of his genuine works were possibly interpolated; and they are difficult of access. Even in the British Museum there is no copy of his work on the Book of Revelation, but I understand there is one at the Bodleian in Oxford. The general student has in the main to depend upon extracts and quotations.

It does appear, however, that at one period at least he expected a literal reign of Christ upon the earth, though his words show some hesitation. He explains Christ's coming in Revelation 19 as a personal coming, but later admits that it may be referred to Christ acting invisibly in His Church militant. According to E. B. Elliott (whose account of Joachim in *Horae Apocalypticae* was evidently based upon direct study of the commentary on Revelation) the abbot equates the Millennium of Revelation 20 with 'that great sabbath which is to be at the end of the world' and says that whether Christ's coming is to be at the beginning of this sabbath time, or the end of it, has seemed to some doubtful; but both St Paul's and Christ's own words seem to fix it at the commencement of the sabbath period.

It is difficult to see how on this view the Millennium could be described as an age of the Spirit. There is no doubt that the main trend of Joachim's teaching suggested to his followers that they stood on the brink of great spiritual developments, an awakening and renovation of the Church, an age of Christian victory and widespread conversion. If we use the terms 'Joachite' and 'Joachism' as referring to the way in which his doctrine was understood by his disciples we may leave on one side the question of the precise distinction between Joachim's own teaching and that of his followers. (For more information on Joachim the general reader should see Henry Bett's *Joachim of Flora*, where the main works on the subject are given. Joachim and his followers are referred to in the majority of extensive works on the Middle Ages; see e.g. those by G. G. Coulton. Two older works, useful for the period we now

approach, are H. C. Lea's *History of the Inquisition*, which gives
a good account of the Franciscan sects, and Neander's great
History of the Church, which, although it is now a hundred years
old and needs checking with more recent works, is of particular
value for its copious quotations, many of which are not readily
accessible elsewhere.)

THE INFLUENCE OF JOACHISM

In the year 1254 a great stir was created at Paris by the
publication of a treatise entitled *The Eternal Gospel*. It consisted of the three genuine works of Joachim together with an
introduction written by a Franciscan, Gherardo da Borgo
San Donnino. Gherardo declared that the Roman Church was
'the carnal Church', the 'whore of Babylon', 'the Synagogue
of Satan'; that the Pope was a mystic Antichrist and a forerunner of the true Antichrist, and that the sacraments were no
longer needful for salvation, for in six years the Holy Spirit
would usher in a new age when the world should be ruled by
poverty and love. The heretical tendency of his work was
immediately seen and Gherardo was consigned to imprisonment in a dungeon where he remained until his death eighteen
years later.

The works of Joachim were very popular among the Franciscans, who arose about the time of his death and regarded
themselves as the fulfilment of his prophecy. It appears that
he had foretold the emergence of two new orders which were
later identified with the Dominicans and Franciscans. Some
think that this prophecy was an interpolation. There is no
doubt that the main lines of his teaching were applied more
particularly to the work of St Francis who was said by some of
his followers to have inaugurated the third age of the Spirit.
After the death of St Francis in 1226 a great dispute arose
among the Franciscans and various parties emerged; the
Spirituals or Zealots held that the rule of absolute poverty
should be enforced, while the Moderates held that some
relaxation of this rule was inevitable. Some of the Spirituals
went to extreme lengths in their fanaticism, exaggerating the
person of St Francis and making him almost a second Christ.
Joachim had emphasized the need for an inward, living
Christianity and had decried confidence in externals; some of
his unguarded statements had given the impression that in the

coming age of the Spirit the outward organization and ordi-
nances of the Church would be abolished and monastic contemplation would be the prevailing characteristic of the faith.
Some of the more extreme of the Spiritual party overemphasized
this mystical note, and Gherardo in the work mentioned above
swept away the whole sacerdotal system, affirming that love
would replace all the sacraments of the Church.

It was remarkable that the strife between the Spirituals and
the Moderates should have reached its height in the course of
the thirteenth century, for Joachim had indicated the year
1260 as one of peculiar importance. He had arrived at this
date on the basis of the ' 1,260 days' of Revelation 11_3 and 12_6,
counting each day as a year. The forty-two months of Revelation 11_2 and 13_5 also produce the number 1,260, reckoning
thirty days for each month. Such passages had produced
the traditional belief accepted by Augustine that Antichrist's
reign would last for three and a half years. The half-week of
Daniel 9_{27}, and the 'time, times, and half a time' (Daniel
7_{25}, 12_7, Revelation 12_{14}) also produce the number three
and a half. Joachim however favoured the day-year interpretation and regarded the 1,260 days as a prophecy of so
many years. The forty-two generations of Matthew 1 would
appear to confirm this, for (counting a generation as lasting
thirty years) the period from Abraham to Christ would also be
1,260 years.

One can understand the immense excitement which would be
produced by the appearance of *The Eternal Gospel*. Its condemnation however led to the downfall of the Spirituals.
But other movements of a heretical kind continued the Joachite
ferment; such were the Fraticelli, an offshoot of the Spiritual
Franciscans, and the followers of Segarelli and Dolcino. (See
Lea's standard work on the Inquisition for details.) It must be
remembered that many spurious works were issued during
this period under Joachim's name.

The connexion which the Joachites saw between Antichrist
and the Papacy was of importance historically. As Bousset
put it:

The belief that the Pope was Antichrist or at least his forerunner
became of world-wide historical importance. This view was
assiduously cultivated by the Franciscans of the opposition, who
had remained true to the original ideal of poverty. From them the
conviction passed over to the pre-Reformation sects. . . .

Hints of this interpretation, connecting Antichrist with the Papacy, have been traced in earlier writers. Anyone who is interested in the question may be referred to a famous speech of Arnulph, Archbishop of Orleans at the Council of Rheims, A.D. 991, as reported by Gerbert, who was later, ironically enough, Pope himself and was known as Silvester the Second. Arnulph refers to recent Popes like John the Twelfth, describing them as 'shameful brutes' and goes on to ask: 'For what do we hold him, who sits blazing with purple and gold, on a lofty throne? If he lacks love, and is only puffed up with knowledge, then is he Antichrist sitting in the temple of God.' The full speech as given in Hefele-Leclercq's *Histoire des Conciles* (Vol. IV, Part 2, pp. 856ff.) was not actually delivered in this form, but Gerbert wove the arguments that were used into a connected whole.

It was, however, through the Joachites that this kind of interpretation gained ground and particularly through the Spiritual Franciscans, and later movements influenced by them. The book of Revelation came to be interpreted in a new way. Babylon was now equated with the Roman Church. The fall of Babylon in Revelation 18–19 is followed by the thousand years of chapter 20; and this meant that the collapse of ecclesiastical Rome would be followed by the reign of Christ. The words of Revelation 18₄, 'Come forth, my people, out of her', were a call to true Christians to leave the Church of Rome. Waldensians and Bohemian Brethren and the others who persisted in spite of the Inquisition were familiar with this general scheme of thought. The present, they felt, is not the Millennium, as Augustine thought; it is the Babylonian Captivity! It is no accident that one of Luther's early works bore the title, *The Babylonian Captivity*. It would be impossible to trace here the varied shapes taken by these new interpretations. The important thing to note is that from the time of Joachim, a new conception of the Millennium as a future period of spiritual victory on earth emerged. The hope of a conversion of the world lived on and was not allowed to fall to the ground. For example, Telesphorus, a Calabrian hermit of the fourteenth century, continued the Joachite tradition in his prophecy that the whole Church would be restored to apostolic poverty and fervour under the leadership of a new Pope, the Pastor Angelicus; the third age would be inaugurated, when all would live the contemplative life. This prophecy of

Telesphorus, it is said, influenced Savonarola in the fifteenth century.

Some of the developments of this Joachite ferment were, as we have seen, definitely heretical. But there were others of a saner type. One recalls the great name of Raymond Lull, whose followers belong to this context. Here it is plain to see that the hopeful attitude concerning the world's future is the inspiration of missionary endeavour—a fact which meets us again and again. Those who believe that God's purpose is to establish His kingdom 'on earth as it is in heaven' will be more inclined to work and pray for the realization of that purpose than those who are obsessed with thoughts of final apostasy and the sway of Antichrist as the culmination of history. The French scholar E. Gilson in his *Spirit of Medieval Philosophy* has a good chapter on the Middle Ages and History. He opposes the common view that the men of this period believed that the world had always been as it was and would remain so until the judgement. He refers to Roger Bacon who looked forward to 'an age of light, in which society, more and more thoroughly Christianized, would become more and more incorporated with the Church', and also to Bonaventura, who said that the final age of humanity would be an era of peace. It seems to me that Gilson is in this section attributing to the Middle Ages generally doctrines that were more particularly held by those Franciscans and others who had come, consciously or unconsciously, under the influence of Joachism. It is significant that Bacon and Bonaventura were both Franciscans.

One of the most interesting of the early Joachites was John Peter Olivi, a Franciscan who lived from about 1247 to 1297. He amplified Joachim's prophetic scheme distinguishing seven ages of the Church, but the main lines were the same. A good account of his teaching is given in Neander's *Church History*, from which the following particulars are taken. The sixth age was the renewal of the evangelical and the extirpation of the antichristian life, with which is connected the final conversion of the Jews and pagans, or at once the reconstruction of the primitive Church. The seventh age is in its relation to this earthly life a sort of sabbath and corresponds roughly with the third era of Joachim's teaching. The sixth age began, in one sense, with the time of St Francis, but more perfectly with the judgements executed on a corrupt Church. Olivi 'supposes a progressive evolution of the antichristian and the Christian principles, both proceeding side by side, to the last decisive struggle'. Ultimately the new age of the Holy Spirit will arrive. The precursor of the new period of genuine life, which consists in following Christ in evangelical poverty, is St Francis. In the period of the Holy Spirit the extensive increase of the Church would proceed from its intensive power. They who exhibited the perfect image of Christ in evangelical poverty, would be employed as the instruments for the extension of God's kingdom through the whole world.

Olivi explicitly equated the Roman Church with Babylon, and his writings were and are still regarded as heretical. But they continued to exert an influence among some of the Franciscans and in other ways. He uniformly represented the Babylon of Revelation as the corrupt Church of Rome hurrying to the judgement. 'And as, previous to her fall, her malice and her power grievously oppressed the spirit of the elect, and hindered the conversion of the world, so will her overthrow be to the saints as *a release from their captivity*.' This imagery of a release from captivity is to be found in Joachim, but he did not equate Babylon with the Roman Church. To his followers however the Babylonian Captivity was a kind of battle cry which continued to sound through the succeeding centuries.

Olivi distinguished a three-fold manifestation of Christ in the history of the world; the first and last, visible; the middle one not sensible, but spiritual. The spiritual advent of Christ is pre-eminently attributed to the sixth period, but it is also applied to the whole process of development of the Church. This spiritual advent of Christ is a noteworthy feature; and it will meet us again at later stages. It had of course been mentioned by Joachim himself.

Neander counts Olivi 'among the prophetic men who bore within them the germs of great spiritual developments in the future, though intermingled with a chaotic mass of heterogeneous elements' (VIII. 450, Eng. Tr.) He refers to the idea of development and growth in the life of the Church as Olivi had expounded it:

For as a tree, so long as it subsists only in its root, cannot as yet unfold its whole peculiar nature, and let every part of it be seen, which can only be done when, in its branches, leaves, blossoms, and fruit, it has reached its complete development; so the tree of the Church . . . neither could nor should unfold itself from the beginning, as it can and must do in its perfection. As the course of development

marked by the Old Testament supposes a gradual progression, so
does the process of the development of Christian wisdom, on the
foundation of the New Testament.

There was a growing illumination from the beginning of the
world up to Christ; and the Christian era displays a similar
process.

It should be made clear that whatever some extreme
Joachites said, Olivi himself made no suggestion that Christianity itself was to be superseded by some new revelation. The
whole process is 'only a progressive, organic evolution of
Christianity itself, through different stadia, starting from that
which Christ has done once for all' (Neander, 446).

The aim of the entire evolution is nothing other than the complete
exhibition of the image of Christ, according to life and knowledge
in humanity; which coincides with the true realization of the image
of God, and of man's destined dominion over the world. So too
the sixth day, on which man was created in the image of God,
corresponds to the sixth period, in which the mass of the Jews and
pagans will be restored to the image of God by Christianity.

After his fine summary of Olivi's writings, Neander concludes:
'We shall perceive the after-workings of them in the succeeding periods.'

LATER DEVELOPMENTS

There is no doubt that Joachim and his followers released a
number of ideas which played a most important part in succeeding centuries. The connexion of the Antichrist conception
with the Papacy was a fantastic piece of scripture exegesis but
it nevertheless helped to alter the history of the world. It may
be said that the Joachite interpretation of Revelation simply
provided the terms and thought forms for the spirit of revolt
and dissatisfaction as it gradually gathered strength. But there
was more in it than that. R. H. Charles is surely right in
maintaining that the Joachite prophecies fomented and
encouraged revolt against Rome; 'statesmen, thinkers, monks,
students, artisans, and men of the world generally drew for
generations strength and courage to press onward toward the
better time, and to resist, in their diverse ways, the claims of
the Papacy, which stood between them and the promised City
of God' (*Studies in the Apocalypse*, p. 23). It was precisely

because they believed that prophecy had foretold the fall of the
Papacy that its enemies were emboldened to withstand its
claims; and the book of Revelation undoubtedly played a part
in the growing ferment which finally boiled over in the Reformation. It was not only the Antichrist doctrine which was
important here, but the very conception of a renovation of the
Church and a spiritual renewal helped forward the cause of
reform. A new interpretation of 2 Thessalonians 2 meets us
in various places. In this passage it is said that 'the man of
sin' will be destroyed by the Lord Jesus with the breath of His
mouth at His coming. Breath is the same word as Spirit; and
some interpreted this passage as meaning that the Spirit of
Christ manifested in the new teaching of the rediscovered
Gospel would destroy the Church of Rome, and the triumph
of Christianity on the earth would follow. In connexion with
this spiritual advent of Christ a Waldensian treatise on Antichrist may be mentioned. This spoke of antichristian tendencies
having their beginning in the time of the apostles and now
reaching a climax. 'We are not therefore to expect Antichrist
as one that is yet to come; so far from that, he is already old.
His power and authority have begun already to diminish, for
already the Lord slays this godless beast by the spirit of His
mouth, by many men of good disposition, sending forth a
power which is opposed to his, and to that of those who are
fond of him.'

Joachism had its negative and positive sides. On the one
hand there was the fall of Antichrist, and on the other the new
age of the Spirit. It should be made clear that the different
parts of the Joachite scheme did not always go together. Thus
there were many who accepted the identification of Antichrist
with the Papacy, who had no place for the new era of Christian
triumph. Some of these felt that though the fall of Rome would
mean the purifying of the Church, the time would not be long
before the end of the world.

Wyclif refers to Joachim but shows no knowledge of his works.
He does not appear to have been directly acquainted with
Gherardo's introduction to *The Eternal Gospel*, which had little
direct influence in England. But as H. B. Workman contends,
in the general atmosphere which this work created, we can see
the source from which Wyclif picked up many of his ideas and
much of his phraseology (*Wyclif*, II. 97–9.) His sympathies
were at first with the Spiritual Franciscans and he agreed with

them that the Roman Church was Babylon. But he did
not adopt the idea that the Holy Spirit would soon usher in a
new age when the world would be ruled by poverty and love.

It is clear that the Joachites touched the Reformation movement in several different areas. Bousset after pointing out the
importance of the Joachite prophecies in connexion with the
pre-Reformation sects, goes on to say:

H. Preuss has shown how important a role the idea of Antichrist
played in the age of Luther among the widest classes of the people—
how the idea gradually dawned on Luther's mind, and became
fixed, that the Pope was the incarnate Antichrist, and how this
conviction led him to more keen and daring opposition to the
Papacy, and filled his soul with all the passion and remorselessness
of battle. (Article 'Antichrist' in *Encyclopedia of Religion and Ethics*.)

The influence of the Joachite doctrine of Antichrist has long
been recognized. The more positive side of Joachism has not
received the same measure of attention. Here there are various
strands which need to be distinguished. The emphasis upon
the inward and the spiritual was at times linked with a disparagement of sacraments and of the outer organization of the
Church. This may possibly have some connexion with the
later rise of the Quaker movement and with some phases of
Puritanism. Again, the idea of a third age of the Spirit was at
times, as we have already seen, pushed to heretical lengths with
the implication that Christianity would be superseded by some
further revelation. St Thomas Aquinas was evidently referring
to something of this kind when replying to 'objection 3' which
had been raised in relation to the question: 'Whether the new
law will last till the end of the world?' (*Summa*, II. 1, Qu. 106,
Art. 4). He states the objection thus:

There was a state corresponding with the Person of the Father viz.
the state of the Old Law wherein men were intent on begetting
children; and likewise there is a state corresponding with the Person
of the Son, viz. the state of the New Law, wherein the clergy who
are intent on wisdom (which is appropriated to the Son) hold a
prominent place. Therefore there will be a third state corresponding to the Holy Spirit, wherein spiritual men will hold the first
place.

It is easy to recognize here some of the more extreme of the
Spiritual Franciscans. Men like Gherardo appeared to be

putting forward the writings of Joachim as a new Gospel, the Eternal Gospel. Joachim had certainly used the phrase 'the Eternal Gospel', which he took from Revelation 14$_6$, but he did not apply it to his own writings. He explained it as being the Gospel of the Holy Spirit; and he made the rather dangerous statement that the Gospel of Christ was transitory and temporal, but its spiritual significance was eternal. The heretical Joachite faction found the Eternal Gospel in his own writings, but this was not the meaning of Joachim himself. Nevertheless, 'it is not to be denied that they found in his books the notion of a final Gospel, a spiritual Gospel, which was to supersede the Gospel of Christ as written in the New Testament, and to be an everlasting Gospel' (H. Bett, *Joachim of Flora*, pp. 49–50). The idea of a third age of the Spirit has cropped up again and again in the history of human thought, and sometimes it has been put forward in a form in which no Christian could accept it. This is the case with the closing paragraphs of Lessing's *Education of the Human Race*; he refers explicitly to certain enthusiasts of the thirteenth and fourteenth centuries, their 'three ages of the world' and their glimpse of a new eternal Gospel.

In spite of these aberrations there were others who were inspired by Joachism to look for the age of the Spirit in a conversion of the world to Christianity, a spiritual reign of Christ in the hearts of men. Some of the Bohemian reformers were evidently attracted to this more positive message. The earliest forerunner of Huss, Milicz, was probably a Joachite himself (so Lea's *Inquisition*, II. 436). He foresaw not only a judgement on the corrupt Church, but also a renovation of the Church, by which it was to be prepared for the Second Advent of Christ. He called not for a crusade to open a way to Jerusalem on earth, but for a spiritual crusade which by the triumphant diffusion of the word of Christ should make the heavenly Jerusalem accessible to all. A later Bohemian reformer, Matthias of Janow, was influenced by Milicz; he declared that before the end of the world the Church of Christ would be reformed, renovated, and more widely extended. Before the Final Judgement Christ would reveal Himself in a multitude of preachers. The spiritual revelation of Christ through His genuine organs, the spiritual annihilation of Antichrist by the same, and a new illumination of the Church, were to prepare it for the last appearance of Christ. In this spiritual sense he understood much of that which is said concerning the victory of Christ over Antichrist and concerning the signs of Christ's appearing. The expression that Christ will destroy Antichrist by the breath of His mouth, is not to be understood literally, but spiritually. The parables of the leaven and the mustard-seed would find their application, as in the primitive, so also once more and pre-eminently in the last times.

Matthias, continuing the work of Milicz, himself influenced John Huss.

CHAPTER 15

THE REFORMATION AND AFTER

APART from the developments outlined in the previous chapter, what we may call the Augustinian view continued to dominate Christian thought throughout the Middle Ages. It was generally held that the empirical Church was the millennial kingdom, that the present time was the fulfilment of Revelation 20, since Christ had bound Satan at His first coming. The world would continue pretty much as it was until the Judgement, which might occur at any time. In this chapter our main purpose is to discover if the Reformation encouraged any hope of a victory for the kingdom of Christ on earth, and to inquire exactly what the Reformers and those who succeeded them taught about the prospects of Christianity in the world.

Sufficient has been said in the previous chapter to show that there was a connexion between Joachism and the movements which prepared the way for the Reformation. When Luther and his colleagues described the Roman Church as Babylon, and the Pope as Antichrist, they were but repeating what had been said centuries earlier by Spiritual Franciscans, Lollards, and the rest. There is a continuous series of links between Calabria and Wittenberg, as far as this negative and condemnatory side is concerned. But what of the doctrine of a coming age of faith and spiritual victory?

It might be expected that if the sixteenth-century reformers perpetuated one element of Joachism, some aspects of the more positive and hopeful side would also be represented. It must be admitted, however, that the 'Augustinian' view continued to prevail in the form in which it had been dominant in the Middle Ages. As we have already seen it was possible for men to follow the purely critical elements of Joachism, and to neglect the more constructive message. This is virtually what Wyclif did in the fourteenth century; and Luther and Calvin did something similar in the sixteenth. They adopted with eagerness the view that the Pope was Antichrist; in fact it has been maintained that after Luther had reached this conclusion his whole attitude

145

L

stiffened. But while the aim of a reformed and purified Church engaged these leaders, they did not look for any world-wide conversion of the human race, or for any widespread development which would be very different from the previous centuries of Christian history.

It is true that the main reformers did not absorb all the teaching which had been circulated by those bodies sometimes known as 'medieval nonconformists'; nor did they gather into their movements all the reforming groups of Europe. Some still remained which were unattracted by Luther and Calvin; and whether among these there lingered the hope of a really Christian world is a question at which we must look at a later stage. That such a hope was still cherished here and there long after the thirteenth century is clear, particularly in the case of Bohemia. Our immediate concern is to illustrate the line taken by Luther and Calvin and the English reformers. A few significant references will be sufficient to indicate the limits of their expectations and hopes.

LUTHER AND CALVIN

Reformation thought was on the whole rather pessimistic in its outlook on the future. Luther in answer to the Bull of 1520 wrote: 'Our Lord Jesus Christ yet liveth and reigneth; who, I firmly trust, will shortly come, and slay with the spirit of His mouth, and destroy with the brightness of His coming, that Man of Sin.' He gave various estimates of the time the human race would endure. Thus at one time he said: 'God forbid the world should last fifty years longer. Let Him cut matters short with His last judgement.' The following is also from the *Table Talk*: 'The wickedness of the world is risen to that height that I dare presume to say that the world cannot continue many hundred years longer.' Again: 'I persuade myself verily that the day of judgement will not be absent full three hundred years more. God will not, cannot, suffer this wicked world much longer.'

Similar are the words of Melanchthon:

The words of the prophet Elias should be marked by everyone . . . 6,000 years shall this world stand and after that be destroyed; 2,000 years without the law; 2,000 years under the law of Moses; 2,000 years under the Messiah; and if any of these years are not fulfilled, they will be shortened (a shortening intimated by Christ also) on account of our sins.

Calvin also appeared to hold out little hope of a conversion of the world. It is interesting to examine his commentaries on the Old Testament prophets to see how he interprets the passages which describe an era of righteousness and peace. His general line is that the promises to Israel are being now fulfilled in the Christian Church. He also explains that for their complete fulfilment we must include the Second Advent of Christ and the consummation in the final state. Thus Isaiah 2, 9, 11, 65, 66, are referred to Christ and His present kingship and to the Church. Christians, he explains, are at peace with one another as well as with God, their evil passions are tamed, the new creation is to be understood as the new age which began with Christ. Isaiah's prophecy of a new heaven and earth includes certain exaggerated modes of expression, but the greatness of the change which Christ brought was such that it could not be described in any other way. The renovation begins with us, and when we shall be perfectly renewed, heaven and earth shall also be fully renewed, and shall regain their former state. On the promise of longevity in Isaiah 65_{20} he writes that the citizens of the Church shall be long-lived; although the majority of believers hardly support themselves through weakness 'yet that promise is not make void; for if Christ reigned truly and perfectly in us his strength would undoubtedly flourish in us and would invigorate both body and soul'. Isaiah 11_9 means that Christians are free from all desire of doing hurt to others; and the reference to the knowledge of God covering the earth foretells the fullness of Christian knowledge as contrasted with the meagre and rudimentary wisdom of the Jews.

ENGLISH REFORMERS AND OTHERS

The English reformers were in the main in agreement with Luther and Calvin as far as the matter we are discussing is concerned. The volumes of the Parker Library, which give the relevant English writings of this period, suggest that they thought the end of the world to be near, or if this is not confidently stated they nevertheless held out little hope of the world's conversion. This at any rate is true for the sixteenth century.

Ridley laments that 'the world without doubt (this I do believe, and therefore I say it) draws toward an end'. Latimer repeats the Elias prophecy about 6,000 years and adds that 'there be past 5,552 years; so that there is no more left but 448 years. Futhermore these days shall be shortened for the elects' sake'. With regard to the Second Advent he says: 'Peradventure it may come in my days, old as I am, or in my children's days.'

John Bradford, who was born about 1510 and martyred in 1555, was connected with Ridley, Latimer, and Cranmer. (This was the man who on seeing evil-doers taken to execution made the famous remark: 'But for the grace of God there goes John Bradford.') He wrote a 'Meditation concerning the kingdom of Christ, and that it is no corporal thing, as the Jews and Anabaptists do feign; to whom the papists in manner assent, making the church so glorious and gay a dame, far unlike to be Christ's spouse, who was here on earth in no such felicity and worldly glory as their church is' (*Works*, II. 359). He quotes various scriptures to prove that in Christ's Church upon earth there shall be good and bad mingled until the Day of Judgement. He is in agreement with the Augustinian view and affirms that

thy church and the true children thereof shall in this world until the last day suffer persecution, and that goats will be amongst the sheep until the day of judgement.

This seems to be the view of most of the English reformers of this period.

A little later a new interpretation of the Book of Revelation arose, but without seriously modifying the general outlook. Whereas Augustine had dated the Millennium from our Lord's ministry some writers now fastened upon the reign of Constantine as marking the beginning of the thousand years, a period which they were inclined (unlike Augustine) to take literally. It is rather curious that Foxe the martyrologist (*Eikasmi*, 1586) equated the binding of Satan with the Church's triumph at the time of Constantine. Unlike some Protestant writers, he spoke well of this emperor; he did not regard the 'donation' as historical. Persecution ceased, he says, for a thousand years (at least in the sense that there was no universal murderous persecution), from Licinius to the time of Wyclif and Huss. Then Satan was released for a time, in fulfilment of Revelation 20$_{7\mathrm{ff}}$. In his *Acta et Monumenta*, Book v, Foxe says that the chaining and closing up of Satan was after the ten persecutions of the primitive Church. The thousand years of Revelation 20 thus began in 294 and ended in 1294.

It may be mentioned here that a few years later Alcasar, a Jesuit priest of Salamanca, in his interpretation of Revelation said that Constantine was the angel who bound Satan, and thereupon the Millennium began. He held that Chapters 1–11 dealt with the Church's victory over the Jews, 12–20 with its victory over Rome and the whole world, the destruction of Babylon (i.e. pagan Rome) being effected by Constantine and his successors; 21–2 he referred to the triumphant state of the Church in heaven. The whole apocalypse therefore showed how Rome, of old the head of pagan idolatry, was to be changed into the metropolis of the Catholic Church.

Later in the seventeenth century the Protestant writers Grotius (in Holland) and Hammond (in England) accepted a similar interpretation in connexion with the Millennium. The first resurrection, they said, was ecclesiastical and began at the time of Constantine with the victory over paganism. The Millennium, which they took as a literal period of a thousand years, lasted from the fourth to the fourteenth century. Then Gog and Magog (the Othman Turks) arose. When they are destroyed and their attack on Christendom is defeated, the Final Judgement will take place. With the lapse of time, this interpretation became difficult to sustain; the 'little time' of Revelation 20$_3$ could hardly be stretched to cover several centuries. (This verse states that 'he should deceive the nations no more, until the thousand years should be finished: after this he must be loosed *for a little time*'.)

On the whole it could be contended that after the Renaissance and the Reformation the general outlook on the future was far gloomier than in the Middle Ages. Through the Renaissance the classical doctrine that decline was inevitable because the world was wearing out affected thinking on the subject; while the Reformation encouraged the view that the Church had become corrupted in the early centuries. Whereas in Augustine's teaching the apostasy was relegated to the last three and a half years of the Christian era, the view now gained ground that 'the mystery of iniquity' (Romanism) was at work from the days of the apostles, in accordance with 2 Thessalonians 2$_7$.

SEVENTEENTH-CENTURY ILLUSTRATIONS

The idea of deterioration and decline is prominent in a work by an Anglican clergyman, Godfrey Goodman's *Fall of Man* (1616). Here it is argued that modern men are weaker than the ancients, the earth is grown barren, the seas do not afford the like quantity of fish, as heretofore they have done. The great wealth of the men of old is contrasted with present conditions. All this is held to prove that 'the Last Judgement approacheth'. All the signs of Christ's coming do already appear; when the hangings and furniture are taken down, it is a token that the king and the court are removing.

Although the work is entitled the *Fall of Man*, this doctrine of a deterioration caused by the lapse of time is pagan rather than biblical, and Goodman refers to the ancient classical writers for confirmation of his contention, and to what they had said about the original age of gold. This pagan theory of inevitable decline—in nature as well as human life— received emphasis on account of the Renaissance. It is sometimes said that the Renaissance gave rise to the doctrine of progress. The opposite is probably nearer the truth. When the classical writings were rediscovered, modern writers and readers were overwhelmed by their consciousness of inferiority to the great figures of the past, Plato, Sophocles, and the rest. The famous struggle between the Ancients and the Moderns (described so well in J. B. Bury's *Idea of Progress*) was the result. It took centuries to gain the point that modern man was not *necessarily* inferior to the men of classical antiquity. The predominance of classical studies in schools, which has lasted almost up to the present time, is again due to the conviction that no modern production could be worthy to compare with the achievements of the Greeks and the Romans. The common idea that the Rennaissance immediately gave rise to boundless self-confidence is wide of the mark; its first effect was often one of despair. This must be remembered in connexion with such works as that of Goodman. This doctrine of inevitable decline had appeared in Judaism about the time of the beginning of our era; but it had not been at all prominent in the great theological systems of the Middle Ages—in Aquinas for example. For ancient Jewish teaching of this kind, see 2 Esdras 4_{55}: 'Creation

is already grown old and is already past the strength of
youth.'

One unusual interpretation from the seventeenth century
which may be included on account of its interest occurs in a
remarkable poem by George Herbert (1593–1633), entitled
The Church Militant. He describes Christianity beginning in
the east, like the sunrise, and spreading westward. But he
brings out the idea that the Gospel is forsaken in each area
in turn as a more westerly land welcomes it.

> . . . so went the Church her way,
> Letting, while one foot stepped, the other stay
> Among the eastern nations for a time,
> Till both removed to the western clime.

The Moslems have now taken possession of the eastern regions.
Soon the western lands will again be covered with darkness:

> Nay, it shall ev'ry year decrease and fade;
> Till such a darkness do the world invade
> At Christ's last coming, as his first did find . . .

> Religion stands on tip-toe in our land,
> Ready to pass to the American strand . . .

> Yet as the Church shall thither westward fly,
> So Sin shall trace and dog her instantly.

And so, finally, when the round of the globe has been accomplished, the Last Judgement will appear in the east, where the
faith first began to make its circuit.

An example from a later period of the seventeenth century is
provided by Milton's *Paradise Lost.* In Book XII he describes
how Michael gives to Adam a résumé of world-history. The
Flood, the story of Israel, the coming of Christ, are dealt with
and then comes a brief account of the course of the Christian
era. It is rather a dismal story. The Apostles, it is true,
'win great numbers of each nation to receive with joy the
tidings brought from heaven'; but on their departure, wolves
make their entrance and the apostasy sets in. Superstition and
greed appear to be the prevailing notes of the professing Church.
A few will rise in protest and will be met with heavy persecution:

> the rest, far greater part,
> Will deem in outward rites and specious forms
> Religion satisfied; truth shall retire
> Bestuck with slanderous darts, and works of faith
> Rarely be found: so shall the world go on,
> To good malignant, to bad men benign;
> Under her own weight groaning till the day
> Appear of respiration to the just,
> And vengeance to the wicked, at return
> Of Him so lately promised to thy aid,
> The Woman's seed; obscurely then foretold,
> Now amplier known thy Saviour and thy Lord,
> Last in the clouds from heav'n to be reveal'd
> In glory of the Father, to dissolve
> Satan with his perverted world, then raise
> From the conflagrant mass, purged and refined,
> New heavens, new earth, ages of endless date
> Founded in righteousness, and peace, and love,
> To bring forth fruits, joy, and eternal bliss!

There is here no hope of the world's conversion, no hint of a Millennium, not even the Reformation is mentioned. The majority of professing Christians through the centuries are regarded as pretenders; and no hope of any renewal or development is held out. The age will end with the Second Advent, and then follow the New Heaven and Earth of the eternal state.

MILLENARIANISM AGAIN

Something should be said here about the revival of Millenarianism (or Chiliasm) and one or two illustrations may be given of its vitality in the Reformation period and later. The main reformers of the sixteenth century rejected it, and the Augsburg and Helvetic Confessions branded it as a Judaistic heresy. But it was adopted by some of the Anabaptists, who were outside the main reformation stream, and in particular by the Anabaptists of Münster who tried to prepare for the reign of Christ by taking military measures against His enemies. It is important to remember that there were many other Anabaptists who held very different views, e.g. Menno Simons. Menno believed that the coming of Christ was near, not however to inaugurate the Millennium, but for judgement.

John Bradford, mentioned earlier in this chapter, found it necessary to write against Anabaptist millenarians; and in his *Meditation concerning the kingdom of Christ* written in the sixteenth century are some words still worth pondering by present-day millenarians:

Whereas the Anabaptists do cite the prophets, who speaking of Christ's kingdom use often figures and similitudes of worldly empires that by temporal and visible things we may arise to a deep consideration of spiritual and eternal things in Christ's kingdom, let us learn so to do. And again let us know that the Gospel is the exposition of the prophets; and therefore these corporal metaphors in the prophets, painting forth the kingdom of Christ, must be interpreted according to the Gospel, which teacheth clearly Christ's kingdom to be a spiritual and no temporal thing.

Nevertheless, millenarianism revived in England, again outside the main Reformation stream, and was strong in the seventeenth century. A chiliastic sect emerged known as the Fifth Monarchy Men. Their name derives from the Book of Daniel; the four pagan empires of Daniel 2 are to be followed by the fifth empire of the kingdom of God; similarly in Chapter 7, the four beasts are followed by the 'one like unto a son of man'. These fanatics believed they were called to represent in advance this Fifth Monarchy of King Jesus. Their leader was Colonel Thomas Harrison, who later became a Major-General, and in 1650 Commander-in-Chief in England. It was maintained that 'the four world-empires of the Book of Daniel covered the whole intervening period down to the Protectorate of Cromwell, with the breakdown of which the fifth world-empire of the full dominion of Christ might be expected. With the Advent of Christ and the establishment of the Fifth Monarchy would come a true Kingdom of Saints, without priest or sacrament, law or oath, king or government' (A. C. Underwood, *History of the English Baptists*, p. 83). Harrison was hanged by the Convention Parliament; and in exasperation the Fifth Monarchy men rose under Venner, a cooper, in January 1661. The trained bands were unable to deal with them, so the regulars were called out. After a fierce encounter the maddest were shot down or disarmed in an alehouse near Cripplegate. 'Thus ended the last politically important wave of chiliasm and the last attempt of Christian social reformers to set up the Kingdom of God in this world by the sword' (Underwood).

Chiliastic interpretations of the Book of Revelation still flourished both on the continent and in this country. Independents like Thomas Goodwin were at times inclined to Chiliasm. The works of Mede had wide influence; he and his followers attempted to fix dates for the setting up of the millennial kingdom.

Millenarianism was represented in this country in the eighteenth century by such men as T. Hartley, Rector of Winwick, of whom mention has previously been made. He wrote on the subject in 1764 but later changed his views and accepted the system of Swedenborg. It will be unnecessary to pursue the later history of Chiliasm as more recent movements have been referred to in an earlier chapter. It is sufficient to say that it has continued without a break to the present time. Last century it was strongly maintained in certain evangelical circles. The great New Testament Greek scholar, Dean Alford (author of the hymn, 'Come, ye thankful people, come',) was a convinced millenarian; 'I do maintain, and receive as an article of faith and hope' the literal resurrection at the beginning of the thousand years.

It is sometimes alleged that the German Lutheran, J. A. Bengel (1687–1752), the famous Abbot of Alpirsbach, textual critic and commentator, was a chiliast; but this is not so. It is true that he worked out prophetic schemes in his interpretation of the Books of Revelation and Daniel, and believed in two periods of a thousand years each, the former of which would begin in 1836, but he did not believe that in either period Christ would personally reign on the earth. It is therefore very unfair to class him as a chiliast and to place him in the same category as Mede. The point which the Reformation Confessions condemned was not the insistence on any length of time but the Judaistic idea of the Messiah's personal reign on the earth; this was the head and front of the chiliast's offending. Bengel believed in the successful evangelization of the world and he thought he had the key to the exact dates when this would take place, but he did not believe in the pre-millennial advent of Christ.

This mention of the evangelization of the world reminds us that the possibilities open to Christian thought were not exhausted by Millenarianism and the traditional Augustinian view. Not all who rejected the 'Judaistic heresy' of Chiliasm were satisfied to expect an ultimate apostasy; not all Anglicans agreed with Goodman and Herbert, nor all Puritans with Milton. How did the conception of a Christian world fare amidst all the changes of post-Reformation times? This is the question to which we now turn, and in answering it we propose to begin at the end and work backward, and in so doing we shall dispel a common delusion.

CHAPTER 16

THE LATTER-DAY GLORY OF THE CHURCH

IT IS frequently taken for granted that it was only in fairly recent times that the Church began to look for the conversion of the world as the fulfilment of the purpose of God. It is even suggested that the Church mistakenly borrowed this idea from Godwinism or Victorian optimism and gave it a Christian colouring. J. B. Bury in his book *The Idea of Progress* (1920), a most fascinating work, is probably right in suggesting that the notion of inevitable progress, so widespread up to the time of the first world war, was originated by deists and French 'philosophes' and later became involved with the doctrine of evolution and the sanguine hopes of the Victorian age. In his *History of Freedom of Thought* he writes that the doctrine of historical progress 'was started in France (1750) by Turgot, who made progress the organic principle of history'.

Christians of course do not believe in progress in the terms in which Bury defined it, and in that form it is generally abandoned at the present time. But this does not mean that we are committed to the belief that history will always be a chequer-board of good and evil. There is a vast difference between the conception of divine purpose and that of an inevitable law of nature. In the following pages a number of quotations from the last few centuries will be given in illustration of the Christian hope in its relation to this world and to the kingdom of Christ on earth; and it will be quite evident that this hope of a Christian world, as the goal of the divine purpose, did not spring from the secular idea of inevitable progress. There will be no need to give illustrations from the nineteenth century, and it is no doubt true that in the Victorian period Christian thought may have become affected by outside influences such as (i) the contemporary hopefulness aroused by scientific and mechanical discoveries, (ii) a misunderstanding of the doctrine of evolution, (iii) the glow of imperial expansion, and (iv) the aforementioned French theory which in various ways had percolated into English thought. While the idea of 'inevitable progress through the mere passage of time' has rightly been abandoned, the Christian hope is far older and need not collapse with it.

THE EIGHTEENTH-CENTURY REVIVAL

John Wesley, preaching before the University of Oxford in 1744, dealt with the subject of 'Scriptural Christianity'. He described its beginnings in the individual soul, then its spread from one life to another, and then its victory in the world. This sermon is included among the *Forty-four Sermons* recognized as indicating the doctrinal standards of The Methodist Church. Some of the other sermons of Wesley, not included in this collection, deal more fully with the subject, particularly one on the theme of 'The General Spread of the Gospel', the text being Isaiah 11$_9$: 'The earth shall be full of the knowledge of the Lord, as the waters cover the sea.' He refers to the evangelical revival as it had developed in England and then envisages its spread to other countries—first Protestant countries, then those partly Protestant and partly Roman Catholic, then to those wholly Romanist such as Spain, Italy, and Portugal. Then he describes the victory of Christ among the Moslems and a passage from this particular section may be quoted:

And then the Saviour of sinners will say, 'The hour is come; I will glorify my Father: I will seek and save the sheep that were wandering on the dark mountains. Now will I avenge myself of my enemy, and pluck the prey out of the lion's teeth. I will resume my own, for ages lost: I will claim the purchase of my blood.' So He will go forth in the greatness of His strength, and all His enemies shall flee before Him. All the prophets of lies shall vanish away, and all the nations that had followed them shall acknowledge the great Prophet of the Lord, 'mighty in word and deed'; and 'shall honour the Son, even as they honour the Father'.

Then come references to the Red Indians, the inhabitants of the East Indies, 'numerous tribes of Tartars, the heathen parts of the Russias, and the inhabitants of Norway, Finland, and Lapland', and more distant nations. Islands at present inaccessible will be reached and 'all Israel too shall be saved'.

At that time will be accomplished all those glorious promises made to the Christian church, which will not then be confined to this or that nation, but will include all the inhabitants of the earth. 'They shall not hurt nor destroy in all my holy mountain.'

The hymns of Charles Wesley proclaimed the same message, and it is of particular interest to note that at times he used Advent language to describe this spiritual victory. This is the case with the hymn, 'My heart is full of Christ'. Another with a similar theme is 'All glory to God in the sky'. John Wesley, the day before he died in his eighty-eighth year, sang the following verses from his brother's hymn:

> All glory to God in the sky,
>   And peace upon earth be restored!
> O Jesus, exalted on high,
>   Appear our omnipotent Lord!
> Who, meanly in Bethlehem born,
>   Didst stoop to redeem a lost race,
> Once more to Thy creatures return,
>   And reign in Thy kingdom of grace.
>
> O wouldst Thou again be made known!
>   Again in Thy Spirit descend,
> And set up in each of Thine own
>   A kingdom that never shall end.
> Thou only art able to bless,
>   And make the glad nations obey,
> And bid the dire enmity cease,
>   And bow the whole world to Thy sway.

Wesley's contemporary, John Newton, best known as a hymn-writer, preached a remarkable series of sermons in the years 1784–5 on the scripture passages which make up the text of Handel's *Messiah*. A number of these are relevant to our present subject. Thus Sermon XXXII on Romans 10_{18} is entitled 'The Progress of the Gospel'. The fulfilment of the promises respecting Messiah's Kingdom is progressive, says Newton. The prophecies of the Old and New Testaments encourage us to hope for a time when the light of Gospel truth will break forth with meridian brightness, the glory of the Lord shall be revealed and all flesh shall see His salvation. In accordance with Paul's words: 'All Israel shall be saved.' In Sermon XXXIV Newton declares that God's truth and honour are engaged for the success of His Gospel, and they must stand or fall together. The kingdoms of the earth shall become the kingdom of our God and of His Christ. Sermon XXXVII is on 'The Extent of Messiah's spiritual Kingdom', the particular part of Handel's libretto in this case being Revelation 11$_{15}$. It is pointed out that such prophecies as Isaiah 2, 11, 60, have not yet been fulfilled. But the promises of the Lord cannot fail. It is not necessary to suppose that every individual shall be savingly converted to the Lord in this future day of His power, but (i) the Gospel shall visit nations now in darkness, (ii) this Gospel shall prevail, not in word only, but in power, (iii) disputes among Christians shall cease, and (iv) it will be a time of general peace. In Sermon XLVIII it is said that 'a time is coming when many (perhaps the greater part of mankind) shall walk in the light'.

CONNEXION WITH THE MISSIONARY MOVEMENT

This belief that the purpose of God for the world was its conversion to Christianity was of very great importance in the development of Christian activity. It was closely connected with the modern missionary movement of the past hundred and fifty years which has led to an enormous expansion of the Church, greater indeed than in any previous period. Men's actions spring from their beliefs. If we believe that the present age will end in apostasy, that the victory of Christianity is not part of the divine purpose, we shall be satisfied with things as they are. But if we believe that the Church is the organ of the divine plan to reconcile all things to God, that a time is coming when through the power of the Cross the knowledge of God shall cover the earth as the waters cover the sea, the whole spirit of our approach and our expectancy will be different. In any case, it is a fact that the roots of the modern missionary movement—a movement which has led to the emergence of the world Church, 'the great new fact of our time' —were connected with a profound faith in the Latter-day Glory of the Church, as it was called. The phrase of course comes from the many prophecies of the glory of the latter days in the Old Testament, such as Isaiah 2.

A book by Jonathan Edwards must be mentioned at this point, *A Humble Attempt to Promote Prayer* (1748). Edwards lived in America and was associated with the 'awakening' in Massachusetts. His call to prayer was taken up in the midlands of this country by groups of Baptists and others; and it was from this circle of prayer that there emerged the work of William

Carey, whose forty years' heroic labours in Bengal virtually provided the spearpoint of the modern missionary movement. Now if we examine this work of Edwards (which may be found in Vol. II of his collected *Works*) we notice that a good deal of it is concerned with prophecy. He calls attention to the numerous passages in the Old Testament which foretell a golden age of peace and righteousness. He then points out that these prophesies have never yet been realized. And he invites Christian people to call upon God in earnest prayer that these divine promises may be fulfilled in the speedy conversion of the world. It is remarkable that while Edwards was a Calvinist he nevertheless looked forward to a time when 'instead of the few true and thorough Christians now in some few countries, every nation on the face of the whole earth shall be converted to Christianity, and every country shall be full of true Christians'. Those who imagine that the hope of the world's conversion is an obsolete and ridiculous by-product of Victorian optimism would do well to study these pages written over two hundred years ago.

It is evident from the scriptures (writes Edwards) that there is yet remaining a great advancement of the interest of religion and the kingdom of Christ in this world, by an abundant outpouring of the the Spirit of God, far greater and more extensive than ever yet has been. . . . It is often foretold and signified, in a great variety of strong expressions, *that there should a time come*, when all nations, through the whole habitable world, should embrace the true religion, and be brought into the Church of God. . . . Christ compares the Kingdom of Heaven in this world to leaven, which a woman took and hid in three measures of meal, till the whole was leavened. . . . It is natural and reasonable to suppose, that the whole world should finally be given to Christ, as one whose right it is to reign, as the proper heir of him who is originally the King of all nations, and the possessor of heaven and earth.

Among the passages of scripture he adduces are Psalm 72, Isaiah 2, 66_{23}, 40_5, Psalm 2_{6-8}, Matthew 13_{33}, John 12_{32}. Paul's words in Romans 11 show 'that the time is coming when the whole world of mankind shall be brought into the Church of Christ; the fullness of both, the whole lump, all the nation of the Jews, and all the world of Gentiles'. The era of the Latter-day Glory is connected with the Millennium of Revelation 20. Once again we find Advent language used to denote a religious awakening, the coming of Christ in Revelation 19 being interpreted spiritually. It is not, says Edwards, a literal coming, but rather a manifestation of Christ 'after long hiding himself', 'a great revival and mighty progress of true religion'.

The links connecting this work by Jonathan Edwards with the missionary activity of William Carey are traced in *The Prayer Call of 1784*, a pamphlet by E. A. Payne published in 1941. Edwards's little book was reprinted in this country (at Northampton) and its suggestion that Christians should join in concerted prayer specifically for 'the extension of Christ's Kingdom in the world' and for the revival of real religion was taken up by the Northamptonshire Association of Particular Baptists. 'It was this American pamphlet that helped to prepare the way for the founding of the Baptist Missionary Society, for the parallel advance in the Northampton Association, and for many another movement of the Spirit of God' (Payne). By a curious coincidence the place in Massachusetts where Edwards lived was named Northampton, and so (as A. T. Pierson observed years ago in *New Acts of the Apostles*) 'Northampton in England echoed the clarion peal of the New England Northampton' and the monthly concert of prayer was established. Pierson also maintained 'that Carey's movements were only the germinating of what Edwards, and others like him, had planted'.

The Baptist Missionary Society, founded through Carey's influence in 1792, was the first of its kind and was followed by a dozen others in the next few years. The London Missionary Society (which sent Morrison to China, and later Livingstone to Africa, and Chalmers to New Guinea) was founded in 1795, the Church Missionary Society in 1799, the British and Foreign Bible Society in 1804. The Methodist Missionary Society was officially founded in 1813 though Methodists had been engaged in missionary work years earlier. These developments were no doubt largely due to the evangelical revival of the eighteenth century, but the vision of a Christian world also played a part. The prayer meetings which have been referred to were not entirely general, they had in view quite clearly a world-wide movement of the Spirit of God. Andrew Fuller, one of those who initiated them, put forward as one of his main points: 'Consider what God has promised to do for his church in times to come.' Carey in his historic *Enquiry* (1792) was mostly concerned to show the religious condition of the world at that time, but he maintained that the intention of God was

M

'to prevail finally over all the power of the Devil, and to destroy all his works, and set up his own kingdom and interest among men, and extend it as universally as Satan had extended his'. Christians must endeavour 'by all possible methods to bring over a lost world to God'.

Edwards of course was not the first to expound the doctrine of a Christian world. In certain circles the Latter-day Glory of the Church was a familiar conception. One thinks of Isaac Watts and his hymn, 'Jesus shall reign', written in 1719. Then there is Matthew Henry whose famous commentary on the Bible appeared in the years 1708–10. In his notes on Isaiah 2, the passage about swords and plowshares, he wrote:

We have reason to hope that this promise shall yet have a more full accomplishment in the latter times of the Christian Church, when the Spirit shall be poured out more plentifully from on high. Then there shall be on earth peace.

The commentator Daniel Whitby (1638–1726), Precentor of Salisbury, is sometimes erroneously described as the first who put forward the post-millennial interpretation of the Book of Revelation; but while he did not originate this view there is no doubt that his work was important in popularizing it. Unlike Augustine, he maintained that the Millennium was future and meant a glorious state of the Church. The fall of Antichrist was interpreted to mean the final collapse of Roman Catholicism, which would be followed by the conversion of the Jews and a flourishing period of spiritual triumph, peace, and plenty.

BUNYAN AND OTHERS

It is most important to recognize that John Bunyan (1628–88) taught this doctrine of a spiritual Millennium and a victory of Christianity on the earth. He is sometimes reproached with attending too exclusively to the individual soul and abandoning the city of destruction to its fate. But those who repeat this charge must be totally unfamiliar with his works on Antichrist and the Holy City. The former of these, *Of Antichrist and his ruin*, treats of the Roman Church along the usual Protestant lines; but it also describes the flourishing state of the true Church after the fall of Papal Rome. The theme of the golden age of the Church is developed much more fully in the *Holy*

City, or New Jerusalem. This fine work was printed in 1665, during Bunyan's imprisonment, and is probably the first extended description of a Christian world in the English language. It is an exposition of Revelation 21_{10-27}, 22_{1-4}. He takes the view (later promulgated by R. H. Charles) that these verses of Chapter 21 deal with the same period as the thousand years of 20_4. These passages are regarded as a description of the Church's final victory on earth, the spiritual reign of Christ. Bunyan refers to an abundance of converts to the Christian faith:

multitudes, and that of all sorts, both of Jews and Gentiles, Moors, Tartars, Turks, and those in the utmost parts of the world, shall now be entangled with the light and truth, with the glory and goodness of the doctrine of the twelve.

. . . a great harvest of sinners shall be gathered by the grace of the Gospel. But the truth is, the Scriptures go with open arms toward the latter end of the world, even as if they would grasp and compass about almost all people then upon the face of the whole earth with the grace and mercy of God. 'The earth', saith God, 'shall be full of the knowledge' of the glory 'of the Lord, as the waters cover the sea.'

This does not mean that every single person on earth will be a true Christian for 'in the midst of all this glory, or while the glorious light of the Gospel shall thus shine in the world, yet even then there will be some also that will not see and rejoice in the glory hereof'. But their power will be small; the governors of all the world at that day shall be Jerusalem men. Again there is special mention of the Jewish people: 'I told you before that the Jews shall at this day be converted to the Christian faith, and shall have a great name and much of heaven upon them in this city.'

It is clear that in the seventeenth century, Milton did not speak for all the Puritans on this subject; nor did all Anglicans adopt the dismal outlook on the future that we found in Goodman's work, referred to in the last chapter. In fact, Goodman was answered by a most interesting writer, Archdeacon Hakewill whose *Apologie for the Power and Providence of God* first appeared in 1627. The opinion of the world's decay, he says, 'quailes the hopes, and blunts the edge of vertuous endeavours'. Prognostications often help to further that which they foretell. In one section Hakewill supports his more hopeful view by producing 'probable proofs . . . that the Church of Christ before the consummation of the world shall yet enjoy a more peaceable and flourishing estate, than at any time hitherto it hath'. As for the idea that the age is to end with Antichrist, he 'is long since come into the world . . . his downe-fall is not far off and thereupon the Church of Christ shall flourish more in peace and power, in doctrine and manners, in lustre and glory than hitherto at any time in former ages it hath done'.

SOURCES AND ORIGINS

In the last chapter it was shown that the main Continental and English reformers did not hold out any hope of a conversion of the world. We now find that from the seventeenth century this hope emerges and plays an increasingly important part, though side by side with more traditional views. How did it originate?

If we refer again to Bunyan's treatise on Antichrist, we find that one notable factor in his exegesis is the parallel drawn between the history of Israel and the history of the Church. The captivity of the Jews in Babylon corresponds to the dominance of the papacy. The deliverance from this captivity answers to the emancipation of the true Church from papal control. The prophecy of Revelation that the fall of Babylon (XIX) would be followed by the Millennium and the New Jerusalem (XX–XXI) meant that the final collapse of Rome would be followed by the Latter-day Glory of the Church.

This series of parallels is not likely to have occurred independently to Bunyan. It resembles the 'concordances' of which Joachim and his followers were so fond. Is it possible that there can be any connexion? If we go back four hundred years to the thirteenth century, we discover a similar outline in the writings of Olivi, whose message of a release from Babylonian captivity was quoted in an earlier chapter. After this release, he continues, the prophecy of Revelation 21 shall be fulfilled, the twelve gates of this chapter standing for the great teachers of this last period, by whose means the kingdom of God is to be extended among the pagans and Jews. The main lines of this interpretation were of course taken from Joachim, who expounded the song of exultation on the fall of Babylon in Revelation 19 as meaning the song of the Church on earth escaped out of, and freed from, the New Testament Babylon; a song which he compares with that of the Jews restored with

Ezra from the ancient Babylon. The song of the twenty-four elders, explains Joachim, is the answering Alleluia in heaven for the liberation of the righteous, the conversion of the Jews, and the bringing in of the fullness of the Gentiles; and so will begin that Kingdom for which we continually pray, Thy Kingdom come. It will be remembered that Joachim did not equate the Roman Church with Babylon, but his language was readily adaptable to this identification.

I have little doubt that the connecting links between the scheme of Bunyan and the teaching of Joachim could be traced through the intervening centuries by anyone who cared to investigate Christian thought as it developed in the interim. We know that Joachite teaching lived on in the Spiritual Franciscans and passed into the medieval anti-papal sects, Waldensians, Lollards, and Hussites revealing its influence in varying degrees. According to Lindsay, the Waldensians of Savoy and France, the Brethren of France, and the Unitas Fratrum of Bohemia all used the same children's catechism; this is an indication of the sharing of ideas which must have taken place and the ease with which their circulation was effected. This is most obvious in the case of the Joachite view of Antichrist, which was common to all these groups and was a dogma of the great Reformers. While the doctrine of a Christian world was not taken up by Luther and Calvin, there is plenty of evidence to show that this particular Joachite idea had been widely scattered, and there is no need to repeat what was said earlier of such men as Milicz and Janow. When we find this idea emerging again in post-reformation times it is difficult to avoid the suspicion that here too there is simply a survival from earlier times, particularly when the teaching is clothed in the same imagery.

One of the most interesting features of the Reformation is the way in which certain groups and ideas by-passed, as it were, the main Reformation movement. This can be illustrated in a concrete way by the fact that pre-Reformation Bibles in German were to be found in use almost two hundred years after the Reformation (T. M. Lindsay, *History of the Reformation*, I. 150). When we remember the connexion which existed between anti-papal movements in France, Germany, and Bohemia, and we remember too how some of these medieval groups had perpetuated Joachism on its positive as well as its negative side, it becomes easy to see how the expectation of a converted world still lived on in spite of the Lutheran rejection of this teaching. Its appearance in the seventeenth century was not an innovation, but the coming into sight of a stream which had long been flowing in obscure places or beneath the surface. This would explain why it was practically absent from the teaching of English Reformers in the sixteenth century and came to its clearest expression with those Nonconformists who emerged in the seventeenth. It is possible that the idea came to England from Holland.

It is a remarkable fact that the General Baptists, the Independents (Congregationalists), and the Pilgrim Fathers who went to America in 1620, all originated from English exiles living in Holland, particularly in Leyden. There they were in touch with Anabaptists and Mennonites, with elements outside the main trend of Reformation thought as represented by Luther and Calvin. Whether the Anabaptists were 'an original growth of the Reformation epoch' as E. A. Payne maintains in his brochure *The Anabaptists of the Sixteenth Century* (1949), or whether they were connected with medieval nonconformists, is a question which need not detain us. The latter opinion was held by Lindsay, and his remark is noteworthy that 'the Anabaptists retained a German Vulgate long after the publication of Luther's version'. K. S. Latourette appears to agree with Lindsay's view in this matter (*Expansion of Christianity*, III. 13, 436). But there is no doubt that all kinds of eschatological ideas, old and new, were freely discussed at this time, particularly in the tolerant atmosphere which Holland provided for so many exiles. One of the Leyden exiles, Thomas Helwys, later formed the first Baptist Church worshipping on English soil. And it is of great interest for our present purpose to find that his famous book on *The Mistery of Iniquity* (1612) has a similar scheme to that of Bunyan. A facsimile edition was published by the Baptist Historical Society in 1935. On the title page are the words: 'Flee out of the midst of Babel, etc.' (Jeremiah 51₆). Again we have Advent language used of a spiritual movement, and again the judgement upon Babylon is followed by Gospel triumphs.

And whereas our Saviour Christ saith, that this his coming shall be as the lightning cometh out of the East, and is seen into the West, this makes it manifest unto us that the glorious overspreading of the Gospel again, shall be as at the first, General over all, and that men shall seek after, and resort unto the light of the truth of God, as

Eagles do to their prey, according to the prophecy of Isaiah 60_4, Lift up thine eyes round about, and behold all these are gathered and come to thee, thy sons shall come from far, and Isaiah 66_{18}, The Lord saith it will come that I shall gather all Nations and Tongues, and they shall come and see my glory.

At this point Amos 9_{11-12}, Isaiah 11_{11-12}, and Revelation 19_{17}, are quoted in full together with Revelation 21.

The Holy Spirit speaking of the glorious exaltation of the Holy City, after the destruction of Babylon, saith, The Kings of Earth shall bring their glory and honour unto it, and the glory and honour of the Gentiles shall be brought unto it. And this yet is the hope and comfort of the Saints of Gods, that it shall come to pass, that they which now come against Jerusalem shall go up from year to year to worship the King, the Lord of hosts, and to keep the Feast of Tabernacles, Zechariah 14_{16} (p. 187).

In another notable passage (p. 84) Helwys deals with the eschatological chapters of the Gospels and says that these places 'must be most carefully and diligently compared together',

because the wise reader shall find (by good observation) that there are four prophecies of our Saviour Christ's, by the Evangelists set down together, which are
  1, the destruction of Jerusalem;
  2, the days of the exaltation of the man of sin, seen and discovered;
  3, the days of the Son of Man, in the brightness of his coming for the consuming and abolishing of the mistery of iniquity, the abomination of desolation, the Man of sin.
  And lastly the day of Christ's coming to judgement.

Bunyan was a Particular (i.e. Calvinistic) not a General Baptist, and may not have read Helwys's book; but both works show the kind of doctrine which was current in these early Nonconformist circles. (The Particular Baptists were an offshoot of an Independent Congregation in London, founded by Henry Jacob who came to London from Leyden about 1616.)
  In the post-Reformation period we have traced three schools of thought, which have continued to the present time: (1) The Augustinian view, adopted by Luther and the English Reformers—this undoubtedly had the largest following; (2) Millenarianism; and (3) belief in the Latter-day Glory of the

Church. The evidence rather suggests that it was mainly through Nonconformists that this new note of hope for the world's conversion was first sounded in England. Hakewill of course was an Anglican; but he belongs mainly to the battle between the Ancients and the Moderns, and mentions the question of world evangelism almost incidentally. He refers in this connexion to a work on missions written by a Dutchman, Julius Heurnius, a Leyden man whose work was printed in that town in 1618.

This doctrine of the Church's glorious future was at first involved in interpretations of the book of Revelation which today are only of historical interest. This is the case with Bunyan and Edwards, as we have seen. But with Wesley and John Newton we have a conception of the victorious spread of the Gospel which has freed itself from these obsolete elements.

The possible links with earlier phases of Christian thought in the Middle Ages are of interest but they are not vital for our present purpose. Sufficient has been said to show that the hope of a Christian world has been held continuously for several centuries, that it is not a by-product of secular thought, and that it has played an important part in the expansion of Christianity.

CHAPTER 17

THE COURSE OF HISTORY

THE QUESTION of Christ's Kingdom as it has developed in the preceding chapters is inevitably bound up with our interpretation of history. It will be helpful at this stage to look first of all at some of the views represented in the ancient classical world, and to see the new element brought into prominence by the Hebrew and Christian teaching. This will enable us to grasp a few of the main trends of thought on the subject at least in outline, and will help us toward a more constructive statement. Some recent pronouncements which tell us to find the meaning of history in the development of the single human soul are far too individualistic; they suggest indeed that there is a meaning in biography (the story of the individual) rather than in history (the story of the race). This certainly fails to do justice to the sweep of Bible teaching, whose themes embrace the redeeming purpose of God for the whole race. Any interpretation which misses the Messianic element in Christianity is obviously incomplete. But let us first look at some representative references from the Graeco-Roman world.

THE ANCIENT WORLD

Aristotle (fourth century B.C.) held that the world had no beginning and would have no end; but he thought the arts of civilization had been discovered and lost again and again. Since the circular motion of the heavens was eternal, human life on the earth would never end. This view, however, was not widely adopted. It is in a sense a variation of the cyclic theory as far as human history is concerned.

That history repeated itself in cycles was widely held, and sometimes this popular conception was carried to pedantic extremes. According to E. Rohde (*Psyche*, p. 342),

in Orphic poetry (and there perhaps for the first time) occurs the despairing thought of the exact repetition of the past; events which have already been lived through once returning again with the convergence of the same attendant circumstances. Thus, Nature, ever reverting to its own beginnings, draws men with it in its senseless revolution round itself.

In modern times this view of exact repetition an infinite number of times has been put forward by Nietzsche. Strangely enough he regarded this nonsense as a brilliant discovery, and was eager to insist that it was all his own work. Some of the Stoics held a view of this kind; and according to their teaching the universe is periodically destroyed by fire and a new beginning made. The cyclic conception did not always, of course, entail the precise recurrence of each event.

The Epicureans (whose teaching may be studied best in the magnificent work of Lucretius, *De Rerum Natura*, written in the first century B.C.) held that our world had a beginning and was inevitably wearing out; it would finally pass away, but there were innumerable worlds, continually coming into being and passing away, each one made like ours by the chance combination of atoms. As the multitudes of atoms fall and swerve in chaotic confusion they here and there congregate in systems of differing size and shape. History, according to Lucretius, is a process of decline. Originally the earth in its fruitfulness produced animals in rich variety; of these some perished and others survived through cunning, swiftness, etc.— an interesting anticipation of 'the survival of the fittest', which Lucretius derived from the Sicilian Greek philosopher Empedocles. But now this period of fertile productivity is over and the earth has ceased to bear like a woman worn out by the lapse of years. The first race of men was hardier by far than the present. With the lapse of time men began to soften, and as nature's powers fail, beasts are feebler, harvests are smaller, and the land is remorselessly washed away by the ocean.

This doctrine of *inevitable deterioration* was very common in the ancient world, whether in association with a cyclic conception or not. The Age of Gold came first, it was thought; then the Silver Age, and according to Hesiod (eighth century B.C. or even earlier) the next in order were the Bronze Age, then the Age of 'the divine race of Heroes who were called the Demigods', and finally the Iron Age in which the poet himself was living. The heroes were those who fought before Thebes and Troy. Homer, too, is at times overcome by this mood of pessimism aroused by the idea of man's gradual degeneration;

he contrasts the heroic life with 'men as they now are' and says: 'How few sons are equal to their fathers in virtue; worse, most of them; few, indeed, are the men who are better than their fathers' (*Odyssey*, II. 276f.)

This is echoed in Horace's *Odes* which refer to the deterioration which time brings. Time, he says, changes all things with decay; we are worse than our ancestors; and our descendants will be worse than ourselves. In the following century, Seneca the contemporary of St Paul wrote in one of his letters that in the childhood of the race, men had lived in innocence nearer to the divine.

One or two other examples may be given on account of their interest. It is instructive to observe that Philo (*c.* 20 B.C.– A.D. 50), although a Jew, adopts this pagan sentiment. Adam, he writes, was better in every way than his descendants. This is not merely a corollary of the doctrine of the Fall; but because the generations are progressively worsening:

Never have his (Adam's) descendants attained the like bloom, forms and faculties ever feebler having been bestowed on each succeeding generation. I have observed the same thing happening in the case of sculpture and painting: the copies are inferior to the originals, and what is painted or moulded from the copies still more so, owing to their long distance from the original. Much the same appears in the case of the magnet: for the iron ring which touches it is held most forcibly, but that which touches this one less so. A third hangs on to the second etc. . . . those removed from the starting-point get looser all the time, owing to the attraction being relaxed and losing its power to grip as it did before. Mankind has evidently undergone something of the same kind. As generation follows generation the powers and qualities of body and soul which men receive are feebler (*On the Creation*, Loeb edition, I. 111f.)

One striking exception to the doctrine of inevitable decline which stands out in classical writings is the Fourth Eclogue of Virgil. Written in the first century B.C. it foretells the birth of one who should bring an age of peace to the world. It is not fully explained by the belief in cycles, as though he were merely saying that with the ever-circling years the turn of the Age of Gold had come again. A number of its phrases are reminiscent of Isaiah, and there is strong probability that the teaching of Old Testament prophecy lies behind it. The Sybilline Oracles contained a large Jewish ingredient and Virgil expressly mentions the Cumaean Sybil in his opening lines. I do not think anyone could read the discussion of J. B. Mayor, W. Warde Fowler, and R. S. Conway, in *Virgil's Messianic Eclogue*, without being convinced of its ultimate dependence upon the prophecies of Isaiah. (The case made out by this book is much more cogent than that given in H. Gressmann's *Der Messias*, in which a special section is devoted to this famous eclogue.) Virgil may have been consulted in connexion with the new selection of Sybilline Oracles which the Emperor Augustus caused to be made. Passages from Isaiah may well have been included and from this source Virgil could easily have derived the Messianic idea without recognizing its Hebrew origin.

It is a striking fact that this exception to the prevailing views of antiquity is linked in this way to the prophecies of Isaiah. It was the Hebrew who put the Golden Age in the future. It was mainly because of this eclogue that Virgil was honoured in later ages by the Christian Church and that the Sybil was included with the prophets. This poem was regarded as a prophecy of the birth of Christ. It is not surprising that its language is included in the mosaic pavement of the Cathedral of Siena.

CHRISTIAN THOUGHT

It was partly because of its heritage of Hebrew prophecy that Christianity brought a new spirit of hope to a dying world, though the main reason was the new life from Christ which surged in the Church's heart. A consciousness of new life and power rather than a carefully reasoned philosophy led the Christians to abandon the despairing mood of paganism. Clement of Alexandria wrote concerning Christ: 'He hath changed sunset into sunrise' (*Exhortation to the Heathen*, xi).

Christianity broke free from the paralysing effect of a belief in inevitable cycles because it maintained that the living God had acted in history and had a purpose for the world, a purpose being fulfilled through Christ and His Church. The phenomenal growth of the early Church in spite of oppression and persecution confirmed this faith. What F. C. Baur said about the second-century apologists is true on a wider scale:

They are always more or less conscious that they are the soul of the world, the substantial centre holding everything together, the pivot on which the world's history revolved, and those who alone have a future to look to. . . . When there are men who feel themselves in this way to be the soul of the world, the time is indisputably approaching when the reins of the government of the world will fall unasked into their hands. (Quoted in J. Orr's *Neglected Factors in the Study of the Early Progress of Christianity*, p. 188).

The words of Origen which were quoted earlier may be recalled; he looked for the victory of Christianity and foretold its triumph as it more and more took possession of men's minds.

However, as we have seen, this sublime faith was obscured from early days by other elements of an apocalyptic kind and it is unnecessary to summarize here what has been said in the preceding chapters of the course which Christian thought has taken through the generations. We have seen that the hope of the world's conversion has had a long history; and that it played a vital part in the beginnings of the modern missionary movement. But it has had to struggle against all kinds of misconceptions and difficulties; and it must be admitted that the despair with which Jewish apocalypses regarded the present age often invaded the Church, and at times even the pessimistic outlook of paganism. If Virgil wrote like a Christian, then St Cyprian wrote like a pagan when he penned the following eloquent lines:

The world itself now bears witness to its approaching end by the evidence of its failing powers. There is not so much rain in winter for fertilizing the seeds, nor in summer is there so much warmth for ripening them. The springtime is no longer so mild, nor the autumn so rich in fruit. Less marble is quarried from the exhausted mountains, and the dwindling supplies of gold and silver show that the mines are worked out and the impoverished veins of metal diminish from day to day. The peasant is failing and disappearing from the fields, the sailor at sea, the soldier in the camp, uprightness in the forum, justice in the court, concord in friendships, skill in the arts, discipline in morals. Can anything that is old preserve the same powers that it had in the prime and vigour of its youth? It is inevitable that whatever is tending downward to decay and approaches its end must decrease in strength, like the setting sun and the waning moon, and the dying tree and the failing stream. This is the sentence passed on the world; this is God's law: that all that has risen should fall and that all that has grown should wax old, and that strong things should become weak and great things should become small, and that when they have been weakened and minished they should come to an end (*Ad Demetrianum*, iii).

One Christian thinker who attempted a kind of philosophy of history was St Augustine. His *City of God* was begun shortly after the fall of Rome in 410, and his original aim was to answer the criticisms of pagans who said that this great disaster was due to the adoption of the Christian religion. Rome had been secure enough under the protection of the old gods; it was ominous that the empire's conversion to Christianity should be followed so soon by the sack of the world's capital. Augustine rebuts this criticism in his first ten books; but he then develops more fully the conception which had already formed the foundation of his argument.

Reference has been made a number of times in the foregoing chapters to this great work, more particularly to its eschatology; and something has been said about its main theme in Chapter 13. Although Rome, the eternal city, had been sacked by the Goths, Augustine reminded his readers that there was one city which would never fall, the city of God, described in the opening sentence as

That most glorious society and celestial city of God's faithful, which is partly seated in the course of these declining times, wherein 'he that liveth by faith', is a pilgrim amongst the wicked; and partly in that solid estate of eternity, which as yet the other part doth patiently expect, until 'righteousness be turned into judgement', being then by the proper excellence to obtain the last victory, and be crowned in perfection of peace. . . .

He shows that through the whole story of man we can trace the rise and continuance of the two cities, the earthly and the divine. On the one side we have the city of man, taking different forms, embodied in empires and civilizations, particularly the world empires of Assyria and Rome 'to which all the other kingdoms are but appendices'; on the other we have the pilgrim city of God, not very impressive on the outside, but nevertheless constituting the society of God's faithful people. Cain was the founder of the earthly city, and he was the first murderer. Romulus, the founder of Rome, appropriately enough also murdered his brother. The Bible is in effect a Tale of Two Cities. And beyond the pages of the Bible we can trace this dual tendency in human affairs.

One serious criticism of Augustine's work is the rather negative attitude to the State and to secular affairs. Nowhere does he explicitly recognize that the State can be the servant of God, that in the divine purpose the earthly and the heavenly cities should be co-ordinated, not opposed. This more comprehensive idea was developed in later periods and found its classical expression in the Middle Ages. When Leo the Third crowned Charlemagne as emperor on Christmas Day 800, a spiritual meaning became attached to the Frankish kingship, which previously had been merely a rule of force. The idea (though not the name) of the 'Holy Roman Empire' which played such a dominant part in the Middle Ages was then born, and the rule of the earthly city was at least in intention hallowed by a sense of sacred responsibility. This is the kind of Christian political thought which does justice to the Incarnation, since it embraces man's bodily life and recognizes human society and government as ideally within the divine order.

P. H. Wicksteed in his fine book *Dante and Aquinas* calls attention to 'Dante's steady assertion of the intrinsic worth of the secular life' (p. 134) and to the parallels between sacred and secular which occur in his teaching. The history of Rome is a sacred history no less than that of Palestine.

And it was no less natural and seemly that Aeneas should be privileged to penetrate the unseen world to receive guidance in the founding of Rome than that Paul should have the like privilege for the confirmation of the saving faith. And this is not a secularizing of the spiritual but a spiritualizing of the secular order of things. It is a systematic attempt to raise this life to the dignity and beauty of the life of Eden, which in Dante's view was not merely a preliminary to the life of heaven, but an integral part of God's scheme for man and a part which was worthily associated with the other.

SPENGLER AND TOYNBEE

A modern philosopher of history who can help us at this point is Arnold Toynbee. But since he himself tells us of the stimulus he received from the work of Spengler, something should first be said of this German writer and his famous *Decline of the West*.

Spengler maintains that each great culture passes through a life-cycle corresponding to the four seasons. He tells us (in a footnote to page 37, Vol. II, Eng. Trans.) that Goethe had characterized the four parts of a culture, its preliminary, early, late, and civilized stages, 'with such a depth of insight that even today there is nothing to add'. Spengler takes eight great civilizations (the Egyptian, Babylonian, Indian, Chinese, Mayan, Classical antiquity, the Arabian, and West European) and shows that in each case there was (1) a Spring, with the rise of a new mythology (e.g. the Vedas, Homer); (2) a Summer of full self-consciousness with the rise of a characteristic philosophy and a new mathematic (e.g. Pythagoras, Descartes); (3) an Autumn, with the loosening of social cohesion, the growth of rationalism and individualism, and great conclusive philosophical systems (e.g. Plato and Aristotle, Goethe and Kant, the Sophists and the Encyclopedists); and finally (4) a Winter, when inner development is complete, and instead of culture there is civilization—which is its fossilized counterpart —finding its spiritual expression in cosmopolitanism and ethical propaganda (e.g. Buddhism, the Stoics, nineteenth-century socialism); in this period racial mixture produces a mongrel population. This cycle, he says, is a fixed law, not a matter of superficial parallels. Thus Alexander and Napoleon appear at the same point of development in the respective cultures to which they belong. The present need, he says writing in 1918, is for a new Caesarism—it is rather striking that this was written a few years before the rise of Mussolini and Hitler. The title of the work indicates Spengler's belief that the collapse of western civilization is inevitable and nothing can be done about it; it is doomed by a law of nature. Here we have a modern form of the cyclic theory of ancient times, and it is significant that when men forsake the Christian faith this is apt to reappear.

Christopher Dawson in his fine book *Progress and Religion* has given an effective answer to Spengler's fatalistic scheme, showing that his brilliant theory breaks down before the historical facts of intercultural relations. There is a continuity of civilization; even those great empires which fall leave something for their successors; something of their art, litera-ture, and spiritual life, endures when the outer structure collapses.

Arnold Toynbee in his monumental *Study of History* has taken up the idea of successive civilizations running their course and ceasing to be. Twenty-six civilizations have come to birth, but of these five were arrested in their development, such as the Spartan and Polynesian, and four have been abor-tive like the Christian Scandinavian. He rejects Spengler's determinism; and like Dawson finds an element of spiritual continuity.

Certainly, in all these movements of the forces that weave the web of human history, an element of sheer recurrence can be detected. Indeed, it stares us in the face. Yet the shuttle which shoots backwards and forwards across the loom of Time in a perpetual to-and-fro is all this time bringing into existence a tapestry in which there is manifestly 'a progress toward an end' and not just an 'endless repetition' in the likeness of the shuttle's own action (Vol. IV, p. 34).

Toynbee in one striking passage of his Burge Lecture, *Christianity and Civilization*, uses the imagery of the chariot to show that a cyclic movement can at the same time be a movement toward a goal, the wheels corresponding to the former and the chariot itself to the latter. Turgot had seen the Physical Universe as the wheel and mankind as the vehicle for which this wheel's vain repetitions provide a means of locomotion along a 'one-way' road. But Toynbee makes a different use of this apt illustration. The wheels represent the 'vain repetitions of the Gentiles', the forward movement of the chariot itself represents a progressive process of religious faith.

If religion is a chariot, it looks as if the wheels on which it mounts toward Heaven may be the periodic downfalls of civilizations on Earth. It looks as if the movement of civilization may be cyclic and recurrent, while the movement of religion may be on a single continuous upward line. The continuous upward movement of religion may be served and promoted by the cyclic movement of civilizations round the cycle of birth-death-birth (p. 22).

This philosophy of history is in some ways in agreement with Augustine's. It is the doctrine of the two cities in a new guise. The earthly city takes different forms, it is Babylon, or Rome; but throughout all the changes the city of God remaineth.

The doctrine of the two cities is a valuable key to the Bible narrative. Early in the Book of Genesis we have the story of Babel, with its tower unfinished and its citizens scattered. But this is followed almost immediately by the story of Abraham's call. Abraham left the earthly city to make a new beginning; he went in search of a city which hath the foundations, whose builder and maker is God. The two-fold development thus begun continues throughout the Bible. Babel is Babylon, and its name persists almost to the last page. Meanwhile the pilgrim city of God continues undestroyed. The Bible is not a

N

compendium of theology; but the story of a community, the people of God, to whom the revelation of God came, Jesus Christ being central to the whole development, for Abraham led on to the Israelite nation and on to Christ. From Him springs the Christian Church, while the revelation too is summed up and embodied in Him. The changing civilizations, Egypt, Babylon, Assyria, Persia, Greece, and Rome, provide the background for the story of the divine society. It is interesting to find that in the closing chapters of the Bible we still have the imagery of the two cities—the destruction of Babylon and the vision of the New Jerusalem coming down out of Heaven from God.

Thus the interpretation of history given by Augustine (and more recently by Toynbee) is essentially that presented in the Bible. Augustine however, believed that the triumph of the Church had taken place and did not appear to look for any intensification of the work of faith within the Christianized peoples of the empire, so that the human story might go on for a long or a short period—it was like so many yards of ribbon which might be cut at any point. Toynbee's interpretation on the other hand, like that of Dawson, does leave room for development, and envisages the divine city as preserving all that is of value in the different human cultures as they in turn cease to be.

In his Burge Lecture, already referred to, Toynbee insists that the Church on Earth will never be a perfect embodiment of the Kingdom of Heaven. He gives more attention to the production of immortal saints than to the establishment of a Christian world-order. But he does show how the Christian Church may ultimately be the social heir of all the civilizations. He points out that through the work of the great Alexandrian theologians valuable elements of Greek philosophy were incorporated into Christianity, and that the same process may be repeated with Oriental philosophy. All that is best in Hinduism and Buddhism may live on in the Christianity of the future, which may thus be left as the spiritual heir of all the other higher religions, and of 'all the philosophies from Ikhnaton's to Hegel's; while the Christian Church as an institution may be left as the social heir of all the other churches and all the civilizations'.

Toynbee insists that the fashioning of immortal souls is more important than the creation of an ideal social order, but (1) this individual spiritual progress in this life will indirectly produce more social progress than could be attained in any other way, and (2) within the Church there is a growing fund of illumination and grace, so that 'in this matter of increasing spiritual opportunity for souls in their passage through life on Earth, there is assuredly an inexhaustible possibility of progress in This World'. The historical progress of religion in This World 'may, and almost certainly will, bring with it, incidentally, an immeasurable improvement in the conditions of human social life on Earth'.

CHAPTER 18

THE END OF THE WORLD

Even those who look for a victory of Christ on the earth must face the question of the earth's duration. Christians have never believed that the present earthly conditions can go on for ever. Aristotle thought that the process of birth and death, generation and decay, would always continue and that the great wheel of the universe would revolve eternally. But even among pagan writers he was in a minority.

The Hebrews believed at one time that the Messianic kingdom on the present earth would continue for ever. But later this view was modified: a renewed earth came into the picture, an earth on which there would be no death and which represented the final state of blessedness. On this view, the present course of human life does come to an end; and this has always been maintained by the Church. But within this general framework a variety of opinions has been developed.

ANNIHILATION OR RENOVATION?

> . . . like the baseless fabric of this vision
> The cloud-capp'd towers, the gorgeous palaces,
> The solemn temples, the great globe itself,
> Yea, all which it inherit, shall dissolve,
> And, like this insubstantial pageant faded,
> Leave not a rack behind.

At one time I thought that these famous words of Shakespeare (so badly misquoted in Westminster Abbey) represented the usual Christian view. To my surprise I find that the prevailing view through the centuries concerning the universe seems to be not that it will finally be annihilated, but renewed.

Most of the early Greek philosophers believed in innumerable worlds (Anaximander, the Pythagoreans, Anaxagoras, Democritus). The Epicureans followed this tradition and held that there was an infinite number of worlds, each containing stars, earth, etc., and terminated by a boundary. The gods were said

to inhabit the lucid interspace of world and world and to be
utterly indifferent to the happenings in any of the systems
around them. The decline and end of our particular earth
would not be more than a trivial event in comparison with the
innumerable worlds which the universe comprised. Continually, new universes were arising and old ones passing away,
and this process would continue for ever just as it had done in
the infinite past. Aristotle denied the multiplicity of worlds, and
it was ultimately due to him that the idea prevailed that there
was only one system in existence. The Aristotelian view was
taken up by Ptolemy the astronomer and held the field for
many centuries with its theory that the one and only universe
revolved around the earth.

The Bible regards the created universe as one system and on
the question of its ultimate fate some passages could be quoted
in support of annihilation while others take a different line.
Some verses say the world will last for ever—Psalm 78_{69}:
'like the earth which he hath established for ever.' Passages
which suggest that the world will be annihilated are as follows:
Psalm 102_{26}, Isaiah 34_4, 2 Peter 3_{10}, Revelation 20–1. These
appear to be definite, and yet when we examine them closely
it is evident that we must not decide on their meaning too
hastily. 2 Peter 3 co-ordinates the two judgements, one in the
past by flood, the other in the future by fire (the final conflagration). Now it is very important to recognize that the
world after the flood is described as a new one, though the
writer obviously did not mean the earlier one had been annihilated. In verse 6 he speaks of 'the world that then was', the
world which 'perished' being overflowed with water; this is
contrasted with 'the heavens that now are, and the earth'.
This must govern the meaning we give to the 'new heavens
and a new earth' of verse 13. In the light of his own usage
this does not mean something entirely new and unrelated to the
present world; but as the world after the flood was a new one,
so it will be after the second judgement of fire. In neither
case is there a completely new creation. (We may compare
the words of Wisdom 19_6 on the Exodus from Egypt: 'For the
whole creation in its proper kind was fashioned again anew.')

The final conflagration was not usually regarded in the
apocalypses as bringing final destruction; it was purgatorial
and followed by universal restoration (see *Sibylline Oracles*,
IV. 171ff., III. 617ff.) The words of St Paul in Romans 8 are

decisive as to his view; the universe is to be renewed, transformed, and delivered from all imperfection.

The conception of the world's final annihilation would seem to be more in keeping with the Gnostic view of matter than the Christian. There is evidence that some of the Gnostics taught that at the end of history the material world would be annihilated and only spirit would remain.

The prevailing teaching of the Church was of a restored and renovated universe. Irenaeus wrote: 'For neither is the substance nor the essence of the creation annihilated (for faithful and true is He who has established it), but "the *fashion* of the world passeth away".' Aquinas in the thirteenth century was merely summing up the orthodox view (see Chapter 2). As he says, there was some diversity of opinion about the extent of the final conflagration; Bonaventura thought that the whole universe needed purifying, while Aquinas restricted the cleansing fire to the earth. Bonaventura's view would appear to be reflected in the '*Dies Irae*' when it speaks of the world being reduced to a cinder; but even here we ought not to speak of annihilation because it was usually thought that from 'the conflagrant mass' new earth and heaven would phoenix-like arise.

The doctrine of annihilation, taught by the Gnostics, was adopted by some Christian thinkers. It seems that it emerged in an unambiguous form after the Reformation and the Renaissance. Some of the most uncompromising and explicit expressions of this view are to be found from the beginning of the seventeenth century. One cannot help wondering whether it was the revival of classical studies (including the study of Stoicism with its final conflagration) which stimulated this tendency. Hakewill in his *Apologie* contends for annihilation and is at pains to refute Suarez, the famous Spanish Thomist, who had supported the traditional view of its renovation; it is significant that most of Hakewill's quotations come not from the Bible but the Greek and Roman classics. Sir Thomas Browne (*Religio Medici*) pointed out that annihilation strictly went beyond the conception of destruction by fire as found in the classics:

Philosophers that opinioned the world's destruction by fire, did never dream of annihilation, which is beyond the power of sublunary causes; for the last and proper action of that element is but vitrification, or a reduction of a body into glass; and therefore some of our Chymicks facetiously affirm, that at the last fire all shall be christallized and reverberated into glass, which is the utmost action of that element. Nor need we fear this term, annihilation, or wonder that God will destroy the works of His Creation; for man subsisting, who is, and will then truely appear, a Microcosm, the world cannot be said to be destroyed (I. 50).

I believe the World grows near its end, yet is neither old nor decayed, nor shall ever perish upon the ruines of its own Principles. As the work of Creation was above Nature, so is its adversary, annihilation; without which the World hath not its end, but its mutation (I. 45).

The words of a prayer by Pascal provide an instance of a Roman Catholic of this period supporting annihilation:

O God, who wilt consume the heavens and the earth at the last day, and all the creatures they contain, to convince men that nothing subsists but by Thy hand, and that nothing besides Thee deserves our love, because besides Thee nothing is fixed and permanent. . . .

It is unnecessary to pursue this interesting subject in detail. Sufficient to say that the two theories of annihilation and renovation have continued to the present time. There is something rather diverting about the Church's indifference on this question. We are so wealthy that we can dispense with the universe. We don't mind either way. Our Father could make another if necessary. Kagawa says: 'The universe is mine. God threw it in when He gave me Christ.' It is a mere make-weight. When someone told Emerson that the world was soon coming to an end, he replied: 'We shall get on all right without it.'

Some Christians in recent days have welcomed the second law of thermodynamics as a confirmation of the Church's doctrine; they are evidently unaware what the predominant Christian tradition is. An eloquent passage in Trench's *Notes on the Parables* gives the more orthodox view. His comment on the word 'nature' is particularly suggestive. He is drawing out the relationship between the seen and the unseen, and after pointing out that at present nature gives only an imperfect reflection of God's truth and love, he goes on:

But one day it will be otherwise; one day it will be translucent with the divine idea which it embodies, and which even now, despite these dark spots, shines through it so wondrously. For no doubt the end and consummation will be, not the abolition of this nature, but the glorifying of it; that which is now nature (*natura*), always, as the word expresses, striving and struggling to the birth, will then be indeed born. The new creation will be as the glorious child born out of the world-long throes and anguish of the old. It will be as the snake casting its wrinkled and winter skin; not the world, but 'the *fashion* of the world', passing away, when it puts off its soiled work-day garments, and puts on its holiday apparel for the great Sabbath which shall arrive at last. Then, when it too shall have been delivered from its bondage of corruption, all that it now has of dim and contradictory and perplexing shall disappear. This nature, too, shall be a mirror in which God will perfectly glass Himself, for it shall tell of nothing but the marvels of His wisdom, and power, and love.

THE ABODE OF THE BLEST

The question of the duration or destruction of the visible universe is interlocked with that of the final destiny of the soul. Two strands have entered the Christian doctrine of the final state; one is Jewish, the other may for convenience be called Greek since it is represented in certain forms of Greek philosophy.

The Jews believed that the eternal Kingdom would come on the earth—a renewed earth, but still the earth. Through resurrection the righteous would return to the earth to share in the Kingdom. They thought of the earth as flat, having heaven arched over it like an inverted basin. *Sheol* was a cavern beneath the surface of the earth. At the resurrection saints would rise from *Sheol* to live the risen life on the transformed earth. There is not a lot of support in scripture for the view that in the final state the saints will live in heaven; this may be traced here and there but the Jewish view of life on a renewed earth seems to predominate. Montefiore's comment on the words, 'Great is your reward in heaven', is: 'This does not mean that the reward will be enjoyed in heaven and not upon the regenerated earth in the Messianic age.'

The Greek view (which is connected with Indian and Persian thought and is reflected in Gnosticism) was of planetary spheres beyond which lay the abode of the divine. Through his body man was for the present tied to the earth. But if he lived properly as a philosopher, his soul would one day escape from its prison and would rise through the spheres to the dwelling of light, leaving earth far beneath him. The actual levels of sea, earth, and sky, corresponded to different degrees of good and evil. Those who loved material things would return as lowlier creatures, the worst as oysters buried in the mud! (so Plato's *Timaeus*, which is not to be taken too seriously). The universe was regarded as a sphere and the heavenly place of glory was on the 'back' or surface of the sphere.

In Christian thought there was a kind of accommodation or compromise between the Greek and Jewish doctrines. The conception of heaven as the place of final destiny ultimately prevailed; but the Jewish idea of a resurrection body was retained. Some Christian teachers were uncertain whether earth or heaven was to be the final dwelling-place of the saints; some imagined that the company of the blest would be graded. Irenaeus writes:

But when this present fashion of things passes away, and man has been renewed, and flourishes in an incorruptible state, so as to preclude the possibility of becoming old, then there shall be the new heaven and the new earth, in which the new man shall remain continually, always holding fresh converse with God. . . . And as the presbyters say, Then those who are deemed worthy of an abode in heaven shall go there, others shall enjoy the delights of paradise, and others shall possess the splendour of the city; for everywhere the Saviour shall be seen according as they who see Him shall be worthy.

They say, moreover, that there is this distinction between the habitation of those who produce an hundred-fold, and that of those who produce sixty-fold, and that of those who produce thirty-fold: for the first will be taken up into the heavens, the second will dwell in paradise, the last will inhabit the city; and that it was on this account the Lord declared: 'In my Father's house are many mansions' (*Adv. Haer.* V. 36).

As late as the seventeenth century Milton seems undecided as to whether eternal life is to be on earth or in heaven:

> To judge the unfaithful dead, but to reward
> His faithful, and receive them into bliss,
> Whether in Heaven or Earth; for then the Earth
> Shall all be Paradise.
> (*Paradise Lost*, XII. 461ff.; cf. V. 496ff., VII. 160f.)

The main Catholic tradition, however, decided for Heaven. If Christians at death went to Heaven to be with God it was difficult to imagine them one day exchanging Heaven for earth again, even a renewed earth. This helped to make the Greek view more and more at home in Christian thought. 'My soul there is a country, afar beyond the stars.' Aquinas is quite clear on the subject; the earth and the heavenly bodies will still exist and while the lost remain in Hell in the centre of the earth, the saints are in the empyrean Heaven beyond the starry spheres. Dante has to pass through all these planetary spheres to reach Paradise. He encounters various saints at each stage of his journey, but this is only a poetic device to illustrate differences of character and degrees of beatitude; it is made plain that the permanent home of all of them is in Paradise.

NATURE AND ETERNITY

That man will still (even after the winding-up of history) have a relationship of some sort with the created universe has been contended by a number of Christian thinkers. According to Aquinas the world will be renewed at the same time as man is glorified. It was made for him, and while he will no longer need its sustenance it will still reveal the Divine majesty. 'This disposition of newness will be neither natural nor contrary to nature, but above nature (just as grace and glory are above the nature of the soul): and it will proceed from an everlasting agent which will preserve it for ever' (*Summa*, III, Qu. 91). The ending of the rotation of the heavens will mean the cessation of all life on the earth; there will be no more flora or fauna. But the main structure of the universe with its sun, planets, and stars will remain as before, though now motionless.

It will be seen that according to this teaching, the function of the universe is to reveal the glory of God and it is related to glorified man as an object of contemplation only.

W. E. Orchard maintains that 'the natural order as created by God is never to be destroyed, but is to continue in a more glorified form, in which redeemed souls are to have a creative share' (*Foundations of Faith*, IV. 64). This reference to creative activity goes further than the teaching of Aquinas. It could be contended that the latter reflects the influence of Aristotle and the Greek disparagement of activity and craftsmanship. To

Aristotle, thought was the highest function of man, for God Himself was the eternal thinker. God's action upon the world was not direct; He moved the world by desire. It was simply the effect of His being which acted upon the world, not anything which He consciously initiated Himself. All action, said Aristotle, is petty and unworthy of the divine; the divine life consists in contemplation, and the greatest human blessedness springs from the same (*Nicomachean Ethics*, X). This whole tendency is probably responsible for the Christian interpretation of eternal life as contemplation, man being assimilated to the Divine. We need to return to the Hebrew conception of God as the mighty worker; this would react upon our interpretation of the heavenly life. This in turn would affect our view of our relation to the created universe. To Aquinas, the universe will exist eternally as a witness to God and a revelation of His glory, so that our attitude toward it would be purely that of contemplation, and strictly speaking, since the saints have direct knowledge of God and 'see all things in the Word', the revelation of God in the creation is redundant. But if we remember that God is the worker, the creator, and that we are called to be co-workers with Him, then we shall be led to expect a closer relation to the universe than that of contemplating it from outside. If God originally called men to have dominion over the earth (as we read on the first page of the Bible), it may well be that in the eternal life He will give men a share in His wider purposes for the universe. Faithful over little things, they will be called to greater responsibility.

One reason why Heaven makes so weak an appeal to many people is that it has been presented too exclusively as consisting of a vast multitude of saints lying prostrate before a throne and gazing upon God. (Faber's lines contain an awkwardly mixed metaphor; men do not prostrate themselves in order to gaze, but to hide their faces in self-abasement; cf. Genesis 42 ₆.) Even Peter on the mount of Transfiguration longed to do something with his hands. If we noticed that in the Bible God is first shown to us as the Creator, His hands soiled with star-dust and with clay from the making of man, we should be encouraged to believe that in the eternal life there will be a place for activity and creativeness, and for artistry of other kinds as well as the musician's. God is spirit, and yet He maintains contact with the universe; surely then it is not impossible that in the heavenly life we may still have some relation with the universe.

It is not being contended, as some have suggested, that our dwelling -place may change from star to star. It is rather that the great God of all may still allow His little children to help Him in His workshop, that He who has manifested part of His glory through material means and has used Mozart and Donatello and hosts of others in so doing, may still employ the sons of men as His co-workers in His dealings with the rest of His vast creation. What of those undeveloped areas we call nebulae? The galaxies may be to the sons of the resurrection as marble quarries to a sculptor.

> If such his soul's capacities,
> Even while he trod the earth—think, now
> What pomp in Buonarroti's brow,
> With its new palace-brain where dwells
> Superb the soul, unvexed by cells
> That crumbled with the transient clay!
> What visions will his right hand's sway
> Still turn to form, as still they burst
> Upon him?
>
> (Browning's *Easter Day*.)

B. H. Streeter says that Heaven will include Love, Work, Thought, Beauty, Humour, and the Vision of God (*Immortality*). C. Ryder Smith discusses the place of Nature in eternity in his *Christian Experience* (pp. 283–90). See also C. S. Lewis, *Miracles*, p. 192; he rejects the wintry idea that Heaven is merely a state of mind, and maintains that Nature 'will be always and perfectly—as present Nature is partially and intermittently—the instrument for that music which will then arise between Christ and us'.

THE CONSUMMATION

So far we have been mainly concerned with the possibility of a place for the universe in eternity. It is clear from the foregoing that by the phrase 'the end of the world', Christian thought has generally speaking meant not the annihilation of the universe but the consummation of the age, or the end of human history. No Christian thinker has ever maintained (as Aristotle did) that human life on its present terms is likely to continue for ever. And so we must turn now to the question of the consummation. Christian thought seems to be agreed that there must be a winding-up of the life of humanity on the earth, a transition to the eternal state. It is unthinkable, on theological as

well as scientific grounds, that human life will just go on and
on. There must be a final reunion of the Church militant and
triumphant, a breaking-down of the barriers between the seen
and the unseen, as taught in the New Testament (Romans 8).

In traditional thought the Second Advent has marked the
term of human history. Even if we reinterpret the conceptions
of Judgement and Resurrection along lines suggested in Part
One, what are we to say of this other important element of
Advent teaching? The various parts of the traditional doctrine
all held together: the return of Christ to the earth, the General
Resurrection and the Final Judgement; and if we reinterpret
the Resurrection and Judgement in the way indicated, it is
hardly possible to leave the return of Christ to the earth in
isolation as a literal event. The origins of the Advent doctrine
encourage us to expect a symbolic rather than a literal fulfilment; but can we say anything of the reality which is sym-
bolized? I do not wish to suggest for one moment that I have
any ready answer to this question. All one can do is to draw out
certain principles.

In the early part of this chapter we were reviewing the teaching of the Church in past centuries and it is obvious that some
of it is quite untenable today. We cannot accept Aquinas' idea
that the circular movement of the heavens will cease, for the
simple reason that no such movement exists. Aquinas made
full use of the scientific ideas available to him in his century and
we must do the same in ours. Many will think here of the law of
entropy. The sun and other heavenly bodies are constantly
giving out energy; and though we are told by some authorities
that the heat of the sun is at present increasing, the time will
come when it will lose all its heat and will no longer give any
light. What is true of the sun is true of every star in the heavens.
The ultimate end of the universe will on this showing be utter
and complete death when all the energy in the cosmos will as it
were be evenly distributed through space so that movement,
light, and life, will be at an end.

This, however, does not take account of the continuing
activity of God. He upholds all things by the word of His
power. 'My Father worketh until now and I work' (John 5₁₇).
God is still at work upon an unfinished universe. He has even
called man to share in His creative activity. We have no idea
what developments may result from the control of elemental
powers which has already passed into man's hands and is doing

so increasingly. Moreover, even the scientist appears to be admitting that new matter is continually coming into existence. Dr E. T. Whittaker, a distinguished mathematician and astronomer, in his work *The Beginning and End of the World*, maintains that there are reasons for supposing that matter is being continually created. What was said in the early part of this chapter, about the long Christian tradition concerning the continued existence of the universe, need not be abandoned. Whatever the ultimate fate of the solar system may be, the cosmos as a whole may still remain when man's earthly story is over.

As far as *human history* is concerned, the idea that everything will just be left to peter out is quite inconsistent with Christian faith. We cannot agree with Troeltsch that 'there is far more certainty about the advent of the last man cooking the last potato with the last fire of coals, than . . . of the Second Coming of Christ'. Such a dismal end would not be consistent with what we know of God's character. Again, the idea that the earth may have a fortuitous end through some fool letting off an atom bomb with overwhelming and universally fatal results, is not compatible with the truth that this is God's world and ultimately He is in control of its destiny.

As to the exact way in which human history will end, we can speak (as Augustine did of the Trinity) only to avoid being silent. It may be that the conditions of human life will in the course of many generations change almost beyond recognition and that the transition to 'the final state' will be prepared for in some way, so that instead of a sudden cataclysm or interruption occurring like a bolt out of the blue there will be a process stretching over a period. Creation is not less divine because we now think of it as a long process filling millions of years instead of as a brief and sudden act completed in six days. Similarly the consummation of the creation and of the human story is not less a divine act if it be reinterpreted in a corresponding way.

Man was not made in an instant by the immediate activity of God. The process was an immeasurably longer one. Yet God was behind it all. The literal account of Genesis says that God moulded an image of clay and blew into its nose. The scientific account is much more wonderful and far less crude than this. If we apply a similar treatment to the end-time, we shall reject the literal events which, like the details of the

Genesis story, are attributed to the immediate activity of God operating in a small stretch of time. Instead we shall think of a long process and God working through slow and intermediate means. But just as surely as in the case of man's creation we shall insist that the religious values are preserved.

The Church must accustom itself to the idea of a vast future on the earth. What is to happen ultimately 'doth not yet appear', as it doth not yet appear what we shall be. Nearer the time those who are then living will know more about it than we do. Our wisdom would be to hold that in a way beyond our understanding, events will move toward some consummation in which God shall be all in all, the present terms of human life will be ended, the righteous judgement of God will be manifest, the children of God reunited in fellowship with one another and with their Lord. If anyone wishes to add with Maldwyn Hughes that 'history will be consummated by some supreme manifestation of the presence and power of Christ' (*Kingdom of Heaven*, p. 181), I shall certainly not quarrel with him.

It is not a reproach that today the Church cannot speak with the old definiteness about the details of the consummation and the future life, that we cannot set out with the exactness of a railway time-table as our grandfathers did the doctrine of the Last Things. We are nearer to St Paul who had the greatness of soul to admit that there were some things seen as in a riddle; for we know in part, and we prophesy in part; but when that which is perfect is come, that which is in part shall be done away.

CHAPTER 19

CONCLUSION

RESULT OF SURVEY

In the foregoing pages we have spent a lot of time in going into the various views put forward by representative Christians and in tracing the developments of doctrine which have taken place. We have been wise in this procedure. Any modern presentation of Christian belief must take careful account of the thought of the past and must seek to preserve those underlying elements which have persisted through all the changing modes of expression.

The position maintained here is that we shall find the way through our difficulties by carrying further certain trends which became manifest years ago. Thus in the matter of Judgement there has been an increasing recognition that we cannot press literally the idea of an enormous hall of justice, as it were, in which the human race is judged one by one, with witnesses giving evidence for and against, and a final pronouncement of sentence. Yet there are some who, while agreeing with this, would still maintain that we must preserve the Judgement as an event of some kind at the end of time. On this matter everyone must follow what he believes to be the truth, recognizing that the fundamental matter is not whether judgement is a collective event or not but the fact that the Judge of all the earth will do right and that we must all face our personal accountability to Him who weighs the spirits and by whom actions are tried.

But on the general question, it is the spiritualizing of the Christian hope which will provide the reinterpretation we so desperately need. In spite of the widely varied eschatological speculations which at some time or other have found a following, there are certain broad trends which can be traced. Again and again while some particular factor has had to be abandoned as far as its literal meaning is concerned, the underlying spiritual meaning has nevertheless been retained. There is an increasing recognition that this spiritualizing process must be applied to traditional eschatological forms. But though the ancient pictures have dissolved in so far as they were taken as actual representations of the future, all the spiritual values which they expressed may still be conserved.

In the early centuries Augustine and others saw that the books of judgement could not be taken as literal record books; men's deeds were rather inscribed in their own minds and memories. Aquinas and others saw that a separate trial for each individual in the presence of a concourse of men and angels was unthinkable; the Judgement would be conducted mentally. Meanwhile the conception of a judgement at death had virtually rendered a Great Assize redundant. In more recent times the idea of a General Resurrection as a reassembling of actual particles has been increasingly abandoned and other ways have been found of expressing our faith in immortality in such a manner that personal identity is not lost. If today we regard the return of Christ to judge the world and to awaken the dead as a pictorial representation of great spiritual issues we are in a sense carrying further those tendencies that have been manifest for a long time in Christian thought; indeed they can be traced in the pages of the New Testament itself.

Again and again fervid apocalyptic expectations have been disappointed; desires for some imminent divine inbreaking have so frequently been discredited by non-fulfilment that the time has come to recognize that those who entertained them misconceived the method of God's action in history. Their impatience must be understood but not emulated. God's ways can be read more clearly in the Cross and Resurrection of Christ than in the pages of Enoch and Revelation.

If a chess-player were to tip up the board or to sweep all the pieces to the floor, you would realize that the game had become too difficult for him to solve. Instead of the hard task of overcoming the problems of the situation, he has taken the easier course of ending the contest, admitting he was unequal to it. And similarly if we say that God at any minute may burst into the word with irresistible might bringing history to an end, is not this equivalent to the suggestion that the situation is beyond Him? It is surely consonant with a nobler conception of God to believe that with infinite patience He will bring about the fulfilment of His eternal purpose and

o

the triumph of good over evil on the chessboard of the world, not suddenly interrupting the process with violence but controlling it and by grace bringing it to a victorious consummation.

We believe that in the Incarnation God did indeed break into the world's life (though not with violence). It is here that we find the irruption of the supernatural, in the Word made flesh. Our view of the course of history is bound to be affected by the fact of the Incarnation. If, as we believe, something new entered the world in the coming of Jesus Christ, the human situation cannot remain as before. 'It is a plain fact of history that in the birth of Christ there entered into the process of human life a spiritual energy of unparalleled power. Into a corrupt society there came silently a new regenerating force greater than any other which history can show' (J. H. Oldham). As surely as the poisoned pot was purified by the ingredient which Elisha cast into it, the new divine life which came to the world in Christ will transform and make wholesome the humanity into which it was introduced and in which it still remains.

As we have seen, it was this faith, that the sure promises of God would find their fulfilment through a world-triumph of Christ's Gospel, which lay at the roots of the modern missionary movement. The future Advent of Christ has always meant among other things His vindication, His triumph in the scene of His humiliation. As He comes more and more fully into the hearts of men and gains more and more control of human affairs, so will His Kingdom attain its sure increase, for the nations are His promised inheritance and the uttermost parts of the earth His possession.

'I COME UNTO YOU' (John 14$_{18}$)

The great truths which the Advent doctrine has preserved through the generations—the final victory of Christ, the fact of Judgement, the certainty of reunion—still remain even if we have to express them today in new ways.

Sufficient has been said already about Judgement and Resurrection in Part One. At this point a number of scattered references to the idea of Christ's spiritual Advent may be gathered up. It is noteworthy that many who have held fast to a final Advent that is to be literal and visible, have also spoken of Christ coming to the world in other ways. This indicates the kind of Advent hope we need to cultivate at the present time.

We recall Augustine's words about 'the Advent whereby He comes daily to the Church, whom He visits spiritually when He dwells in us by faith and love'. We remember too that Advent language has often been used of spiritual conquest, and even eschatological passages of the New Testament have been applied to some great Christian advance in the present or the future. This sort of reinterpretation is of great service to us today; and if we find it difficult to retain the conception of a literal descent to the earth, or are willing to leave as an open question the kind of consummation which may lie in the distant future, we have here an Advent hope which is linked more closely with our present situation and our spiritual needs.

We remember how Olivi spoke of an Advent of Christ which was to be distinguished from the final consummation, a spiritual Advent which could be equated with the whole process of development of the Church. Helwys understood the coming of Christ in Luke 17 as a great spiritual movement, a 'glorious overspreading of the Gospel'. Many of the Reformation writers gave the eschatological language of 2 Thessalonians 2 a spiritual interpretation; Christ would accomplish what was there described 'not by Himself immediately, but by His Spirit and word in His Church'. Edwards explained the Advent passage of Revelation 19 as meaning not a literal coming but a manifestation of Christ, 'a great revival and mighty progress of true religion'. Charles Wesley in a number of hymns used Advent imagery to express Christ's conquest of the souls of men and His reign of love in their hearts. When we speak of Christ coming into His own, or into His kingdom, we are perpetuating this usage. Most important of all, there are the chapters in St John's Gospel which give us the Last Discourse. The evangelist while making quite explicit the final return at the end of time, appears to be telling his readers that the real meaning of Christ's coming is not exhausted by a single interpretation; He visits the hearts of His disciples in mystic fellowship, He came back at Easter, He comes through the Holy Spirit.

If we find the real fulfilment of the Advent hope in a growing spiritual triumph of Christ we are therefore not without precedents which suggest this reinterpretation. We have maintained (Chapter 1) that the Old Testament prophecies of a great theophany appear in a Christian dress in the New Testament in the form of an Advent of Christ; it is noteworthy that devout Jews have found in some of the Old Testament theophanic passages symbolic language which is not to be taken in a literal manner. We are following a similar reinterpretation in suggesting that Christian thought must take the same course when it speaks of the coming of Christ.

The use of Advent language to describe some spiritual movement has become almost conventional. The saint at prayer in the gloom of a dark age prays: 'O that thou wouldest rend the heavens and come down.' 'Even so, come, Lord Jesus', cries a great Christian leader in modern times as he longs for revival in the great city (Dr Scott Lidgett in *Christian Commando Communiqué*, p. 5).

Arnold Toynbee has some interesting remarks on the Second Advent in his *Study of History*, Vol. Three. It comes up in his treatment of Withdrawal-and-Return, and also in the matter of 'Etherealization'. He traces the way in which notable men have in many instances had a period of obscurity or withdrawal, sometimes after failure on the practical plane. From this withdrawal they emerge with new powers and immeasureably wider influence and greater success. With communities, too, the same process may be traced. Toynbee shows that in the case of our Lord we can see this law in operation. 'In the story of Jesus, the Withdrawal-and-Return *motif* perpetually recurs.' He withdraws into the wilderness and returns from the Temptation in the power of the Spirit. He withdraws to the mount of Transfiguration and returns resolved to die. 'He descends into the tomb in order to rise immortal in the Resurrection. And, last of all, in the Ascension, He withdraws from Earth to Heaven in order "to come again with glory". . . . In the concept of the Second Coming, the motif of Withdrawal-and-Return attains its deepest spiritual meaning.'

But this process often means a return with new powers, and activity on another plane. The temporary withdrawal of the creative personality makes possible the development of potentialities and is followed by his subsequent return transfigured— 'in a new capacity and with new powers'. Toynbee calls this an instance of the law of 'etherealization' and it is along this line that he deals, in an appendix, with the Second Coming. He admits that

the doctrine of the Second Coming was conceived in the Primitive Christian Church at a time when the Church was oppressed by a sense of weakness and failure, and when even its keenest minds had as yet no inkling of the tremendous victories which Christianity was to win in the fullness of time on the strength of the First Coming alone.

He maintains that enthusiasm for this doctrine is most evident among frustrated sects and societies. But he nevertheless finds the real key in his concept of etherealization. The Advent promise is

a mythological projection into the future, in physical imagery, of the spiritual return in which the Apostles' vanished Master reasserts His presence in the Apostles' hearts when the Apostles take heart of grace to execute, in spite of the Master's physical departure, that audacious mission which the Master, when He was actually present in the flesh, had once laid upon them.

Though Toynbee only touches on this subject incidentally, these suggestive references are in harmony with the development of thought of which we have already spoken. His remarks point to an interpretation of the Advent as a spiritual one, as activity on another plane.

FACING THE FUTURE

The Church should recognize the likelihood that a long future lies before the human race. We ought not to be unduly disturbed if we cannot yet envisage the precise way in which history will reach its climax. We ought, however, to be more concerned with the prospect for Christianity in the intervening time. A certain indifference about this question prevails in some quarters. Some tell us that we must not expect anything vastly different from the present situation; that we must be satisfied to see a few in each generation saved from worldliness and sin; that no extensive victory for the Cross is to be anticipated. It is easy to understand why so many are losing hope in a world whose very foundations seem at times to be breaking up. But those who believe that this is God's world and that the living Christ is still in the midst of His people, can never abandon themselves to final despair. Even the century which has suffered two fearful world-wars has also witnessed a phenomenal expansion of the Christian movement in new territories and the emergence of a World Church conscious of its divine mission (see A. M. Chirgwin's *Under Fire*). We must also learn to take the long view and remember we are living in the days of the early Church.

At the birth of the Church the proportion of the world-population that was Christian was less than one per cent. The proportion is very much greater today, though it would be rash to make an attempt to calculate it. But it is self-evident that there is no fatal figure beyond which there can be no further advance. Moreover Christ counts for more now in influence and in those matters which lie beyond our calculation. If we believe that the growth of the Church is desirable, we must not limit the power of God by saying that the world now has as much Christianity as it can take.

At the same time, remembering the doctrine of the Two Cities, we must not expect a steady and inevitable advance all along the line. There is a sense in which 'the world' (in its New Testament meaning of life organized without God) is displaced rather than improved. The picture which emerges from our previous discussions is certainly not a Christianized form of the modern doctrine of Progress. It is rather that of a struggle between the Church and 'the world' in which the latter continually expresses itself in new shapes while the former with its indestructible life continues to provide the true home for the spirit of man, to assimilate and gather into itself all that is of value in the secular kingdoms as they pass by, and finally succeeds in bringing every part of life beneath the control of Christ. There may be setbacks here and there but the ultimate issue is sure. This is the kind of philosophy of history we find in the Bible, a story of contest and survival, a process in which the world is not improved but superseded. The cities of human pride and imperial splendour disintegrate while the city of God remains as the residual legatee. Some of those who speak of an apocalyptic element in the Bible really mean this element of struggle and judgement running through its story. There is nothing here which forbids the hope of ultimate victory for the divine purpose of righteousness and peace. Indeed the Latter Day Glory of biblical prophecy is often presented as the culmination of strife and judgement. As Matthew Henry once wrote: 'The kingdom of Christ shall wear out all other kingdoms, shall outlive them, and flourish when they are sunk with their own weight, and so wasted that their place knows them no more.'

Part of the prejudice of many Christians against all hopes of the coming of the Kingdom on the earth is due to the spate of secular Utopias which have appeared in recent generations. These really lie outside our subject; and in any case Christianity is mainly concerned with people and their relation to God, not with systems and their relation to the earth. Something, however, may be said about this class of speculation. It should be noted that the earliest descriptions we have of a Golden Age are in the Old Testament, e.g. Psalm 72, Isaiah 2, 11. And while Plato and others thought of an ideal order controlling one city or nation, Isaiah and his friends thought of all humanity, a far wider conception than that of Plato or Aristotle, Campanella, Bacon, or Sir Thomas More. In recent times anything less than the whole world has become unthinkable in this connexion, and so there has been unconsciously a return to the comprehensiveness of the Old Testament visions.

At the time of the Deistic movement the idea of inevitable progress by the lapse of time and the growth of knowledge became popular; and later the curious teaching of such men as Fourier and Godwin emerged. Fourier thought that the discord in the animal world was a reflection of the discord in the human soul; if the latter were remedied, the fiercest of animals would cease to fight and even the sea would turn to lemonade! Godwin in *Political Justice* (which influenced Shelley so deeply) said that a half-hour's toil from every man would suffice to produce the necessities of life; man's influence over bodily laws would increase so that ultimately sleep would be unnecessary and life would be prolonged by intellect. When the limit of population is reached men will refuse to propagate themselves further and death, it seems, will be no more!

In the present century the question of the control of other planets and stars has emerged. The concept of Utopia is now applied, not to Athens or to some imaginary island in the sea, nor merely to the whole globe, but to the heavenly bodies. H. G. Wells says through one of his characters, 'I remember one night, I sat up and told the rascal stars very earnestly how they should not escape us in the end' (*Modern Utopia*). Here J.B.S. Haldane's essay on 'The Last Judgement' may be mentioned (in *Possible Worlds*, 1927). In the golden age millions of years ahead, the life of the individual lasts about 3000 years; and men spend their time cultivating personal relationships and enjoying art of all kinds. The human body is pretty much as at present, but teeth have disappeared. The earth finally threatens to become uninhabitable and a migration to Venus takes place. Olaf Stapledon's *First and Last Men* (1930) is similar. The migration to Venus is, in this work, followed millions of years later by another to Neptune. But, less ambitious than those who dream of the conquest by man of the whole universe, the author tells how at long last the human race comes to an end.

Great are the stars, and man is of no account to them. But man is a fair spirit, whom a star conceived and a star kills. He is greater than those bright blind companies. For though in them there is incalculable potentiality, in him there is achievement, small, but actual. Too soon, seemingly, he comes to his end.

'He is only a fledgling caught in a bush-fire.'

These speculations are interesting and I do not think that the Christian should ignore them altogether. Christians like Cowper two hundred years ago sneered at man's attempts to fly; and yet today it is they who look ridiculous. (Cowper on aeronautics: 'But he has been a groveller upon the earth for 6000 years, and now at last, when the close of this present state of things approaches, begins to exalt himself above it.') If man was made to have dominion, as stated on the first page of the Bible and in the 8th Psalm, then such fulfilments would merely provide a wider illustration of the divine purpose for man.

But attempts to forecast the kind of future which may ultimately await humanity are hazardous. However greatly the conditions of man's life and his habitat may change, the fundamental realities of divine and human relationships will be the same.

As for the way in which human history will be consummated, it is unnecessary to go beyond what was indicated in the previous chapter in the section on 'The Consummation'. Questions concerning the end will become clearer when the time approaches. 'We know not with what we must serve the Lord until we come thither' (Exodus 10$_{26}$). An illustration by T. H. Barratt on this point has brought help to many:

Perhaps we may come nearest to essential truth about the matter (i.e. the earthly end of human story) by a simple human parable.

Imagine a fevered little child in bed, in a darkened room. Now try to describe that little child's 'world'. There are the aching limbs, the throbbing head, the pillows and the bedclothes; strange shadows in the darkened room cast by a flickering fire or perhaps a hidden night-light; dim shapes of furniture or pictures on the walls; the rain beating on the window; and outside, black night and the infinite unknown. That and that only is the child's 'world'. And now imagine that a strange and sudden thing occurs. The electric light is switched on! The shadows vanish, the dim shapes disappear, the old 'world' has passed away; and there, sitting, watching, all the time, close by is—'Mother!' She had never really gone away, but the child's first thought is—'She has *come*!' And with her coming all things have become new. The old world of shadows has gone, swallowed up in the new wonder of reality and love.

That little child is our humanity, fevered and ill at ease, conscious only of dim shadows and flickering lights, of mystery and unintelligible pain, of homelessness and night. And then something happens, something for which we mortals have no name, but the one and only thing which ultimately matters—and men become aware of things unseen, of spirit, love, reality, and God. We say: 'Lo! He comes with clouds descending.' But He has never really gone away. He has been there all the time, for Christ is never an absentee (*Methodist Recorder*, 12th December 1935).

It is in parables and symbols that we can best think of the End. But meanwhile we must not forget that Christ is indeed with us 'all the time'.

He is not only the One who has come; He is always the coming One. He came back to His own at Easter; He came in a new and more intimate way at Pentecost. He came in the early triumphs of the Gospel, and He still comes in the judgements and revivals of history. He comes into the hearts of those who receive Him, and to the dying bed of His people. We must live in constant watchfulness, as men who look for their Lord, lest His coming in some crisis or opportunity should find us unready or asleep.

In our prayer that He may come more and more in spiritual power into the life of men, we may well make use of the verses of Charles Wesley's great hymn:

Gird on Thy thigh the Spirit's sword,
 And take to Thee Thy power divine;
Stir up Thy strength, almighty Lord,
 All power and majesty are Thine:
Assert Thy worship and renown;
O all-redeeming God, come down!

Come, and maintain Thy righteous cause,
 And let Thy glorious toil succeed;
Dispread the victory of Thy Cross,
 Ride on, and prosper in Thy deed;
Through earth triumphantly ride on,
And reign in all our hearts alone.

INDEX